*Preludes to Vision*

# PRELUDES TO VISION

*The Epic Venture in Blake, Wordsworth,
Keats, and Hart Crane*

## Thomas A. Vogler

UNIVERSITY OF CALIFORNIA PRESS
BERKELEY, LOS ANGELES, AND LONDON

*1971*

University of California Press
Berkeley and Los Angeles, California
University of California Press, Ltd.
London, England

Copyright © 1971, by
The Regents of the University of California

ISBN: 0-520-01687-4
Library of Congress Catalog Card Number: 70-107662

Printed in the United States of America
Designed by Dave Comstock

Anon I rose
As if on wings, and saw beneath me stretch'd
Vast prospect of the World which I had been
And was; and hence this Song.

—Wordsworth

What we must understand is the reason why
the soul's wings fall from it, and are lost.

—Plato

# Preface

This book grew from musing in solitude over a number of years. During those years there were many who helped make my life, the context of those musings, rich in the kinds of experience that enable one to recognize in a poem the completion of a human relationship. I have been fortunate to have among my friends Larry George, Jerome Schneewind, Gladden Schrock, Harold Bloom, Frances Beasel, Gabe Berns, Rich Randolph, Harry Berger, Jr. and Hank Swartwood. I have benefited from many teachers and been inspired by a few, but by none so much as by the example and teaching of Christian Mackauer, for whom everything mattered. My own students have enriched my life and sharpened my impressions, listening and sharing and questioning, keeping my thoughts—and me—alive long after the completion of this book. If I could name them all I would, but John Wilkes, Pat Gallagher and Sharon Moorhead would come first.

T.V.

Santa Cruz, 1970

# Contents

# Contents

# Chapter 1

# In Search of the Epic

A Heroic Poem, truly such, is undoubtedly the greatest work which the soul of man is capable to perform.

—Dryden, "Dedication of the Aeneid"

We cannot possibly understand the change and growth of art-forms without following the change of the idea of the soul in human history.

—Rank, *Art and Artist*

Looking at Dryden's "Dedication of the Aeneid" from the vantage point of over two and a half centuries, we find a strange suggestiveness both in the ease of the "soul of man" phrase and in the "truly such" qualification, which for Dryden was little more than a matter of poetic and critical common sense. One of the best critical glosses of Dryden's "truly such" qualification may be found toward the end of the eighteenth century in a statement by Samuel Johnson. "By the general consent of criticks the first praise of genius is due to the writer of an epick poem, as it requires an assemblage of all the powers which are singly sufficient for other compositions. Poetry is the art of uniting pleasure with truth, by calling imagination to the help of reason." [1] The authoritative, self-confident tone of both of these pronouncements, and of many similar ones that came between, was possible because of the unquestioned connection between poetry and truth, a connection which Johnson made explicit. For the modern reader, poet or critic, the connection is neither so inevitable nor are the terms so readily definable as

1. "Milton," *Lives of the English Poets*, ed. George B. Hill (Oxford: Clarendon Press, 1905), p. 170.

they seem in Johnson's capable hands. Something has happened to the metaphysical status of poetry since his time, inclining many toward the attitude of Byron—"Another Epic! Who inflicts again / More books of blank upon the sons of men?"—or even that of Poe—"I hold that a long poem does not exist."

By almost common consent, this change in status is ascribed to the rise of the Romantic movement in the late eighteenth and early nineteenth centuries. Something happened during this period that crystallized the impossibility of writing the epic poem that a whole century of criticism had been concerned with defining. The epic genre, as formally defined, ceased to be viable after Milton; and in spite of all attempts to be prescriptive, the Neo-Classic theory remains descriptive. The demise of a genre is not in itself a new phenomenon, but the demise of a genre for so long considered a philosophic and moral justification for poetry is not only new, it is of fundamental significance.

It has become increasingly obvious to critics of the genre that the *desire* to write an epic must be examined as part of what the epic *is*. Thomas Greene describes the desire as "historical fact—that the legendary epic ideal was like a spirit that seized and rode great men, haunting and exhausting them, driving them sometimes to misdirect their gifts, but also, in some few cases, to surpass them." Jeremy Ingalls has pointed to epic motive as "the defining factor" from which any "functional definition" of epic must be derived. The point is considerably less redundant than it might appear to be on first sight, especially when an historical change in the nature of attempts to write epics can be dismissed as a failure of that desire. According to E. M. W. Tillyard, "in the eighteenth century the epic impulse left poetry for the novel." [2] This statement seems clearly false if by "epic impulse" he means what he later calls the "epic urge," and describes as one of the four essentials in the composition of a true epic poem. Whatever the novelists may have been doing, or trying to do, the poets continued to be haunted by the epic ideal and the desire to continue and redefine the tradition of which Milton was the last great English embodiment.

Tillyard's statement is also puzzling if we understand it to imply something more like the historical movement toward representational or "realistic" writing that accompanied and stimulated the growth of

2. Thomas Greene, *The Descent from Heaven* (New Haven: Yale Univ. Press, 1963), p. 9; Jeremy Ingalls, "The Epic Tradition: a Commentary," *East-West Review* 1, no. 1 (Spring 1964): 44; E. M. W. Tillyard, *The English Epic and Its Background* (London: Chatto & Windus, 1954), p. 14.

the novel in the eighteenth and nineteenth centuries. There was an indisputable movement during this period toward the kind of realism in which the novel surpassed even narrative poetry; but that movement was only part of the history of the novel, and the assumption that the urge to write epic poetry somehow left poetry for the novel is essentially a narrow and misleading one. If anything, the history of the novel since 1800 shows less and less concern with any kind of conventional realism, more and more tendency to become like the poems I shall discuss in this study—more autobiographical, more poetic in language, and more metaphysical in depth. In Ernest Baker's words, there was "a change [in] fiction corresponding to the earlier change in poetry, a change of attention from outer to inner, a concentration of vision, a sudden illumination." [3] The only novelist who deliberately tried to embody as much of the epic in a novel as possible was Fielding, and both his career as a writer and his thoughts on the epic problem point to the conclusion that the novel is not in any simple historical sense a continuation or development of the epic.

The epic did survive for a period as a foil for mock epics (*Rape of the Lock, Hudibras, Tom Jones, Don Juan*) and even as a recipe (as in *Peri Bathous*) for a Blackmore's *Prince Arthur*. Although any highly formalized genre lends itself to parody, the unique pretensions of the epic add an inevitable dimension of seriousness to good parodies of the form. The mock heroic thrives, as Samuel Butler observed, on the contrast between real life and heroic fiction, using the form of the heroic poem as a foil against which a comic/serious vision of reality can be played. For Butler this was the only way the epic conventions could be used to approach the truth.[4] Defoe and Richardson rejected the epic writers as models primarily on moral grounds. Because of their bourgeois morality, they refused to accept what they saw as the ethical implications of the works of Homer and Vergil. Fielding, who had a more conventional Neo-Classic respect for the status of Homer and Vergil, still found nothing viable for the novel in the formal nature of the epic except the burlesque and parody of applying epic conventions to low characters and ordinary events. How whole-heartedly serious were Fielding's attempts to create a comic epic is not at issue here, although it could be argued that the Preface to *Joseph Andrews* and the introduc-

3. Ernest Baker, *History of the English Novel*, 10 vols. (New York: Barnes & Noble, 1936), 8:19.
4. *Characters and Passages from Note Books*, ed. A. R. Waller (Cambridge: Univ. Press, 1908), p. 278.

tory chapter to the eighth book of *Tom Jones* are not really adequate explanations of the works they comment on. Only in his last novel, *Amelia*, does Fielding seem to have achieved a wholly serious *modus vivendi* with an epic work, the *Aeneid*. In this novel, anticipating Joyce's technique in *Ulysses*, Fielding creates parallels with the *Aeneid* that in effect are "a kind of narrative metaphor which assists the imagination of the writer to find a pattern for his own observation of life." [5] Here the parallels enrich rather than qualify the basically realistic imitation of nature which Fielding is attempting, and there is a marked contrast with his earlier attempts to create a comic epic.

For whatever it is worth, Tillyard's generalization is typical of the kind of critical commonplace that so frequently commemorates the passing of the epic genre in the eighteenth century. There are similar observations based on various social, philosophical, psychological, and historical conjectures, but surprisingly little attention has been given to the poets themselves. Critics have condemned poets for their failure to attempt or to achieve poems comparable to the great epics of the past, although some have partially exonerated the poets by pointing out that there are no longer the philosophical or social bases on which to write an epic. Few critics, however, have directly confronted the unavoidable fact that poets have not given up the attempt to write epic poetry. From Blake's wish to succeed Milton as the epic poet of England, and Wordsworth's great attempt to write Coleridge's "long, philosophical poem," to Ezra Pound's epic claims for his *Cantos*, most poets have agreed with Keats. "A long poem is a test of invention, which I take to be the Polar star of Poetry, as Fancy is the Sails—and Imagination the rudder. Did our great poets ever write short pieces?" [6]

Not all poets, however, have shared Keats's commitment to greatness even at the risk of failure. Beginning as early as Dryden and Pope, many poets have left only projected plans or incomplete attempts to write epics. Others, with feebler powers of self-criticism, have left completed "epics" as testimony of their high regard for the epic and as evidence of their lack of ability to write one.

It is easy to disagree in detail with most generalizations about the fate of the epic, but a few valid general conclusions have emerged from all the historical discussion of the problem. The genre of the epic, in the

5. Ian Watt, *The Rise of the Novel* (Berkeley & Los Angeles: Univ. California Press, 1957), p. 255.
6. *The Letters of John Keats*, 2 vols., ed. Hyder E. Rollins (Cambridge, Mass.: Harvard Univ. Press, 1958), 1:170.

limited and formalized Neo-Classic sense, had its last rites early in the eighteenth century, and was followed by little mourning until the revival of genre criticism beginning with Arnold in the nineteenth century.[7] Certain novels have taken on something of the scope and function of the epic, but this has been a development within the history of the novel and must be described by analogy rather than by the comparison of formal structure. The recognition of this trend has led to increasing recognition of the possible epic function of the novel.

The poets, meanwhile, are still compared with Homer, Vergil, Dante, Spenser, and Milton. Their epic pretensions are therefore dismissed because of the obvious differences between their works and those of the earlier poets who have already earned the title of epic poet. In the epic competition between Wordsworth and his avowed rival, Milton, Wordsworth has always lost because the rules of the game have been those used by Milton and his commentators. Yet Milton and Wordsworth are in many significant ways much more alike than Homer and Milton.

The only way to eliminate this kind of competition is to find a context in which the epic possibilities of the modern long poem can be realized. To do this we must begin with a fundamental distinction in the elements of an epic poem. The distinction is often crudely treated in terms of form and content, but is more adequately suggested by the terms "inner form" and "outer form" as they are used by Wellek and Warren. "Genre should be conceived, we think, as a grouping of literary works based, theoretically, upon both outer form (specific meter or structure) and also upon inner form (attitude, tone, purpose—more crudely, subject and audience)."[8] The distinction is essential in thinking about the continuity of epic poetry for several reasons. First, the genre has most often been treated in formal and structural terms (outer form), and this is precisely the approach that is least likely to lead us to the nature of the modern mode of epic. The second reason is more complex, for the inner form of epic has remained essentially the same, while the problems of that inner form have changed, and changed in a qualitative rather than merely quantitative fashion. In an analogous way, it can be argued that the inner form or function of tragedy has remained the essential core of the genre, while the outer form of tragic conventions and tech-

7. See Donald M. Foerster, *The Fortunes of Epic Poetry* (Washington, D.C.: Catholic Univ. of America, 1962) for a more specific discussion of changes in the concept of epic as genre.
8. René Wellek and Austin Warren, *Theory of Literature* (New York: Harcourt Brace, 1949), p. 221.

niques which Aristotle describes at such length has largely changed.

The one constant feature of epics is that they are poems of man in the fullest sense, facing the ultimate challenge of his time, responding with the fullest energy and endurance of his faculties, and achieving some kind of victory over the circumstances that constitute a challenge to his society's continued existence. The trouble with an attempt to formulate the inner form of epic in a few words is that any description of the epic on a highly general level will also sound like a description of tragedy. Both tragedy and epic have been called the highest or noblest of all the genres because they are, in different ways, concerned with man in the fullest sense. It is impossible to distinguish the inner forms of tragedy and epic by a categorical or prescriptive approach because the two genres represent different responses to, or different visions of, the same kind of experience. *Job* can be read as a tragic drama or as a "brief epic" (Milton's term), depending on whether we are reacting to the sense of despair in the early part or to the triumph of the fulfilled covenant at the end.

Since the epic is in some sense encyclopedic, it can include tragedy, or the tragic vision, as something that must be transcended; for epic is concerned, where tragedy is not, with finding or perceiving a vision of ultimate justice and acceptable human destiny. It must go beyond the tragic vision of man defeating himself and finding a triumph in his ability to accept defeat. If tragedy gives us "the thing itself," or "unaccommodated man," epic attempts to give us man in a special kind of context, exploring the totality of responses to the social and historical dimensions of the human situation in an attempt to find an alternative to the tragic vision. Tragedy sees and accepts a sense of ancient and permanent evil, recognized in moments of truth and avoided only through deception. The epic intuits a golden age and a fall from that age, and on the basis of this intuition searches for a vision of change, a prophecy of a better future state. The theme, goal, and motive of the poet merge in a vision of spiritual regeneration that will lead to a state of permanent enlightenment.

Although this common denominator of all poems that we call epic is the same, the factors that produce a true epic can and do change radically. What changes is the poet's conception of man, and perhaps even the very nature of man as his relation to his world changes. The challenge to and response of Odysseus is not that of Beowulf, although there are strong similarities on a general level of comparison. The challenge to and response of Dante in the *Commedia* and of Milton's Adam are not the same, although again, there are obvious and significant similarities. In his response to the challenge, whatever it is, the epic hero ideally embodies to the maximum degree the values held by his society, striving both to overcome the immediate challenge and to achieve a satisfactory relationship between those values and something beyond, some ultimate order, whether the gods of the Greeks or the Christian God or even some prophesied future curve of history—that eventual benign outcome clarifying the present and justifying the suffering we undergo in it. The epic hero never acts purely from personal motives, and it is this aspect that gives the epic much of the social and historical dimension in which its greatness lies. Inevitably, as both the challenges and values change, the problems of the inner form which the poet must solve to write a full epic will change.

In the earliest examples of epic poetry, what are often called "folk epics," the challenge is always some form of potential destruction of the tribe or state. The hero must be potent both in war and love to overcome the challenge; he must overcome the physical threat of destruction or loss of tribal identity and secure the future of the race through his own fruitful sexual union or the preservation of some other union. The hero's epic stature is achieved by making the hero a god, or as near in power to the gods as possible. As a man he epitomizes and embodies the fullest possible range of social values. Even for Vergil, who is not purely a folk-epic poet, the heroic plot must include the founding and peopling of a city.

After the folk epic, the next great period of epic poetry is that of the Christian epic. The challenge to man in the Christian epic is the temptation of sin and the threat of damnation. To meet this challenge, the heroic virtues of earlier epics are either irrelevant or dangerous. Thus Milton, although devoting much of his life to creating a true epic, repudiated military adventure and exploits, "hitherto the only argument heroic deemed," in his desire to give epic treatment to a more spiritual conflict. In the Christian epic the individual human protagonist cannot stand alone as a full embodiment of all values or as the sole compositional center of an epic poem. The hero's intrinsic worth becomes secondary to some form of mystery or grace without which he can never achieve full value. Satan ironically has all the heroic virtues of an earlier age, but he lacks the will to please God, without which the greatest challenge to man, his state of disharmony with God in a fallen

world, can never be overcome in Christian terms. In spite of the absence
of the power struggles that characterize earlier epics, the Christian epic
hero is presented as an embodiment of the heroic qualities of energy
and vitality. Although energy and vitality in the Christian epics are not
expressed in the traditional modes of action, they are ultimate in the
same sense of being all-out responses to the greatest challenge man faces.

There is no generally recognized modern epic, but the attempts poets
have made to find an adequate inner form for epic poetry have produced works among which we may eventually find the epic for our time.
The difficulty, both in creating and in recognizing a modern epic, is
that our culture does not provide the essentials with which earlier epic
poets began. There is no common ideology, no vital, central source for
universally acceptable concepts of authority and value. No culture has
ever been complete enough in this sense for the poetic purpose; part of
the epic poet's task has always been to give to his race or age a completion and embodiment of the meaning of life that he finds in the accepted but not necessarily conscious metaphysic of the time. Both Dante
and Milton brought to completion different elements of the Christian
culture and produced epic expressions of the validity of life on which
both the poet and audience could agree. In spite of Milton's problem
with his own and the prophet's place in society, he shared a sense of
order and value with other members of the Christian tradition.

> O *Adam,* one Almighty is, from whom
> All things proceed, and up to him return,
> If not deprav'd from good, created all,
> Such to perfection, one first matter all,
> Indu'd with various forms, various degrees
> Of substance, and in things that live, of life;
> But more refin'd, more spirituous, and pure,
> As nearer to him plac't or nearer tending,
> Each in thir several active Spheres assign'd
> Till body up to spirit work, in bounds
> Proportion'd to each kind. So from the root
> Springs lighter the green stalk, from thence the leaves
> More aery, last the bright consummate flow'r
> Spirits odorous breathes: flow'rs and thir fruit
> Man's nourishment, by gradual scale sublim'd
> To vital Spirits aspire, to animal,
> To intellectual, give both life and sense,

Fancy and understanding, whence the Soul
Reason receives, and reason is her being,
Discursive, or Intuitive.[9]

The ability to make a firm, unquestioning statement of this sort, based on a faith with the strength of knowledge, is in a very important sense an enabling power, a necessary element in the composition of an epic. Although lacking the explicit metaphysical orientation so prominent in Milton's thought, the Homeric simile fulfilled a similar function in symbolizing a calm background of known permanence and continual, harmonious existence.

In the absence of an accepted spiritual orientation of the collective consciousness and of a shared sense of value, the nature of achievable epic poetry must change; but the possibility of epic poetry does not necessarily disappear. The nature of the epic challenge to man becomes that of finding, rather than preserving, an acceptable collective ideology of some kind. The poet must, in Joyce's words, forge in the smithy of his soul the uncreated consciousness of his race. Before a poet can do this, he must have a firm faith in the power of poetic vision as a mode of finding ultimate truths about the nature of man; he must have the highest possible estimate of the powers of the poetic imagination and complete faith in that estimate.

The problem I have attempted to describe is obviously not only the poet's problem, but the basic problem of our culture. We are haunted by inadequate solutions to the need of the individual mind to reach beyond itself. In this sense the poet's problem is also the religious problem and the philosophical problem of our time. The greatest universal challenge to man is the need to find the kind of convention or attitude toward life which was formerly the enabling cause of epic poetry, the base from which a culture could be brought to poetic completion, and the source of value that was threatened yet could still conceivably be rescued.

The whole problem of writing an epic is thus forced back to a more primary and problematic stage. The poet himself is in a position where he could be his culture's epic hero, if he could achieve a vision of the meaning and significance of life that would demand acceptance, if he could create or find a myth that would awaken and unify the collective

9. *Paradise Lost*, bk. 5:469–488, ed. Merritt Y. Hughes (New York: Odyssey Press, 1935).

imagination—as the great religious myths of the past have done—
thereby living up to Coleridge's ambitious claims. "Idly talk they who
speak of poets as mere indulgers of fancy, imagination, superstition, etc.
They are the bridlers by delight, the purifiers; they that combine all
these with reason and order—the true protoplasts—Gods of Love who
tame the chaos." [10] A heroic claim is put forward even more explicitly
by Wordsworth in his "Prospectus" to *The Recluse*.

> O Heavens! How awful is the might of Souls,
> And what they do within themselves, while yet
> The yoke of earth is new to them, the world
> Nothing but a wild field where they were sown.
> This is, in truth, heroic argument,
> And genuine prowess.[11]

If poets are motivated in their desire to write epics by the basic human need for myth, then the poet's problem might seem to be difficult
but precise: to formulate a myth, newly created or synthesized, in which
he could believe, and which would demand acceptance and belief on
the part of society. But this simple approach is not possible. The great
creations of popular force, the larger religions, customs, and laws, are
not the outcome of individual effort. It is possible, without being overly
mystical, to speak of a national consciousness, or soul, which the individual imagination can bring to completion but cannot itself create.
The very awareness of the problem makes it impossible to write a myth
unconsciously. Furthermore, the challenge of science to poetry as a
mode of knowing has forced poets, even though they resist the challenge, to consider the nature of myth, especially how the poet finds or
creates myth. The problem is to understand poetic vision before—or
while—presenting a myth in the form of a vision.

Faced with the absence of accepted collective beliefs on the basis of
which to write and the impossibility of single-handedly creating them,
poets have turned to the most basic epistemological problems of vision
and perception, and especially to the problems of prophetic vision or
future perspective that can foresee a way out of the present situation.
The prophecy must encourage and support faith and provide a recon-

---

10. *Anima Poetae*, ed. E. H. Coleridge (Boston, 1859), p. 81.
11. Prospectus to "The Recluse," in *The Poetical Works of Wordsworth*, ed.
Thomas Hutchinson, rev. E. de Selincourt (London & New York: Oxford Univ.
Press, 1950), p. 590.

ciliation with death, the real and metaphoric antithesis of poetic creation. Yet it is a mistake to attempt to approach such poems through
religious terminology and concepts alone. Similarly, it is a mistaken ap-
plication of erudition to attempt to read the poems solely as epistemology or metaphysics. The poets are attempting poetic solutions to problems of perception and we must honor their attempts if we wish to
understand their work as poetry.

The problem of poets has been not merely how to write a good rather
than a bad long poem, but how to write one at all; and the first step
is to become a theorist of vision, of the human power of imagination.
Before he can establish his own authority to teach the nation, or to
reveal to it its traditions and future possibilities, the poet must establish
the nature and authority of the poetic imagination. The authority can
be found only through an exploration of the nature and possibility of
poetic vision.

> with the thing
> Contemplated, describe the Mind and Man
> Contemplating; and who, and what he was—
> The transitory Being that beheld
> This Vision.[12]

The result has been poets whose subject is poetry, whose notion of
significant action is the poet in the process of ordering his experience of
reality into the poetic fabric. It is in this direction that the possibility
of a poetic epic with a heroic action began to emerge in the nineteenth
century. If there is to be an epic, it will be of significance to the degree
that the problems of the poet, facing experience, are the problems of
his community. In highly simplified terms, there may be an epic potential in the search for an adequate and comprehensive view of life and
art. The search is a fundamental, available, and even heroic subject with
which the poet can perform the function of expressing in imaginative
form the experience potentially common to all.

The problem of finding a subject, in the conventional sense, has been
a reflection of the increasing importance of the search itself. Wordsworth had a list of possible epic subjects, as did Milton, Dryden, and
Pope. In Book 1 of *The Prelude* he does not reject them; he flees from
them and the "vain perplexity" he falls into when contemplating the

12. Prospectus to "The Recluse," in *Poetical Works*, p. 590.

task of embodying them in a poem. Instead, he turns to a "theme / Single and of determined bounds"—the growth of his own mind—and the subject becomes the history of a mind looking for a subject. In the presence of the heroic frame of mind, which seems to come early in a nation's history, a merely historical event or situation takes on an aura of epic glory; life is interpreted heroically because individual action is naturally and inevitably put into an epic frame, divorced from the complexity of the historical context in which it occurs. This epic frame of mind clearly does not exist today, and it had already disappeared in England in the sixteenth century. Although there are a profusion of theoretically possible subjects for an epic poem and an abundant variety of possible models for limitation or development, there have been almost no modern examples of the earlier heroic view of life.

We do have, however, a number of poems that express a view of the life of the imagination that is heroic in the sense that I have been describing. I have deliberately postponed the introduction of specific poems as examples, because the attempt to relate a number of poems to each other must begin with a rather vague impression of similarities either in form or, in this case, in effect or function. The important thing in attempting to establish such relations is to distinguish between valid, significant similarities and similarities derived by a methodology that imposes on everything a predetermined scheme. We must not accept all resemblances as important, nor reject them as coincidence. If there are laws or forms or trends, they must be discoverable within the works and in terms that do not distort the basic conception of the works. The selection of poems to be used in such a comparative study is a crucial factor, yet one that can never be reduced completely to objective criteria. How could Aristotle have inductively arrived at his definition of tragedy without first having some kind of operative definition that told him which works were pertinent to his study? Similarly, I have my own set of intuitive criteria which has led me to exclude such long poems as Southey's "epics," Tennyson's *Idylls of the King*, Browning's *Ring and the Book*, Morris's *Island*, and Hardy's *Dynasts*, while including Blake's *Four Zoas*, *Milton*, and *Jerusalem*, Wordsworth's *Prelude* (but not *The Excursion*), Shelley's *Prometheus Unbound* and *Triumph of Life*, Keats's *Fall of Hyperion* (but not *Hyperion*), Byron's *Don Juan*, Browning's *Sordello*, Tennyson's *In Memoriam*, Whitman's *Leaves of Grass*, Stevens' *Comedian as the Letter C*, Williams's *Paterson*, Pound's *Cantos*, and Hart Crane's *Bridge*. The final selection of examples for analysis from these poems was determined both by my own preference and by limitations of space. I have chosen Blake's *Milton*, Wordsworth's *Prelude*, Keats's *Fall of Hyperion*, and Crane's *Bridge* because I see each of them as a significant attempt to write modern epic poetry. Clearly and directly expressed in them are the elements which I find inevitable in a poem that is a prelude to vision.

In these poems the traditional assumption of a union between poetry and significant truth, even though it is asserted, is no longer an easy one to make. Before these poets can achieve with confidence an epic synthesis of life, they must have confidence in poetry as a valid mode of perceiving reality and in the finished poem as an embodiment of truth. The epic problem is no longer that of recreating the outward history of man or a nation, but of creating the inward history of man, by moving to levels of generality through the concept of the individual as psyche rather than the individual as action.

Augustine refers in *The Confessions* to a "no space-occupying place" into which we sink and out of which we rise again. The realm of these poems is that no-space-occupying place, namely the mind and memory— the consciousness—of the poet, the world in which Wordsworth "must tread on shadowy ground, must sink / Deep—and, aloft ascending, breathe in worlds / To which the heaven of heavens is but a veil." [13] The movement of these poems is a continual sinking and rising within this space in the attempt to avoid the ambiguous hovering of the final image in *The Bridge*. It is too easy and too common a mistake to take the exploration of this internal space as a form of Romantic egotism, for the ultimate "rise" or rebirth the poets seek is always viewed as leading to an awakening and rebirth of man as well as the poet. The movement itself, in its uncertainty and exploratory nature, achieves universal scope, because the attempt to find a vision is presented as a universal problem of the human imagination.

Because of the primarily internal nature of these epics of consciousness, the objective element of the earlier epics, or the usual concern with natural incident, is eliminated. The subject of the epic story becomes the history of the poet's attempts to find a vision. Dante made it clear that the *Commedia* is in part at least a presentation of his own visionary perspective, but there is so much else in the poem that it may be read with little or no reference to that element. For Coleridge, "the sublimist parts" of *Paradise Lost* are "the revelations of Milton's own

13. Prospectus to "The Recluse," in *Poetical Works*, p. 590.

mind, producing itself and evolving its own greatness." [14] In saying this, however, he was well aware of the other parts and that this view reflected primarily his own way of reading. The poems that I shall be looking at in detail are written so that they must be read primarily as attempts to find a personal visionary perspective.

Neither Milton nor Dryden nor Pope nor Johnson considered the poet's private life or the emotions, conflicts, and turmoils of youth appropriate material for truly serious poetry. Contrarily, the last century and a half has set high literary value on personal revelations of childhood and early youth. Artists have become increasingly more aware of the complex totality of influences that go into their poetic development and into their finished works of art. The discovery of the unconscious has been a part of this movement, but only a part. It was primarily the questioning of the status of art as a mode of knowledge which led to the thoroughgoing self-analysis of the artist and to the view made explicit by Rimbaud. "La première étude de l'homme qui veut être poète est sa propre connaissance, entière. Il cherche son âme, il l'inspecte, il la tente, l'apprend. Dès qu'il la sait, il la doit cultiver." [15]

Tillyard has presented a case for reading *Paradise Lost* as a poem about the state of the author when he wrote it. This can be done, in more or less obvious ways, with almost any poem. In some poems this is the primary sense, or the mode they most properly display. This is a view we are all conditioned to accept in the reading of lyric poetry, or shorter poems expressive of easily recognizable emotions. Critics seem less willing to see the lyric mode as valid in a longer poem, even when the poem is primarily concerned with subjective problems of perception. It would be as easy to apply Tillyard's approach to Dante as to Milton, but in each case there is an inevitable distortion, for there is so much more in the *Commedia* or in *Paradise Lost* than the state of the author. It is a distortion of emphasis to take this limited aspect of the two works as their primary mode, whereas in a poem like *The Bridge* we are forced to follow the poet's attempts to expand the lyric into a poem of epic scope.

The traditional distinction between lyric and epic is one that Blake, Wordsworth, Keats, and Crane, in different ways, all attempted to overcome. The lyric moment of inspired vision, with its direct intuition

14. *Coleridge's Miscellaneous Criticism*, ed. T. M. Raysor (London: Constable & Co., 1936), p. 164.
15. *Lettres de la Vie Litteraire d'Arthur Rimbaud*, ed. Jean-Marie Carre (Paris: Gallimard, 1931), p. 61.

of reality, was the beginning of poetry for these poets, the only mode of knowledge whose validity could not be doubted because of the sheer intensity of the vision. Yet ordinary lyric poetry, however good, lacked the scope and significance of the long poem which these poets felt was needed as a genuine justification for poetry. Somehow, the immediate impact of poetic vision characteristic of the lyric and of the young poet, had to be retained in a longer poem that avoided the fleeting, sporadic nature of lyric insight. Implicit in this problem is the basis of a new poetic canon of development, beginning with lyric poems and progressing, finally, to an epic that would retain the intensity and subjectivity of the lyric while achieving the scope and universal reference of the epic. The classic canon was similar in that it began with the pastoral lyric and required the epic performance to be a later product of a gradually developed poetic maturity. In the new canon, however, the whole concept of poetic maturity has been radically changed, so that chronological age and acquired objective knowledge are no longer the important criteria they once were. A Miltonic breadth of intellect and erudition is perhaps no longer possible, as is often suggested; but even if it were, it may no longer be a part of the definition of an epic poet.

The attempt to move from a lyric to an epic mode without losing the vividness of the lyric; the urgency of the challenge to man which the modern epic poem must somehow solve; the constant pressure to discount poetry—these factors help explain why so many poets have not waited until they were fully mature in the traditional sense before attempting to write long, philosophical poetry. They see the great poem they hope to write as a means of clarifying their vision and of achieving the kind of poetic maturity formerly an enabling power for writing an epic poem. Here again, many critics with preconceived notions of what it means to be an epic poet have refused to consider the possibility that a young poet could write anything that might properly be called an epic. But when age is seen as a threat to vision, both in the individual and in the historical movement toward the decay of vital communal myths, the young poet with his intense, lyric, but sporadic glimpses of poetic truth, may be the only one who has a chance, however small and desperate, of finding the vision that will lead to maturity.

> I see by glimpses now; when age comes on,
> May scarcely see at all.[16]

16. *The Prelude* (text of 1805), bk. 11:338–339, ed. E. de Selincourt, rev. Helen Darbishire (London & New York: Oxford Univ. Press, 1960)

Any attempt to describe the general nature of the prelude poem must eventually come to Wordsworth's own comments on the relation his *Prelude* had to his concept of a poetic career. These comments are worth special attention because they relate to what Wordsworth was attempting in *The Prelude* and because they illustrate some of the main points essential to an understanding of *Milton, The Fall of Hyperion,* and *The Bridge.* In his Preface to *The Excursion,* Wordsworth recalls and reflects on the place *The Prelude* had in his poetic development.

> Several years ago, when the Author retired to his native mountains with the *hope* of being *enabled* to construct a literary work that might live, it was a reasonable thing that he should take a review of his own mind, and examine how far Nature and Education had qualified him for such an employment.
>
> As subsidary to this preparation, he undertook *to record, in verse, the origin and progress of his own powers, as far as he was acquainted with them.*
>
> That work, addressed to a dear friend, most distinguished for his knowledge and genius, and to whom the Author's intellect is deeply indebted, has been long finished; and the *result* of the investigation which gave rise to it, was a determination to compose a philosophical Poem, containing views of Man, Nature, and Society, and to be entitled the "Recluse"; as having for its principal subject the sensations and opinions of a poet living in retirement.
>
> The *preparatory poem* is biographical, and conducts the history of the Author's mind to *the point when he was emboldened to hope that his faculties were sufficiently matured for entering upon the arduous labour* which he had proposed to himself.[17]

I have already tried to suggest some of the more general factors that led to the very real need, expressed here by Wordsworth, for a preparatory poem, or prelude. One of the more interesting ambiguities of Wordsworth's statement is the uncertain place "hope" has in the course of the project. The retirement and composition of the poem began with a hope that the outcome would enable him to write the great poem he needed and desired. Yet the final "point" of development is itself still described as a hope—a hope that he *has* achieved the desired preparation, and a hope that can be fulfilled only by the actual composition of the poem he was preparing to write, by the actual embodiment of the

17. *Poetical Works,* p. 494. Italics added.

vision for which he was preparing himself. The structural implications of this ambiguity—the beginning that is a hoped-for end, and the end that is a hoped-for beginning—will be discussed in detail later with relation to particular poems. In the "Advertisement" the ambiguity is emphasized by the unexpected use of "result" in the third paragraph. We know that the very idea of writing *The Prelude* rose from Wordsworth's determination and hope to write the "philosophical Poem," not the other way around as he seems to be suggesting here. Furthermore we know, however painful it is to admit, that *The Excursion* does not fulfill the anticipations of the preparatory poem, either in quality or in the nature of vision. If the view of the human and poetic imagination Wordsworth tried to establish in *The Prelude* constituted an adequate preparation for a later poem, we should expect in *The Excursion* the apotheosis of man as a creative personality, continuing the transfer of the religious ideology, which emphasized the glory of God, to man himself, especially creative man, the poet. Yet we must share Coleridge's disappointment at not finding in *The Excursion* the poet whose imagination is explored in *The Prelude*. Both *The Prelude* and Blake's *Milton* end on notes of expectancy, with an intensely ambivalent sense of simultaneous completion and anticipation. Neither *The Excursion* nor *Jerusalem* is a direct fulfillment of the creative power of the imagination to remake the world; instead, those poems return to survey the remnants of the fallen and fragmented world that *The Prelude* and *Milton* had pushed to the brink of regeneration. This does not mean the later poems are failures because they do not directly fulfill the earlier; nor are the preludes failures because they are not directly fulfilled in succeeding works. I shall try to follow the efforts of the poets to avoid narrow notions of linear development and the inevitable judgment of failure passed on prelude poems when measured by such standards. There is an important sense in which failure is built into a poem aspiring to be a prelude to vision; for the moment of vision, no matter how extended, must fail in time—and the anticipation of that failure is a realistic and high form of poetic success.

The deliberation behind these introductory remarks has been to wring from the freedom of an introduction the opportunity to provide an intuitive context in which the rather detailed readings of specific poems may achieve a broader significance. I have been proceeding so far on two assumptions. First, almost all great poets have had and still have a desire to write a long, serious poem, a total embodiment of their poetic vision. The desire or urge is constant in the abstract, but it is obviously conditioned by current ideas and beliefs in the poet's environment. Second, the ideal basis of an epic, or of any long serious poem, is an adequate view of life and art. The view does not have to be formulated in a critical theory; it can be, and perhaps in part must be, unconscious. By "adequate" I meant to imply that the view be both comprehensive in scope and acceptable or believable; not a wished-for, but a firmly held view. An adequate view of life is one that provides a meaningful context for whatever experience is met in imagination or in fact; an adequate view of art is one that finds a meaningful and significant place for art in the view of life, that gives art, in other words, a centrally significant function.

The prelude is primarily a poem concerned with attaining a perspective from which a fuller, more adequate poetic vision can be achieved. The topographic figure is woefully inadequate as an expression of the spiritual and artistic problems that hinder attainment of the vision. In its broadest sense all poetry is concerned with perspective, with putting in order or relating various elements of experience so that one sees a whole where before there was none. But the perspective sought in these four poems, and in others like them, is a perspective of the poet and his art, of the poet creating his art. Attaining this perspective is necessary before the fullest scope of poetic creativity will be open to the poet, before he can write the "philosophical Poem" (Wordsworth) or a "myth to god" (Crane), before he can see with the godlike eyes promised Keats by Moneta, or before he can find with Blake a vision in which are

> All Human Forms identified even Tree Metal Earth & Stone. all
> Human Forms identified, living going forth & returning wearied
> Into the Planetary lives of Years Months Days & Hours reposing
> And then Awaking into his Bosom in the Life of Immortality.[18]

In the studies which follow, Blake is necessarily first, for chronological reasons, and because he so clearly illustrates the attempt to find and follow the canon that will lead to the creation of the new epic poem. Blake hoped, first in his epics and then in his later paintings, to give his nation an archetypal vision of its identity and future. In this attempt he has also given us the archetypal elements of the poet seeking a vision.

18. "Jerusalem," ch. 4, pl. 99:1–4, in *The Poetry and Prose of William Blake*, ed. David V. Erdman (Garden City, N.Y.: Doubleday & Co., 1968).

# Chapter 2

# The Holy Vessel

In faith, I said, every thing depends on the fact
of believing; what is believed is perfectly indifferent. Faith is a profound sense of security in regard
to both the present and the future. . . . Faith is
a holy vessel into which every one stands ready to
pour his feeling, his understanding, his imagination, as perfectly as he can.

— Goethe, *Dichtung und Wahrheit*

All symbolic art should arise out of a real belief,
and that it cannot do so in this age proves that
this age is a road and not a resting-place for the
imaginative arts.

— Yeats, *The Cutting of an Agate*

But the Eternal Promise
They wrote on all their tombs & pillars & on every Urn
These words If ye will believe your Brother shall rise again
In golden letters ornamented with sweet labours of Love
Waiting with Patience for the fulfilment of the Promise Divine

— Blake, *Four Zoas*, Night VII

Writing in the latter half of the eighteenth century on the nature of
religious belief, Hume suggested that the "first and most essential step
toward being a sound believing Christian" was a thoroughgoing scepticism that rejected the metaphysical problem of the existence of God.
Otherwise, the implications are, the result of needing proof of the existence will inevitably lead to disillusionment in the absence of any possible proof.

> So that, upon the whole, we may conclude, that the *Christian Religion* not only was at first attended with miracles, but even at this day cannot be believed by any reasonable person without one. Mere reason is insufficient to convince us of its veracity: And whoever is moved by *Faith* to assent to it, is conscious of a continued miracle in his own person, which subverts all the principles of his understanding, and gives him a determination to believe what is most contrary to custom and experience.[1]

Hume was never able to find this "miracle in his own person," so his statement was in the nature of a preference, a feeling that the open avowal of faith supported by its own intensity was somehow more honest than the attempt, through reason and logic, to give the pretensions of science to a natural religion. Thus he might well have approved the intellectual honesty of later thinkers such as Kierkegaard, with his "Christian Leap" into faith, or James with his "will to believe"— thinkers who, unlike Hume, could not be relieved of their insecurity by indefinitely suspending judgment about Christianity.

In most of his discussions of faith and belief, Hume had in mind a fairly clear object of faith: the Aristotelian God and the traditional Christian doctrine and practice. In addition to rejecting even the possibility of establishing a metaphysical basis for this object, Hume denied the existence of any moral grounds for making the necessary exertion of will in order to maintain the determination necessary to keep alive an unhypocritical belief. On objective moral grounds the Christian religion must be rejected, according to Hume, because its arbitrary system of duties weakens man's attachment to principles of justice and humanity. Hume dismissed all religious "principles," in fact, as "sick men's dreams." [2] Hence the irony in the statement, quoted from *An Enquiry*, that only a continued miracle could subvert understanding and experience to produce genuine faith. An announced faith, firmly held, could represent only hypocritical zeal or a kind of pathological deviation from experience.

It is clear that Hume's lifelong concern with the problem of religious belief was due to an absence of a ready willingness to believe. He was not only unwilling to admit a metaphysical basis for religion, he also emphatically denied this order of reality to science in his famous rejec-

1. David Hume, "An Enquiry Concerning Human Understanding," in *Essays*, 2 vols., ed. T. H. Green and T. H. Grose (London, 1875), 2:108.
2. Hume, "The Natural History of Religion," in *Essays*, 2:362.

tion of deterministic, causal relationships. As Alfred N. Whitehead points out, some form or variation of Hume's philosophy has generally been held since his time by men of science. "But scientific faith has risen [it did not have to leap] to the occasion, and has tacitly removed the philosophical mountain." [3] Scientists, including Hume, have thought it quite practical to act as if there were natural connections between events, even though there is no ultimate proof for such connections. In other words, they have demonstrated faith in causes and effects as part of an Order of Nature. "Science repudiates philosophy. . . . it has never cared to justify its faith or to explain its meanings; and has remained blandly indifferent to its refutation by Hume." [4] It may well be possible to trace the eighteenth-century scientist's faith in an Order of Nature back to the medieval belief in the all-encompassing providence of a rational God, as Compte suggests in his description of the shift from theological to metaphysical thought. What I want to emphasize, however, is the moral-aesthetic dimension of this shift in faith which qualitatively separated religion and science in the eighteenth century. [5]

The shift was made inevitable by the historical and scientific orientation of the psychology of myth, which Hume subscribed to, and which he outlined at length in the *Natural History of Religion*. Although science too is dependent on faith, for Hume it was infinitely superior to the ignorant, vulgar, and uncritical thought that preceded it. He saw religion as necessarily beginning in a "natural" polytheistic form that fulfilled a definite psychological need in primitive man. It began, not in reason, but in fear of the unknown which the primitive mind attempted to explain by personifying natural forces. Hume, like Compte and Frazer after him, viewed the personifications of myth from so firmly scientific a perspective that he attributed the same limited motives to both the myth makers and the scientists. [6] And if myth (or religion) is examined as a science according to scientific criteria, it inevitably becomes a pseudoscience, infinitely inferior to the real thing. The theory that myth was primarily limited to primitive man, a product of his weakness rather than of his strength, has lost many supporters in recent

3. Alfred N. Whitehead, *Science and the Modern World* (New York: Macmillan Co., 1964), p. 4.
4. Whitehead, *Science and the Modern World*, p. 17.
5. See Ernest Tuveson, *Millennium and Utopia* (Berkeley & Los Angeles: Univ. California Press, 1949) for a fuller discussion of this general topic.
6. Cf. J. G. Frazer, *The Golden Bough*, 3d ed., pt. 1, vol. 1, *The Magic Art and the Evolution of Kings* (New York: Macmillan Co., 1955), pp. 61ff., 220ff.

years. Debates about whether particular myths were historically astronomical, vegetative, or sexual in origin have continued, mainly by an-
thropologists.[7] Meanwhile, Blake's observations on the history of myth
are still valid and fully as cogent in the twentieth-century context as
they were in the eighteenth.

> The ancient Poets animated all sensible objects with Gods or
> Geniuses, calling them by the names and adorning them with
> the properties of woods, rivers, mountains, lakes, cities, nations,
> and whatever their enlarged & numerous senses could perceive.
> And particularly they studied the genius of each city & coun-
> try. placing it under its mental deity.
> Till a system was formed, which some took advantage of &
> enslav'd the vulgar by attempting to realize or abstract the men-
> tal deities from their objects; thus began Priesthood.
> Choosing forms of worship from poetic tales.
> And at length they pronouncd that the Gods had orderd such
> things.
> Thus men forgot that All deities reside in the human breast.[8]
>
> (The Marriage of Heaven and Hell, pl. 11)

Although seeking to discredit religion and, by extrapolation, myth in
general, Hume can be seen as occupying a key position in the substitution of one mythology (science) for another (religion). For many in the
eighteenth century, cultural expediencies were met by an alliance between science and religion in which science explained religion in its own
terms and reduced it to a tolerable deism. Such a substitution, however,
could not take place without threatening those who felt their own
values and immediate psychological experience challenged by the new
view. This was the century of Whitefield and Wesley and Fox as well
as of Hume, and it was the century that produced William Blake.

7. With the notable exception of those like Levi-Strauss (The Savage Mind [Univ.
Chicago Press, 1966]) who are seeking a more fundamental explanation of differ-
erent modes of consciousness.
8. The Poetry and Prose of William Blake, ed. David V. Erdman (Garden City,
N. Y.: Doubleday & Co., 1968). All subsequent quotations of Blake are from this
edition; citations refer when appropriate to title, chapter, plate, and lines. The
alternative standard edition of Blake's works is The Complete Writings of William
Blake, ed. Geoffrey L. Keynes, 2d ed. rev. (London: Nonesuch Library, 1966)
For the convenience of the reader, whenever lines quoted from the Erdman edition
have been presented differently by Keynes, I have included a reference (K) to his
edition.

I have presented a greatly oversimplified view of the intellectual environment Blake found toward the end of the century because he and many poets after him were so significantly poets of reaction. "I must Create a System or be enslav'd by another Mans / I will not Reason & Compare: my business is to Create" (*Jerusalem*, ch. 1, pl. 10:20–21). Not all felt the urge with Blake and Yeats to raise competing systems. Some were mainly repelled by a vision of science peeping and botanizing on a mother's grave; others, like Keats, were for the most part indifferent; still others—Clough, Tennyson, Arnold, to name a few—were perplexed as much as repelled by the implications of scientific discoveries. Only Shelley, and in a different way Coleridge, seem to have felt consistently the urge to domesticate science by using its results for poetic purposes.

For Hume moral and aesthetic grounds had been among the most important reasons for cultivating an already thriving scepticism. Blake can be seen as a turning point in a similar moral-aesthetic reaction, but one against religion and science both. He reacted against religion as shaped by the compulsive illusion that facts about God were qualitatively equal to other facts in nature and history—the very word "facts" is a word of science, a word that seems to insist on considerations of existence and proof as defined by the scientific method.

Blake reacted even more strongly against the materialism of the "new science," against "the fixed scientific cosmology which presupposes the ultimate fact of an irreducible brute matter, or material, spread throughout space in a flux of configurations. In itself such a material is senseless, valueless, purposeless. It just does what it does do, following a fixed routine imposed by external relations which do not spring from the nature of its being." [9] There were very real merits to this mechanical view of nature as evidenced by the spectacular scientific progress between the time of Newton's *Principia* (1687) and Lagrange's *Méchanique Analytique* (1787), but poets saw the deficiencies as well.

By now we are all familiar, through the revival of interest in Donne, with the resistance to the new science that appeared among poets of the early seventeenth century. This resistance was, again, a moral and aesthetic reaction to a new mode of vision, not a matter of intellectual sloth. The shift from perceptions of the cosmos and logos, to the study of the heat from dung (which was necessary, according to Bacon, for an understanding of the nature of heat), was seen as a shift from a more perfect, more moral world to a less perfect one. The shift was from

9. Whitehead, *Science and the Modern World*, p. 18.

an ideal reality, created in part through desire, to a physical reality. Milton, who was relatively well informed about the significance of the new science and its discoveries, nevertheless chose the Ptolemaic system as a matrix for the physical coordinates of his spiritual epic, and he included his reasons for doing so in the poem itself. When Raphael refuses to satisfy Adam's curiosity to know more about cosmology, he does so because Adam's ordeal will be spiritual, and his desire should be for a realization of himself as a potential bearer of the Word of God within himself. If what one sees in the world as reality depends on how one looks at it, then the spiritual state of the observer is the proper subject of poetic exploration. This is the point of Satan's sin, his self-inflicted punishment, and the promise of a "paradise within" for the descendants of Adam. For this ordeal, and this goal, concentration on the works of God in physical nature is irrelevant or secondary.

The reaction to science of a poet like Blake is analogous to the moral-aesthetic resistance to the new science of the seventeenth century. But the lines of difference are drawn this time in much clearer and more adequate terms. If faith in science demands faith in a vision of the world that is unacceptable morally, aesthetically, and psychologically, then one is predisposed to seek another mode of vision. "Predisposed," for the desire to believe in poetic myth as a mode of knowledge is different from a firmly held faith in an achieved poetic vision. And the desire for a sustaining myth has been a common theme in poetry since Blake, while the attempts to present fully achieved visions have been few and tentative.

Blake's theory of vision, and of the teleology of vision, is worth special notice at this point for several reasons. Historically, Blake represents the beginnings of a turn from the Christian epic (Dante, Spenser, Milton) to what may best be called the epic of consciousness. Blake is simultaneously poet and theorist of vision, examining in his poetry the basis of poetic or mythical knowledge of the world. His epics attempt to show man awakening to full realization of his creative personality in an apotheosis meant to work a similar change on the reader. For Blake the defects of the scientific or natural vision, as opposed to the imaginative vision, consisted mainly in its limitations and wrong emphases. He was never concerned with the truth or falsity of a particular theory of natural science, but with the erroneous mental attitude that saw the beauty of nature's mathematical order as the ultimate order and language of reality, which reduced the heavens to an elaborate geometrical machine.

> Others triangular right angled course maintain. others obtuse
> Acute Scalene, in simple paths. but others move
> In intricate ways biquadrate. Trapeziums Rhombs Rhomboids
> Paralellograms. triple & quadruple. polygonic
> In their amazing hard subdued course in the vast deep

> (*Four Zoas*, 2:32–36, MS p. 33) [10]

For Blake, such a vision of reality was the result of being in a fallen state, a state of somnolence or even death when compared with the more comprehensive vision of a higher state of consciousness or the "Divine Vision" of man's ultimate realization of spiritual potential. Given the alternative of seeing the sun as "a round disk of fire somewhat like a Guinea," he prefers (and therefore "sees") "an innumerable company of the Heavenly host crying 'Holy, Holy, Holy, is the Lord God Almighty.'" Descartes, in a comparable situation, made a "choice" which Blake would have utterly rejected. "I find present to me two completely diverse ideas of the Sun; the one in which the Sun appears to me as extremely small is, it would seem, derived from the senses . . . ; the other, in which the Sun is taken by me to be many times larger than the whole Earth, has been arrived at by way of astronomical reasonings. . . . Certainly, these two ideas of the Sun cannot both resemble the same Sun; and reason constrains me to believe that the one which seems to have emanated from it in a direct manner is the more unlike." [11]

In the historical part of Blake's theory of vision, the dominant mode of vision at the end of the eighteenth century was still Newton's "single vision." Thus in *Jerusalem*, Albion "the perturbed Man" is portrayed as a "sleeper of the land of shadows" who refuses the poet's "mild song" of love urging him to awake.

---

10. K2:282–286. The incomplete and problematic state of the *Four Zoas* MS makes interpretation and citation particularly difficult. Erdman edits the text by giving MS p. number and lines for each page. Blake at one point counted the lines for each Night, and Keynes has followed this method in his edition. As examination of the MS facsimile *Vala or The Four Zoas*, ed. G. E. Bentley, Jr. (Oxford: Clarendon Press, 1963) is advisable before reading any edition or interpretation of the poem.
11. Descartes, "Meditations on First Philosophy," in *Descartes: Philosophical Writings*, trans. N. K. Smith (New York: Random House, 1958), pp. 198–199.

Phantom of the over heated brain! shadow of immortality!
Seeking to keep my soul a victim to thy Love! which binds
Man the enemy of man into deceitful friendships:
Jerusalem is not! her daughters are indefinite:
By demonstration, man alone can live, and not by faith
My mountains are my own, and I will keep them to myself:
The Malvern and the Cheviot, the Wolds Plinlimmon & Snowdon
Are mine. here will I build my Laws of Moral Virtue!
Humanity shall be no more: but war & princedom & victory!

(*Jerusalem*, ch. 1, pl. 4:24–32)

Albion here represents the scientific preoccupation with a method, "demonstration." He illustrates the limited part of experience subject to logical and experimental treatment, and an attitude which Blake saw resulting in the denial of humanity and the acceptance of a "Moral Virtue" that dictated aggression as the norm of human action.

There are many passages in Blake's three epics that illustrate the historical, social, and spiritual consequences of the same error of vision. One of the most vivid is from the first chapter of *Jerusalem* in what Blake calls his "awful Vision."

I see the Four-fold Man. The Humanity in deadly sleep
And its fallen Emanation. The Spectre & its cruel Shadow.
I see the Past, Present & Future, existing all at once
Before me; O Divine Spirit sustain me on thy wings!
That I may awake Albion from his long & cold repose.
For Bacon & Newton sheathd in dismal steel, their terrors hang
Like iron scourges over Albion, Reasonings like vast Serpents
Infold around my limbs, bruising my minute articulations

I turn my eyes to the Schools & Universities of Europe
And there behold the Loom of Locke whose Woof rages dire
Washd by the Water-wheels of Newton. black the cloth
In heavy wreathes folds over every Nation; cruel Works
Of many Wheels I view, wheel without wheel, with cogs tyrannic
Moving by compulsion each other: not as those in Eden: which
Wheel within Wheel in freedom revolve in harmony & peace.

(*Jerusalem*, ch. 1, pl. 15:6–20)

"Eden" here is not a different place and not necessarily even a different time; but it is a different and higher order of reality from that woven on the "Loom of Locke." The creative power of the artist—his ability to make imaginative patterns—enables him to take an ordinary sensory experience and see in it a different reality, and in Blake we see *through* rather than *with* the corporeal eye.[12]

It is impossible to read far in Blake without finding an expression of the dependent relation between reality and the perceiver. In *Jerusalem* we find very precise formulations.

> If Perceptive Organs vary: Objects of Perception seem to vary:
> If the Perceptive Organs close: their Objects seem to close also.

> (Ch. 2, pl. 30:55–56; K34:55–56)

> Then those in Great Eternity who contemplate on Death
> Said thus. What seems to Be: Is: To those to whom
> It seems to Be, & is productive of the most dreadful
> Consequences to those to whom it seems to Be: even of
> Torments, Despair, Eternal Death

> (Ch. 2, pl. 32:50–55; K36:50–55) [13]

The most succinct formulation of all, as well as the most often repeated, is found both in *Jerusalem* and *The Four Zoas*: all who see become what they behold. Because man is not passive material to be formed by external forces but imaginatively forms his own world, there are different potential mental forms that sense experience may take. It is the creative artist's task to realize the whole range of potential forms and their proper hierarchical ordering. It is this sense that he must create a system. Furthermore, the artist realizes that man sees what he wants to see, that vision is dependent on desire which in turn is dependent on an awareness of alternatives. If Albion is able to see only the prostitute beauty of nature's mathematical order, this will be the only object of his desire, and his limited vision will dictate a narrow, tyrannical, ethical concept of "Moral Virtue."

There is a certain order, then, to a poet's career, following from the relation of reality to vision, which might be called the teleology of vision. First, the poet must discover within himself the potentialities of

12. See Peter Fisher, "The Critique of Vision," in *The Valley of Vision* (Univ. Toronto Press, 1961) for an excellent discussion of the contrast between Blake's and Locke's theories of perception.
13. Erdman uses the text of MS copies A, C, and F for Chapter 2 of *Jerusalem*, whereas Keynes uses D and E, in which the plates are arranged differently.

alternative visions, a discovery which obviously cannot be made fully until the poet has a vision of the highest order of reality the imagination can create.

> Even I already feel a World within
> Opening its gates & in it all the real substances
> Of which these in the outward World are shadows which pass away
>
> (*Four Zoas*, 7:7–9, MS p. 86; K364–366)

In its fullest realization this was for Blake the "Divine Vision," because the power of the creative imagination that produces it is godlike. For Blake this discovery entailed a mission, for it is accompanied by an acute sense of the restricted vision of other men—a sense gained by the poet from his own periods of non-vision—and is reinforced by a sense of the poet's isolation from those whose vision produces a reality different from his own.

> But Los beheld the Divine Vision among the flames of the Furnaces
> Therefore he lived & breathed in hope. but his tears fell incessant
> Because his Children were closd from him apart: & Enitharmon
> Dividing in fierce pain: also the Vision of God was closd in clouds
> Of Albions Spectres, that Los in despair oft sat, & often ponderd
> On Death Eternal in fierce shudders upon the mountains of Albion
> Walking: & in the vales in howlings fierce, then to his Anvils
> Turning, anew began his labours, tho in terrible pains!
>
> (*Jerusalem*, ch. 3, pl. 62:35–42)

Although Plato subjected Desire to Reason in *The Republic*, in a vision of the human soul quite contrary to Blake's, his analogy of restricted vision in the cave and the high sense of mission the Philosopher must have to return to the darkness is remarkably similar to Blake's sense of mission as a poet. For Blake all true poets were prophets, and Jerusalem could not be built until "all the Lord's People were Prophets." The poet must therefore create prophets, must "awake Albion from his long & cold repose" through his own powers of poetic prophecy. Like Milton, and in a deliberate echo of the opening of *Paradise Lost*, Blake begins *Jerusalem* with a statement of its theme—"Of the Sleep of Ulro! and of the passage through / Eternal Death! and of the awaking to Eternal Life"—and with an emphasis of his dedication.

> I rest not from my great task!
> To open the Eternal Worlds, to open the immortal Eyes
> Of Man inwards into the Worlds of Thought: into Eternity
> Ever expanding in the Bosom of God. the Human Imagination
>
> (Ch. 1, pl. 5:17–20)

The poet's goal and task was to awaken and develop a visionary imagination in his fellow man, and Blake attempted to fulfill this goal in *The Four Zoas* and *Milton* as well as in the final *Jerusalem*.

Any attempt to cope with Blake's preliminary treatment of his theme in *Vala or The Four Zoas* must begin with the manuscript itself, now available in G. E. Bentley's magnificent full-size facsimile edition. The manuscript resists anything like a final interpretation but is illuminating as a glimpse of a natural process or organism seeking its own form, anticipating Dylan Thomas's intuitively Blakean sense of form, which came more than a hundred years later. "Poetry finds its own form; form should never be superimposed; the structure should rise out of the words and the expression of them." [14] In Blake's case the illustrations too are seeking their form, rising restlessly and confusedly from the page, showing simultaneously alternative positions of limbs and a tentative exploration of space rather than the articulation of "minute particulars" so characteristic of Blake's finished work.

In spite of the structural and compositional confusions that surround *The Four Zoas*, its general sense of scale and purpose clearly reflect Blake's notions of a theodicy as the goal of the poetic imagination. The first six Nights are a recapitulation of the history of man's visionary fall and a survey of the fallen world. The end, especially in Night 9, reaches toward an apocalyptic recovery of the fallen visionary powers as they can be embodied in the spontaneous activity of Los, the figure of the imagination.

> And Los & Enitharmon builded Jersualem weeping
> Over the Sepulcher & over the Crucified body
> Which to their Phantom Eyes appear'd still in the Sepulcher
> But Jesus stood beside them in the Spirit Separating
> Their Spirit from their body. Terrified at Non Existence
> For such they deemd the death of the body. Los his vegetable hands

14. *Selected Letters of Dylan Thomas,* ed. Constantine Fitzgibbon (New York: New Directions Publishing Corp., 1966), p. 24.

Outstretched his right hand branching out in fibrous Strength
Siezd the Sun. His left hand like dark roots coverd the Moon
And tore them down cracking the heavens across from immense to immense
Then fell the fires of Eternity with loud & shrill
Sound of Loud Trumpet thundering along from heaven to heaven
A mighty sound articulate Awake ye dead & come
To judgment from the four winds Awake & Come away

(*Four Zoas*, 9:1–13, MS p. 117)

But there is no continuity between the dedicated labors of Los in Night
8 and the final realignment of the fallen powers in Night 9. As epic
statement, the conclusion of the poem lacks the didactic power of the
epic tradition and of Blake's own concept of the poet as prophet; it is
a "visionary" statement in something like the popular derogatory sense
of the word. The poet asserts the reality of the conclusion, but there is
no satisfactory connection established between its reality and the reality
we think we know. The only way to avoid this lack of connection was
to discover the beginning point of regeneration, to turn from a poetic
and inevitably abstracted prefiguration of the apocalypse to the self-
creation of the poet who could awaken man to a real and present
Jerusalem.

Bentley's argument that the last three Nights approached final shape
early, before the poetic transition to them was fully thought out, is
based largely on manuscript evidence but is compelling for other reasons
as well.[15] The visionary goal of this kind of poetic enterprise is intuited
fairly early. In Crane's case, the *Atlantis* part of *The Bridge* was actually
the first part of the poem completed, but that is only the extreme example of a general tendency. The poetic struggle in this context is twofold: to hold the visionary climax in mind, as a *terminus ad quem*; and
to sustain faith in the poetic imagination as a means of getting there
while the means themselves are explored and established. Before going
on to *Milton*, I propose to look briefly at some passages in *The Four
Zoas* that seem to anticipate the special emphasis of *Milton* on the
internal working of the poetic imagination, the struggle to discover the
Last Judgment working within rather than in idealized dramatic images.
Although *Milton* is a much fuller and clearer example of a poem that is
a "prelude to vision," some insight into *The Four Zoas* can serve as a
useful base from which to approach the later poem. In general, Blake's

15. *Vala or The Four Zoas*, ed. Bentley, p. 163.

changes in the overall conception of the work while writing it, and the structural inconsistencies that prevent it from being a whole in its own right, suggest a growing awareness of the necessity for a preparatory prelude—the same necessity that Wordsworth realized early in his career and that impelled Keats so suddenly and intuitively to turn from his *Hyperion* to *The Fall of Hyperion.*

The ambition evident in the proposed scope of *The Four Zoas* seems to indicate that, at least for a while, Blake thought the poem was potentially a fully comprehensive epic.[16] The primary emphasis of the poem as it now stands, however, is on the fall, which for Blake was man's loss of Divine Vision. Although an account of the fall and the fallen state of man is certainly a part of the didactic mission an epic poet in the tradition of Milton must take upon himself, such an account does not necessarily lead to an awakening or regeneration of fallen man. As Night 6 ends with Urizen returning into his "dire Web" of religion, the first six Nights of the extant poem have all been devoted to the fall and a survey of the fallen world. From a purely didactic viewpoint, part of the lesson has been thoroughly covered, but no adequate prophetic strain has emerged. The poem is projected as a vast dream of Albion, who remains off-stage and asleep throughout. The absence of a first-person Albion—or man—from the poem is not necessarily an obstacle to achieving a prophecy of his awakening, because he is present in a composite sense in the Zoas who are in every man. Yet so far there has been no clear indication of the means of regenerating the fallen man, nothing functionally equivalent to the Fate of Vergil, the Grace of Spenser and Dante, or the Divine Providence of Milton. Blake did not need to go outside the potential of man as he saw it, but he did need to find within man the source of a possible regenerative power.

Night 7 exists in two versions, neither of which Blake finally adopted. Whenever Night 7b was written, it is relatively weak and lacking in what we would expect to be the central focus on the means of regenerating fallen man. It ends with only a tiny mustard seed of hope offered by the mourning daughters of Beulah.

> But the Eternal Promise
> They wrote on all their tombs & pillars & on every Urn

16. The first title given the poem by Blake was *Vala, or the Death and Judgement of the Ancient Man a Dream of Nine Nights.* The poem as we now have it is revised from its earlier form and bears the full title, *The Four Zoas, the Torments of Love & Jealousy in the Death and Judgement of Albion the Ancient Man.*

These words If ye will believe your B[r]other shall rise again
In golden letters ornamented with sweet labours of Love
Waiting with Patience for the fulfilment of the Promise Divine

And all the Songs of Beulah sounded comfortable notes
Not suffring doubt to rise up from the Clouds of the Shadowy Female

(*Four Zoas*, 7b:4–14, MS p. 95; K291–301)

The only truly hopeful sign in Night 7b is the birth of Orc, an event cancelled by the death of Luvah. The "hope" is that Luvah will return six thousand years hence, but there is little or no suggestion of regeneration to accompany the return. The "Eternal Promise" is given in completely objectified and abstracted form, and does not actually inspire living hope in Tharmas. The slight progression in the earlier nights toward deeper internalization of the action in the poem disappears in this version of Night 7; and the expected beginning of a regeneration of the fourfold fallen man does not appear, either in external machinery or internal principle.

In Night 7a there is an alternative to the hope in a second coming of Luvah. It lies in the redefined powers of Los's vision and in an active image of Los laboring to build Jerusalem. In Night 7b the poet (Blake) offers an "Eternal Promise" and a hint of the power of the will ("If ye will believe"). In 7a the poet (Los) undergoes changes that will enable him to actively pursue his vision and, through achieving his vision, to bring about the awakening of Albion for the Last Judgment. The more personal note of 7a may suggest an inner crisis in Blake's life, one that reorganized his conceptions of the possibilities of the poetic imagination and of his role as didactic poet. I shall discuss the crisis, however, only as a shift in the function of Los within the poem and as the symbolic expression of the self-creating poet whose will to believe is replaced by an apocalypse-generating desire for vision. This shift in focus, barely discernible in the confusion of Night 7a, resulted finally in *Milton*, in which the symbolic union of Los and the Spectre of Urthona is fully realized in the union of Milton with Blake in the rebirth of Blake as epic poet.

Before Night 7 the completion of the fourfold fall came in Night 4 when Los took on the form of what he beheld in the fallen world around him. In a simple-minded way it would seem that regeneration of the fallen man might begin with Los in a reversal of the fall of the

Zoas. If Los could find some vision outside the fallen world, some glimpse of the Eternal World, his own form would change toward the new vision in a new becoming following the new beholding. However, as is so often the case, what seems a simple idea produces a complex poetic problem.

From Night 5 on, the reign of Urizen over fallen man is strengthened by the enmity between Los and Orc, which represents the conflict between fallen vision and physical life. Fallen vision binds and constricts life soon after childhood, just as Los chains Orc—because "Orc plotted his death"—when Orc is fourteen, the age at which awareness of death begins to restrict the imaginative freedom of youth. Blake describes death as a "plot" of physical life against the potentially eternal, but presently fallen, imaginative consciousness. Wordsworth was obsessed with the same problem, and his question to the child in the *Intimations Ode* might well be asked of Los.

> Why with such earnest pains dost thou provoke
> The years to bring the inevitable yoke,
> Thus blindly with thy blessedness at strife?

As long as Los is jealous of Orc and both hates and fears the potential Luvah in him, no regeneration can begin. Yet Luvah, desire-generating passion, is ever reborn in the form of Orc and thus continually presents the possibility of a change in the relationship between Los and Orc.

Night 7a begins with the Spectre of Urthona hiding beneath a rock and Tharmas fleeing "thro' the deeps of immensity." Urizen descends to the "Caves of Orc" where, while trying to cool the flames of Orc's burning desire, a deadly "root of Mystery" begins underneath his heel. In great pain Urizen is forced to escape momentarily from the "intricate labyrinths," at which point he addresses Orc. The intensified association of Orc with Prometheus here seems especially significant because we anticipate Orc's important role in the restoration of consciousness to fallen man. The role is Promethean only in its passive dimension, however, because of the shift to Los as active instrument of regeneration.

Orc answers Urizen, pointing to his frigid and constricted state, accusing him of existing (like Jupiter) "in horrible fear of the future." Urizen once more urges "Words of Wisdom" on Orc, this time suggesting it is Orc's moral duty to help him defeat Los, whom Urizen recognizes as the main danger to his reign. If the Spectre of Urthona can, with Orc's help, gain dominion over Los, he will be reduced to Urizen's will. Under the dominion of the Spectre of Urthona he would suffer a complete and enervating limitation of vision to the level of physical experience. He would lose his rage, as Orc is in danger of losing his. With difficulty Orc preserves his wrath, answering Urizen in a confrontation that produces a final recognition.

> Avaunt Cold hypocrite I am chaind or thou couldst not use me thus
> The Man shall rage bound with this Chain the worm in silence creep
> Thou wilt not cease from rage Grey Demon silence all thy storms
> Give me example of thy mildness King of furious hail storms
> Art thou the cold attractive power that holds me in this chain
> I well remember how I stole thy light & it became fire
> Consuming. Thou Knowst me now O Urizen Prince of Light
> And I know thee is this the triumph this the Godlike State
> That lies beyond the bounds of Science in the Grey obscure
>
>                          (7a:34–42, MS p. 80; K142–150)

The avowed hypocrisy of Urizen's moral duty reveals to Orc the true value of Urizen's sympathy for his fettered condition. Urizen is the real enemy acting through Los, who in his fallen state actually forged the chains. Orc metamorphoses into a flaming serpent, and Urizen lets him climb the tree of Mystery, thinking that thus "he might draw all human forms / Into submission to his will," yet not knowing the "dread result" to follow. At this point whether we take Orc's metamorphosis as a cruci-fixion—comparable to that of Luvah in 7b—or as a deliberate surrender to mystery, a cyclical process has once more entered to shape the poem and to qualify the prospects of any regeneration of fallen man.

Beginning with line 166, the action of Night 7a shifts to the brooding Los, "producing Eggs that hatching / Burst forth upon the winds above the tree of Mystery." Los laments his inability to enjoy the beauty of the lovely Enitharmon.

> All things beside the woful Los enjoy the delights of beauty
> Once how I sang & calld the beasts & birds to their delights
> Nor knew that I alone exempted from the joys of love
> Must war with secret monsters of the animating worlds
> O that I had not seen the day then should I be at rest
> Nor felt the stingings of desire nor longings after life
> For life is Sweet to Los the wretched to his winged woes
>
>                          (7a:4–10, MS p. 82; K198–204)

In these lines is a lyrically effective hint of the emotional atmosphere in which Blake was working, a glimpse of the isolation and frustration that Milton also found room for in his greatest work. I am not suggesting that we take every passage of heightened subjectivity in *The Four Zoas* as a direct intrusion of the author's voice, nor am I concerned with Blake's biography at all at this point. But it must be emphasized that Blake in Night 7a is leading up to a crisis in Los who, as the fallen consciousness trying to regain his powers of vision, is in part a poetic counterpart of the would-be visionary poet trying to pass the threshold from desire to achieved vision.

While Los laments, the Shadow of Enitharmon slips away to an encounter with the Spectre of Urthona. In their exchange a new version of the fall is outlined in which man's desire for Vala as temptress was the originating cause, their union having brought forth Urizen and clouded man's faculties so that he could no longer find his way "back into heaven." As if in confirmation of this reshaping of the fall, the embraces of the Spectre and the Shade of Enitharmon result in a new Vala.

> the immortal shadow shuddering
> Brought forth this wonder horrible a Cloud she grew & grew
> Till many of the dead burst forth from the bottoms of their tombs
> In male forms without female counterparts or Emanations
> Cruel and ravening with Enmity & Hatred & War
> In dreams of Ulro dark delusive drawn by the lovely shadow
>
> (7a:16–21, MS p. 85; K326–332)

Almost immediately after this prodigious birth the Spectre, without preface or explanation, enters the bosom of Los who "embrac'd the Spectre, first as a brother, / Then as another self." Just what the Spectre of Urthona is has not been fully indicated before this union; and it is mainly from the effects of this union, and from the nearly simultaneous union with the shadow of Enitharmon, that we may surmise what the Spectre represents. As the union takes place, the Spectre speaks in words which convey instant and "irresistible conviction" to Los.

> Thou never canst embrace sweet Enitharmon terrible Demon. Till
> Thou art united with thy Spectre Consummating by pains & labours
> That mortal body & by Self annihilation back returning
> To Life Eternal be assurd I am thy real Self

Tho thus divided from thee & the Slave of Every passion
Of thy fierce Soul Unbar the Gates of Memory look upon me
Not as another but as thy real Self I am thy Spectre
Tho horrible & Ghastly to thine Eyes tho buried beneath
The ruins of the Universe. hear what inspird I speak & be silent
Thou didst subdue me in old times by thy Immortal Strength
When I was a ravning hungring & thirsting cruel lust & murder
If we unite in one[,] another better world will be
Opend within your heart & loins & wondrous brain
Threefold as it was in Eternity & this the fourth Universe
Will be Renewd by the three & consummated in Mental fires
But if thou dost refuse Another body will be prepared
For me & thou annihilate evaporate & be no more
For thou art but a form & organ of life & of thyself
Art nothing being Created Continually by Mercy & Love divine

(7a:32–47, 1–3, MS pp. 85–86; K342–360)

Northrop Frye has developed a comprehensive explanation of the
Spectre in 7a which has the abstract perfection of a mathematical equation.[17] He sees the union of the Spectre and Los as "the tradition of
art and prophecy which reaches its culmination in Jesus." In his view
the other union produces a "fallen perspective of life [Vala], the combining of its two great categories time and space," which Blake saw
culminating in his own lifetime with eighteenth-century deism. The
Zoas, however, are the living forms of the individual man as well as of
the race; and a particular man is in his fallen state because of his own
contracted powers of vision as well as those of his historical era. To
achieve the full breadth of reference that Blake was continually seeking, the culmination of the visionary will in Los (representing the
prophetic tradition in art) should also express the culmination of an
individual visionary will. That is, the self-annihilation of Los should
also represent the genesis of a prophetic poet as well as the genesis of the
tradition. That this double reference was intended can be seen from the
effects of the union on Los. His vision is internalized and expanded.

17. Northrop Frye, *Fearful Symmetry* (Princeton Univ. Press, 1947), pp. 292–299
There are actually two equations given in the poem: Spectre + Enitharmon = Vala;
Spectre + Los = Prophet. The solution is a question of finding the unknown, the
Spectre, from the combinations given. Blake's later treatment of the necessity for
poetic control over time and space (*Milton*, bk. 1) is both clearer and more com-
prehensive.

>     Even I already feel a World within
> Opening its gates & in it all the real substances
> Of which these in the outward World are shadows which pass away

                    (7a:7–9, MS p. 86; K364–366)

This enlargement of vision takes Los to "the limit of translucence," which is the "Consummating by pains & labours / That mortal body" which the Spectre commanded. The "limit" is the fullest development of the fallen power of imagination in man, a limit which must be reached before man can change toward his Eternal Form. The dedication and labor of the visionary poet are represented in the actions of Los in the remainder of the poem.

To return now to the admonitions of the Spectre, the expression of the nature of the change Los undergoes, significant as it is, seems inadequately treated. We expect more insight into the change itself because of the inherent importance of the change as a turning point in the life of a poet and a potential turning point in the history of the race if the poet fulfills his prophetic mission. Instead, we have the bare framework of a rebirth in which the poet undergoes "Self-annihilation" in order to return to "Life Eternal." This is the symbolic death of the old self, necessary for the poetic rebirth of the new self as poet; and it is also destructive of the old, narrow concept of selfhood that was both consequence and cause of the fallen state. The former self is nothing "but a form & organ of life," in itself "nothing, being Created Continually by Mercy & Love divine." Thus the elements of the change are present, but in a way that gives us little more than the fact stated, as if in anticipation of the central problem of *Milton*. The question we have been trying to answer unsuccessfully from Night 7a will be answered in full in the later poem, in which the "Stern desire" here announced by Los is followed by the internal struggle to transcend Urizen as the limiting principle of vision within the poet.

>                     Stern desire
> I feel to fabricate embodied semblances in which the dead
> May live before us in our palaces & in our gardens of [pleasure *del.*] labour
> Which now opend within the Center we behold spread abroad
> To form a world of [life & love *del.*] Sacrifice of brothers & sons & daugh-
>     ters

To comfort Orc in his dire sufferings look my fires enlume afresh
Before my face ascending with delight as in ancient times

(7a:8–14, MS p. 90; K439–445)

I have indicated the deletions in brackets because they so nicely illustrate
the still-developing sense of mission that Blake was realizing in his own
life and transferring to the figure of Los. The changes from "pleasure"
to "labour" and from "life & love" to "Sacrifice" anticipate the changes
we shall trace in *Milton*. As an awakening or birth of the Los who
"enter'd the Door of Death for Albion's sake Inspired" in order to
awaken Albion, Night 7a is not a failure so much as a beginning attempt.[18] While still working on this section of the poem, Blake realized
that the coming-into-being of the poetic imagination of Los demanded
fuller poetic treatment; and it is to *Milton* that we must turn for a full
embodiment of the theme.

18. From the inscription on the archway through which Los passes, carrying his
light, in the frontispiece of *Jerusalem*.

# Chapter 3

# Blake: Mental Fight

What the mind at home, in the spacious circuits
of her musing, hath liberty to propose to herself,
though of highest hope and hardest attempting.

—Milton, *Reasons of Church Government*,
Preface to the Second Book

*The Four Zoas* remains basically a preliminary work, giving a background of the fallen condition of all men as the base from which the poet must break free into his self-creation and the condition from which, as prophetic and visionary poet, he can release man. Blake depicted the fall as a failure of perception, represented in its fullest scope by the sleeping Four-fold Man, who was as helpless and lacking in self-determination as a sleeper while dreaming. It is clear that Blake's conception of the poem changed radically during his composition of it, and that the focus of the change was the crucial Night 7. The change, as Night 7 indicates and *Milton* confirms, was toward an expansion of the scope to include more of the process of writing poetry and, even more important, more of the coming-to-being of the fully realized poetic imagination in an individual. *Milton* is thus a study of the birth of a poet and of the preparatory cracking of the "Mundane Shell" of the "Egg form'd World of Los," a shell which can be broken only by the strength of the inspired poetic imagination. Although the poem is in part a purification and re-creation of the poet Milton, it is more basically an expression of the self-creation of the poet, embodied in Blake, and can be read as a poetic expression of the act of will and imagination that constitutes self-election to the rank of poet.

It is part of the nature of a prelude poem that in it we can never fully separate the art from the biography. This is no reason for feeling uneasy in attempting to read *Milton*. In all art there are biographical facts that enable, or even compel, a writer to write a particular thing in a particular way at a particular time. Blake shared with Keats the knowledge that "A Man's life of any worth is a continued allegory," embodying a "mystery" which "very few can see." Without giving way to psychological determinism, it is quite possible to see that Blake's growing conception of the self-elective role of epic poet, and his realization of increasing powers of vision within himself, made the theme of *Milton* almost inevitable. In *Milton* Blake is attempting to separate from the psychological background of composition the universal process which he had in common with all poets and with all men of fully developed imaginative faculties. In this sense *Milton* is deliberately both archetypal and biographical.

In a letter written while he was still working on *The Four Zoas*, but had probably already started *Milton*, Blake gives us a hint of the enthusiasm and feeling of personal self-renewal he was experiencing during the period. "Excuse my enthusiasm or rather madness, for I am really drunk with intellectual vision whenever I take a pencil or graver into my hand, even as I used to be in my youth, and as I have not been for twenty dark, but very profitable years. . . . In short, I am now satisfied and proud of my work, which I have not been for the above long period.[1] The satisfaction and pride he refers to fit the full-scale conception of the mission of the epic poet that Blake had by now formed, and the feeling of renewal, presented in *Milton* in terms of the growth of the imagination, is here given direct emotional expression.

*Milton* has been discussed as a prelude before, primarily in the musical sense of the word, as a thematic statement and preparation for what is to follow, in which the poet is both finding and beginning to present his theme.[2] In this sense it definitely is a prelude, as the minor prophetic poems were preludes for *The Four Zoas*, announcing and exploring in preliminary form themes to be treated at length in the later poem. In discussing *Milton* as a prelude I shall emphasize a somewhat different and fuller sense of the word: a prelude not only introduces the subject

1. Blake to William Hayley (Oct. 23, 1804), in *The Poetry and Prose of William Blake*, ed. David V. Erdman (Garden City, N.Y.: Doubleday & Co., 1968), p. 703. Wordsworth returned to *The Prelude* in January of the same year and finished it in February, 1805.
2. See Harold Bloom, *Blake's Apocalypse* (Garden City, N.Y.: Doubleday & Co., 1963), p. 365; Peter Fisher, *The Valley of Vision* (Univ. Toronto Press, 1961), p. 246.

but also shows the poet's preparation for it. This is the sense in which
*The Prelude* is so fitting a title for the poem that Wordsworth himself
referred to simply as "the poem on the growth of my own mind," and
ended with the hope for "a work . . . surely yet to come." For a work
to be called a prelude, it must be an enabling work, one that must be
written before the poet can feel completely confident of his powers to
treat his theme. That Blake was, in fact, able to go on and complete
*Jerusalem* gives *Milton* a unique status among other poems that suggest
consideration as preludes. Wordsworth stretched his *Prelude* far beyond its originally conceived bounds, spending the greater part of a
lifetime writing and revising it. Keats's *Fall of Hyperion* remains a fragment, even though we can read it as a "finished fragment." Crane had
neither the desire nor the hope of producing another long poem after
the equivocations and ambiguities of *The Bridge*, which attempted to
be both prelude *and* vision.

To return to Blake's prelude to vision, why should he use Milton as a
persona to express his own poetic rebirth? To avoid for a moment the
theoretical reasons pertaining to Blake's idea of the continuity of vision,
the return to one's epic predecessors for inspiration and example is one
of the most consistent traditions of the epic genre. The image of Vergil
leading Dante by the hand through the *Inferno* was echoed centuries
later by the would-be Vergil of the new world, Hart Crane, turning to
his own inspiration and asking:

> —No, never to let go
> My hand
> in yours,
> Walt Whitman—
> so—[3]

Within the English tradition, Blake turned to Milton as Milton had
turned to Spenser, and Spenser to Chaucer. Milton recognized his in-
debtedness to Spenser, even though he avoided in *Paradise Lost* the
ancient British mythology that gives the *Faerie Queene* so rich an historical dimension. And Spenser saw himself as a "reborn" Chaucer,
carrying on the spirit and adding to the vision of his greatest predecessor
as Blake was to do with Milton.

3. Crane, "Cape Hatteras" part of *The Bridge* (New York: Liveright Publishing
Corp., 1966); reprinted by permission of the publisher. For Crane this was not so
much a sustaining inspiration as one he sought.

> Ne dare I like, but through infusion sweete
> Of thine owne spirit, which doth in me survive,
> I follow here the footing of thy feete,
> That with thy meaning so I may the rather meet.[4]

In addition to a feeling of tradition and his own belief in the continuity of vision, there was for Blake, as for Wordsworth, an identification on a more personal level with Milton. The figure of Milton in *Areopagitica*, a rebel and prophet trying to awaken a hostile and ignorant English nation to a sense of its own best interest and true potential, is close to Blake's image of himself and his mission as the true epic poet. In the advertisement of his Exhibit of Paintings in Fresco (1809), it is not surprising to find him turn to Milton for a motto which fits all of his later work equally well: " *'Fit audience find tho' few'* MILTON."

If for Blake the self-creation of the poet was also to be the rebirth or re-creation of a predecessor, this did not imply that the rebirth was a simple case of reincarnation. Blake's theory of the continuity and unity of all genuine prophetic visions also demanded the increased comprehensiveness of vision with an advance through time and the corollary that each return to genuine vision produces a poet one step closer to the full embodiment of the creative imagination. Although Wordsworth was not concerned so directly as Blake with the historical traditions of prophecy, his own ideas are close to the core of Blake's beliefs.

> I, who long
> Had harbour'd reverentially a thought
> That Poets, even as Prophets, each with each
> Connected in a mighty scheme of truth,
> Have each for his peculiar dower, a sense
> By which he is enabled to perceive
> Something unseen before.[5]

Blake's use of Milton, in addition to continuing the spirit of Milton's search for prophetic vision, also gave him a chance to "correct" Milton who died with his vision still clouded. Blake saw Milton as "a mixture of Christian vision with the sterility of moral virtue and rationalism," [6]

4. *Faerie Queene*, bk. 4, canto 2, st. 34, ed. R. E. Neil Dodge (Boston: Houghton Mifflin Co., 1908). The pun on metrical feet is not to be read into Blake's "Jerusalem" lyric in *Milton*.
5. *The Prelude* (1805), bk. 12:299–305, ed. E. de Selincourt, rev. Helen Darbishire (London & New York: Oxford Univ. Press, 1959).
6. Northrop Frye, *Fearful Symmetry* (Princeton Univ. Press, 1947), p. 337.

in need of a reorientation of his vision of the field of experience, especially with regard to time and sexual relationships.

Finally, the theoretical reason behind Blake's use of Milton, underlying the other reasons I have suggested, was the conviction that the continuity of vision must itself be a part of any significant vision. As the child is father of the man, separate and yet part of the same one man, so Milton and Blake are both parts of the same one man. As the "Four Faces of Humanity" in *Jerusalem*, so they walk "To & fro in Eternity as One Man, reflecting each in each & clearly seen / And seeing, according to fitness & order" (ch. 4, pl. 98:39–40). Insofar as the vision they behold is the same eternal vision of the eternal One Man, they become each other as they become what they behold, partaking of the unity of the Divine Vision.

Within the system of vision that Blake had to evolve to avoid slavery to the "Loom of Locke," *Milton* functions as epistemology. Locke had posited and described the essentially passive development of natural consciousness from a *tabla rasa* in a theory or system that made knowledge "nothing but *the perception of the connection of and agreement, or disagreement and repugnancy, of any of our ideas.*" [7] In *Milton* we are shown the development of a higher state of consciousness made possible by an active imagination that uses, but is not controlled by, the senses. The slavery to Locke, which reduced man's potential to mere survival as an organism through a finite term, is countered by an example of the birth of the transforming power of active perception.

The poem begins almost immediately with a "Bard's prophetic song." All we know about the song, except for the fourteen pages of its text, is the remarkable effect it has on Milton, who hears it in heaven. The effect on Milton is *the* effect desired by a prophetic visionary: an awakening. In content, the Bard's song is a recasting of the fall, returning again to the original problem of the disruption in the harmony of man's faculties which produces a loss of vision. The parallels connecting Palamabron and Satan with Blake and Hayley are in part a return to the ethical and psychological implications of friendship that Spenser was concerned with in Book IV of *The Faerie Queen*.[8] But when Blake's "friends profest are changed to foemen fell" there is a different emphasis

7. Locke, *Essay Concerning Human Understanding*, 2d ed., 2 vols. (New York: Dover Press, 1959), bk. 4:172.
8. The biographical implications have been pursued in Frye, *Fearful Symmetry*, pp. 325–332; and Bloom, *Blake's Apocalypse*, pp. 314–322.

suggesting the internal harmony of the soul's faculties and the social
balance between the Elect, Redeemed, and Reprobates as well as the
ethical norms of interpersonal relationships. For my purposes, however,
the actual content of the Bard's song is not so significant as the implications that follow from the idea of the song as a brief example of genuine
poetic inspiration, illustrating the purpose and the desired effects of
the true poetic mission. As an example of inspired vision, the Bard's
song is both the beginning and the end of the whole poem. It serves to
awaken Milton—the first step in awakening the sleeping man—and it is
an example of what the poet (Milton-Blake-Los) at the end of the
poem is prepared to do.

The song is introduced initially as "what mov'd Milton," and the
structure of the poem is designed to emphasize the effects on Milton—
and Blake as well—of a glimpse of pure poetic inspiration. The song
reveals two aspects that, insofar as they are separable at all, may be
called function and content. A complete study of the content *per se*
would involve recourse to the biographical facts mentioned above and a
reexploration of the presentation of the fall in *The Four Zoas*. Without
so thorough an analysis of the song, however, it is still possible to see
the point of the song that suggests to Milton the need for returning to
mortality. The conclusion that emerges from the Palamabron-Satan
encounter is that "Satan is Urizen." From this Milton realizes that the
temptations overcome in *Comus, Paradise Lost,* and *Samson Agonistes*
were only partial victories, that his Urizenic Selfhood was not a triumph
but a perversion. "I in my Selfhood am that Satan: I am that Evil One!"

The consequences of Milton's failure to achieve this recognition during his own lifetime were twofold for Blake. Historically, Milton must
bear a great deal of responsibility for the development of European history. As the last great prophetic poet of England, what he said and,
even more, what he left unsaid, profoundly affected the development of
the national consciousness. Within the poem, Milton's incomplete development as a poet has left him unsatisfied with his vision. He has become what his distorted powers of vision caused him to see as desirable,
and he is "Unhappy tho' in heav'n."

The distinction between the content and function of the song is primarily one of asking different questions about the song, rather than iso-
lating different elements. Like the play-within-a-play, the implications
of form raised by a poet speaking a poem within a poem suggest the
most basic problems of art and imagination. But the implications reveal

themselves only if we ask the right questions: Who is speaking the song? Who is the audience? What is the effect on the audience, and especially on Milton? How is the effect achieved? A partial answer to the last question is indicated in the content itself, in Milton's recognition of the truth and relevance of the Bard's message to his own life. For the full answer we must explore the other questions and establish, as well as we can, the "mode of existence" of the Bard's song.

The poet speaking, the Bard, is quite clearly meant to be inspiration personified, for his song is a direct reply to Blake's invocation of his own source of inspiration, the Daughters of Beulah. Like the Bard in *Songs of Innocence and Experience*, he exists only as a voice.

> Hear the voice of the Bard!
> Who Present, Past, & Future, sees;
> Whose ears have heard
> The Holy Word
> That walk'd among the ancient trees.

> (Introduction: 1–5)

At the end, when asked "Whence hadst thou this terrible Song?" one answer alone is sufficient. "I am Inspired!" The mysterious Bard has no existence outside his song, for in the uproar in heaven following his claim of inspiration he disappears in terror, taking refuge in Milton's bosom. Thus the inspiration enters Milton, is his inspiration, and in a definite sense never really existed outside Milton at all. The beginning of Milton's awakening is his own poetic inspiration, and Blake is suggesting, in the broader implications of the poem, that his and any true poet's mission must begin with a direct gift of inspiration. Inspiration in poetry, like coincidence in the novel, is something that must always leave the critic feeling a bit uneasy. But this is, finally, one of the most significant aspects of the Bard's song. Yet isolated inspiration is never enough in itself, as Blake had already revealed in *The Four Zoas*. The rest of *Milton* explores what is needed in addition to inspiration for the poet to reach a point of complete readiness for his mission: the overcoming of Selfhood and the Female Will, and the proper ordering of the four Zoas within the perceiving mind.

This view of the Bard's song, as an exemplification of poetic inspiration, gives us one mode for its existence within the poem *Milton*. Yet if we step back and attempt to gain a perspective which includes Blake writing the Bard's song, we multiply the complexities. As a review of the fall, as an example of inspiration, and of his own inspiration for *Milton*, the song is fairly easy to follow. But Blake actually wrote it, and even though it is a pure example of poetic inspiration and vision, it is also his vision. The situation is one in which a poet, in a poem, tries to create the relationship that ideally should exist between a poem and the reader. Wordsworth was doing much the same thing, only on a more explicit level, with the Wanderer's tale in the first book of *The Excursion*. The didactic reasons for this kind of example are fairly obvious, for the awakening of Milton is the kind of awakening Blake ultimately hoped to achieve for all his readers and for the whole nation. Crane, in writing about one of his own poems, indicated some of the complexities that can accompany this kind of structure. "Imagine the poet, say, on a platform speaking it. The audience is one half of Humanity, Man (in the sense of Blake) and the poet the other. ALSO, the poet sees himself in the audience as in a mirror. ALSO, the audience sees itself, in part, in the poet. . . . In another sense, the poet is *talking to himself* all the way through the poem." [9] In *Milton* the situation is, if anything, more complex, for we must consider it as a poem about Blake's preparation for his poetic mission.

The poet (Milton in the poem, and Blake writing it) must have the suggestion of a vision before he can complete the internal process of self-dedication to poetry. The contradiction of the poet having to achieve a vision before he can establish his own qualifications for poetic vision is only a verbal one. Crane was attempting to follow Blake's steps, though in a completely different structural pattern, when he put the *Atlantis* part of *The Bridge* at the end. *Atlantis* represents Crane's initial inspiration, his equivalent of the Bard's song, and was in fact the first part of *The Bridge* that he wrote. In *The Bridge* Crane is attempting to achieve a development of the poetic consciousness that can hold *Atlantis* as a final vision; and in this sense I have spoken of the Bard's song as the end or goal of *Milton*, an example of poetic vision as well as the essential stimulus for attaining a poetic vision. In this view the inspiration, or vision, is a constant, the change being within the poet and affecting his receptivity to the inspiration and to his vision. It is for this reason the Bard's song is inevitably biographical, as is Crane's

9. Crane to Alan Tate (March 1, 1924), in *The Letters of Hart Crane*, ed. Brom Weber (New York: Hermitage House, 1952), p. 176.

*Bridge*. It is a vision of Blake's own struggle with the Urizenic Satan within himself which is objectified in Hayley.

The shift in perspective which I have indicated, from inspiration in the Bard's song to inspiration in Milton and, finally, inspiration in Blake, is the shift demanded again and again by a careful reading of the poem as a prelude. The Bard's song opens into a cosmic and prophetic perspective of history, but it returns to the bosom of Milton and the poetic imagination of Blake. Similarly, the end of the first book opens into a perspective of the world as the realm of the Sons of Los, only to return to a single instant of poetic inspiration.

> For in this Period the Poets Work is Done: and all the Great
> Events of Time start forth & are concievd in such a Period
> Within a Moment: a Pulsation of the Artery.
>
> (Bk. 1, pl. 29:1–3)

The second book is still about the same instant of time in which Milton (in Blake) is "a State about to be Created," just as the initial struggle between Milton and Urizen continues in the second book because there has been no change in time. The whole action of the poem, at the end, can be seen to have been a series of perspectives achieved during the instant Blake lay on the path in Felpham's Vale, even though he rises from that moment of inspiration reborn as a poet.

> Terror struck in the Vale I stood at that immortal sound
> My bones trembled. I fell outstretchd upon the path
> A moment, & my Soul returned into its mortal state
> To Resurrection & Judgment in the Vegetable Body
> And my sweet Shadow of Delight stood trembling by my side
>
> (Bk. 2, pl. 42:24–28)

Although the whole poem is about a single instant of time, it contains an ordered and rhythmical series of perspectives, and there are a number of distinct steps in the regeneration of Milton (and Blake) which may be followed in a determined order. Immediately after his inspired recognition that in his Selfhood he is Satan, the Evil One, Milton enters a dream state in which "His real and immortal Self" sees his other self "entering his Shadow." At this point his consciousness is limited so that "to himself he seem'd a wanderer lost in dreary night."

The change in consciousness is followed by a disquisition on the vortical nature of infinity which establishes a perspective of the earth as "A vortex not yet pass'd by the traveller thro' Eternity." These changes are essential for Milton to return from eternity to the world of time and space, and they are also necessary for the complete union with Blake.

As the Bard entered the bosom of Milton, so Milton enters the tarsus of Blake's left foot. From this point on the poem's action must be read as indicative of changes taking place within Blake. At those places in the poem where the perspective opens out Blake is not changing the subject, but showing historical events as parallels to and potential effects of changes in the microcosm of his imagination. The unity of time is not yet completely established, but a later echo ("But Milton entering my Foot") indicates that the action between plates 15 and 21 is simultaneous with Milton's entering Blake. With the union of Milton and Blake established, Blake announces the problem of the rest of the poem: "To Annihilate the Self-hood of Deceit & / False Forgiveness" (bk. 1, pl. 16). In connection with the full-page illustration of plate 16 this line serves as a motto for the rest of the poem.

Milton journeys above the Mundane shell (but within Blake) and is viewed at a distance by the Six-fold Female, historically represented by Milton's wives and daughters. The significance of his journey is not fully clear to Los, Enitharmon, Urizen, Tharmas, and Orc as they, in turn, see him making his way. Los, not recognizing that Milton is now inspired and not to be completely identified with Satan, attempts to stop him, but Milton presses on directly to his first goal, Urizen. The struggle that follows is inevitable after Milton's recognition that himself is Satan. The dominion of Urizen must be overthrown by the imaginative powers of the newly aware Milton before the harmony of the Four Zoas can be reestablished. Like all of Blake's symbols, the Zoas have both an internal, individual existence and an external, racial-historical existence. The Urizen in Milton-Blake must be humanized before Blake can be fully human and fully a poet. The historical struggle between the prophetic poet and the forces of Urizen in society must follow the internal struggle.

> Urizen rose,
> And met him on the shores of Arnon; & by the streams of the brooks
>
> Silent they met, and silent strove among the streams, of Arnon
> Even to Mahanaim, when with cold hand Urizen stoop'd down

And took up water from the river Jordan: pouring on
To Miltons brain the icy fluid from his broad cold palm.
But Milton took of the red clay of Succoth, moulding it with care
Between his palms; and filling up the furrows of many years
Beginning at the feet of Urizen, and on the bones
Creating new flesh on the Demon cold, and building him,
As with new clay a Human form in the Valley of Beth Peor.

(Bk. 1, pl. 19:4–14)

As Blake, at a point when he felt ready to dedicate himself fully to his epic, met the Urizenic force of Hayley and society, so Milton encounters Urizen directly after his inspiration. Blake realized that the real struggle was not with Hayley, but with himself, and the encounter between Milton and Urizen is another version of that encounter. Urizen attacks the poetic inspiration of Milton with his characteristic frigid sterility and attempts to constrict his consciousness with the baptism of "icy fluid from his broad cold palm." But the inspired Milton humanizes the cold Urizen with red clay, and instead of baptizing Milton, Urizen himself is reborn in the burial place of Moses, who represents the worst aspects of the Urizenic moral virtue. The struggle continues through the poem, but not without leaving Milton free to continue toward the realm of Los and Enitharmon. The Female Will tries "to entice Milton across the river" where he can be "King / Of Canaan and reign in Hazor where the Twelve Tribes meet." But Milton-Blake is now able to resist the temptation of founding a new church, a temptation Blake thought the historical Milton had not resisted strongly enough.

After this extreme close-up of internal perspective, we are again forced back to a larger view of the internal struggle in preparation for a shift from Urizen, whom Milton had to humanize, to Los, who must be awakened. While Milton shapes Urizen with clay, his mortal part is frozen in the rock of Horeb, and his redeemed portion forms the humanizing clay; within the redeemed portion, his "real human" walks above. It is impossible to visualize the total activity here, as it was impossible not to visualize the image of physical combat with Urizen; but it can be seen as a concerted effort leading toward "the Four-fold Man in starry numbers fitly order'd." Albion the sleeping Four-fold Man stirs in his sleep as a tentative indication of Milton's success. "Now Albions sleeping Humanity began to turn upon his Couch; / Feeling

the electric flame of Milton's awful precipitate descent" (bk. 1, pl.
20:25–26). There is no awakening yet, but Albion's stirring emphasizes
the nature of Milton's activity. Blake goes on to reemphasize the internal nature of the struggle between Milton and Urizen.

> Seek not thy heavenly father then beyond the skies:
> There Chaos dwells & ancient Night & Og & Anak old:
> For every human heart has gates of brass & bars of adamant,
> Which few dare unbar because dread Og & Anak guard the gates
> Terrific! and each mortal brain is walld and moated round
> Within: and Og & Anak watch here; here is the Seat
> Of Satan in its Webs; for in brain and heart and loins
> Gates open behind Satans Seat to the City of Golgonooza
> Which is the spiritual fourfold London, in the loins of Albion.
>
> > (Bk. 1, pl. 20:32–40)

The gates to Golgonooza, the City of Los, are figuratively behind
Satan's seat, which is why Milton had first to encounter Urizen before
entering the realm of Los.

Los had continued to oppose Milton's journey, still mistaking his
identity. As long as Los in him remained unreceptive to the inspired
Milton, Blake could not be significantly affected by the union with
Milton, even though he had begun the process of humanizing the
Urizenic Zoa within himself. But when Los in desperation recalls "an
old prophecy in Eden recorded" that Milton will free Orc, Blake is
ready to consummate the union with Milton.

> But Milton entering my Foot; I saw in the nether
> Regions of the Imagination; also all men on Earth,
> And all in Heaven, saw in the nether regions of the Imagination
> In Ulro beneath Beulah, the vast breach of Miltons descent.
> But I knew not that it was Milton, for man cannot know
> What passes in his members till periods of Space & Time
> Reveal the secrets of Eternity: for more extensive
> Than any other earthly things, are Mans earthly lineaments.
>
> And all this Vegetable World appeard on my left Foot,
> As a bright sandal formd immortal of precious stones & gold:
> I stooped down & bound it on to walk forward thro' Eternity.
>
> > (Bk. 1, pl. 21:4–14)

Even though he still doesn't know that it is Milton who has entered his foot, or the nature of the changes the entry has stimulated, the effects of Milton's journey are apparent in Blake's increased powers of vision. The image of the sandal in the vision suggests the real beauty of the Vegetable World when properly perceived by the imagination; the binding on of the sandal suggests both control and acceptance of that world even though the poet's journey is one through eternity.

At this point we are given a glimpse of Ololon's resolution to emulate Milton by leaving Eden for death in Ulro among the shadows. The consequences of this resolution do not appear until the second book, for Milton has not yet put off his Selfhood, which he must do before Ololon can purge herself of the Female Will and unite with him. Inclusion of the passage here emphasizes the simultaneity of all the action and also maintains anticipation for the final step of the regeneration. The actual encounter between Milton and Ololon must wait, because the simultaneity is like that of a logical proposition in which all the steps exist at once yet have a definite order of priority.

After Los recollects the old prophecy and Blake binds on the sandal gaining the increased powers of vision that have followed from the initial poetic inspiration, the Los within Blake is fully awakened, and we are given an image of the union between Milton-Blake and Los.

> While Los heard indistinct in fear, what time I bound my sandals
> On; to walk forward thro' Eternity, Los descended to me:
> And Los behind me stood; a terrible flaming Sun: just close
> Behind my back; I turned round in terror, and behold.
> Los stood in that fierce glowing fire; & he also stoop'd down
> And bound my sandals on in Udan-Adan; trembling I stood
> Exceedingly with fear & terror, standing in the Vale
> Of Lambeth: but he kissed me, and wishd me health.
> And I became One Man with him arising in my strength:
> Twas too late now to recede. Los had enterd into my soul:
> His terrors now posses'd me whole! I arose in fury & strength.

> (Bk. 1, pl. 22:4–14)

The union with Los firmly establishes in Blake the power of poetic imagination and the consequent control over time and space. The perspective shifts, opening out into an historical view of the eighteenth century, with Rintrah and Palamabron asserting the miracles of Whitefield and Wesley and calling on Albion to awaken instantly. But Los calls for patience with a double warning. They have appealed to him as "strong and mighty to destroy," not realizing that "we live not by wrath, by mercy alone we live." Like Calvin and Luther, their fury is premature, their perspective wrong. The return of Milton signals the approach of the Last Vintage, but the final harvest is not yet here. The emphasis in this section is on Los as the historical or temporal faculty of perception, for the essential accomplishment of the prophetic poet is a knowledge of his time in relation to the past and future. "I the Fourth Zoa am also set / The Watchman of Eternity, the Three are not! & I am preserved" (bk. 1, pl. 24:8–9). As "Watchman of Eternity" Los must recognize the birth of a true prophetic poet, and his recognition of Blake as the true poet—the signal for the Last Vintage—is stressed at several points. It is also clear that the rebirth of Blake as poet represents Los's own return from a fallen state.[10]

> I am that Shadowy Prophet who Six Thousand Years ago
> Fell from my station in the Eternal bosom. Six Thousand Years
> Are finishd. I return! both Time & Space obey my will.
>
> (Bk. 1, pl. 22:15–17)

Los's regeneration is followed by Blake's description of the realm of Bowlahoola, "the Stomach in every individual man," as the site for the anvils and furnaces of Los. It seems obvious that the physiological functions of respiration, circulation, and digestion are brought in at this point as the physical or Vegetable measure of time over which Los exercises imaginative control.

> Los is by mortals nam'd Time Enitharmon is nam'd Space
> But they depict him bald & aged who is in eternal youth
> All powerful and his locks flourish like the brows of morning
> He is the Spirit of Prophecy the ever apparent Elias
> Time is the mercy of Eternity; without Times swiftness
> Which is the swiftest of all things: all were eternal torment:
> All the Gods of the Kingdoms of Earth labour in Los's Halls.

10. The regeneration of Los in bk. 1, in connection with Milton's abandonment of Selfhood in bk. 2, means that when Los becomes prophet, loss becomes profit. There is no obvious evidence of an intended pun in the text, but the movement of the poem strongly suggests it.

> Every one is a fallen Son of the Spirit of Prophecy
> He is the Fourth Zoa, that stood arou[n]d the Throne Divine.
>
> (Bk. 1, pl. 24:68–76)

The awakening of Los within Blake has been established, and the nature of Los thoroughly explored. Therefore, what follows this last exposition by Blake as narrator of the poem is a great opening-out of perspective, from the individual changes necessary for Blake to achieve imaginative control over time to an example of visionary perception. The whole world is seen as the realm of the Sons of Los who are trampling out the Last Vintage, preparing for the Apocalypse. The vision ranges from "War on Earth" to the minutest forms of life "Visible or invisible to the slothful vegetating Man."

The poem then returns to the problem of time and space and to a final emphasis, in the magnificent image of the "red Globule of Man's blood," on the single moment of illumination within the perceiving mind of the poet, the single moment in which the vision of eternity is achieved.

> For in this Period the Poets Work is Done: and all the Great
> Events of Time start forth & are conceived in such a Period
> Within a Moment: a Pulsation of the Artery.
>
> (Bk. 1, pl. 29:1–3)

The pulsation of the artery is the temporal measure of the vision, and the globule of blood is the spatial measure or image, opening inward into a visionary infinity which it warms and illuminates like a sun.

> As to that false appearance which appears to the reasoner,
> As of a Globe rolling thro Voidness, it is a delusion of Ulro
> The Microscope knows not of this nor the Telescope. they alter
> The ratio of the Spectators Organs but leave Objects untouchd
> For every Space larger than a red Globule of Mans blood.
> Is visionary: and is created by the Hammer of Los
> And every Space smaller than a Globule of Mans blood. opens
> Into Eternity of which this vegetable Earth is but a shadow:
> The red Globule is the unwearied Sun by Los created
> To measure Time and Space to mortal Men. every morning.
>
> (Bk. 1, pl. 29:15–24)

An understanding both of how the awakening of Los within the human mind has been achieved through poetic inspiration, and how the imagination can transcend the temporal and spatial limitations of the senses, have been fully presented as the first steps essential to the creation of a visionary poet.

Book 1 is concerned primarily with the problems of inspiration and perception which the poet must solve within himself before he can begin to fulfill the mission Blake saw as the role of the fully developed poet. Whereas Book 1 is concerned with the theoretical aspects of inspiration and perception, Book 2 turns to the spiritual problem of dedication, which Blake sees in terms of a need to purge the Selfhood and the Female Will. The theme is clearly announced in Book 1, and it must be seen as developing in simultaneous events during the "single moment" of the poem. The events of Book 1 are presented first because of the priority of inspiration as generating cause, not because of a chronology.

Book 2 begins with a vision of Beulah, a region or state of "pleasant Shadow" that offers a temporary relaxation from the efforts of creativity. This is the state that was to be so great a temptation for Keats, even though he recognized its incompleteness. For Blake it was never more than a "Temporal Habitation," even here, where he gives his most complete presentation of the nature of the region.[11]

Ololon descends into Beulah to consummate the preparation of Book 1. All Beulah weeps at Ololon's great sacrifice, and Satan and Rahab, who "know not of Regeneration, but only of Generation," wail in their inability to understand the meaning of her descent. After the "Vision of the lamentations of Beulah over Ololon," the focus shifts to Milton, who is now ready for regeneration, receiving instructions from Hillel and the Seven Angels of the Presence. The condition of Milton, as a "State about to be created," establishes anticipation of the following movement of the poem, as the isolated motto on plate 16 in Book 1 announced and directed what was to follow.

The conditions of change preceding knowledge of the world are, as before, internal exploration and self-understanding.

> Judge then of thy Own Self: thy Eternal Lineaments explore
> What is Eternal & what Changeable? & what Annihilable!

11. See Northrop Frye, "Notes for a Commentary on *Milton*," *The Divine Vision*, ed. V. de Sola Pinto (London: V. Gollancz, 1957).

> The Imagination is not a State: it is the Human Existence itself
> Affection or Love becomes a State, when divided from Imagination
> The Memory is a State always, & the Reason is a State
> Created to be Annihilated & a new Ratio Created
> Whatever can be Created can be Annihilated Forms cannot
> The Oak is cut down by the Ax, the Lamb falls by the Knife
> But their Forms Eternal Exist, For-ever. Amen Halle[l]ujah
>
> (Bk. 2, pl. 32:30–38)

The Divine Voice speaking in the Songs of Beulah analyzes Milton's regeneration into its essential steps, giving the necessary order of priority for what are nevertheless simultaneous elements.

> When the Sixfold Female percieves that Milton annihilates
> Himself: that seeing all his loves by her cut off: he leaves
> Her also: intirely abstracting himself from Female loves
> She shall relent in fear of death: She shall begin to give
> Her maidens to her husband: delighting in his delight
> And then & then alone begins the happy Female joy
> As it is done in Beulah, & thou O Virgin Babylon Mother of
>     Whoredoms
> Shalt bring Jerusalem in thine arms in the night watches; and
> No longer turning her a wandering Harlot in the streets
> Shalt give her into the arms of God your Lord & Husband.
>
> (Bk. 2, pl. 33:14–23)

The destruction of Selfhood will end the fatal and perverse crippling of perspective by the Female Will and will restore the "Female joy" of giving and completing to the natural relationship.

As Ololon descends through Beulah to Los and Enitharmon, following Milton's descent, internal implications of the action are explicitly emphasized. "And he whose Gates are opend in those Regions of his Body / Can from those Gates view all these wondrous Imaginations" (bk. 2, pl. 34:17–18). The temporal dimension of the regeneration is emphasized in accordance with the time theory of Book 1.

> There is a Moment in each Day that Satan cannot find
> Nor can his Watch Fiends find it, but the Industrious find
> This moment & it multiply. & when it once is found
> It renovates every Moment of the Day if rightly placed[.]

In this Moment Ololon descended to Los & Enitharmon
Unseen beyond the Mundane Shell Southward in Miltons track

(Bk. 2, pl. 35:42–47)

Finally, with the appearance of Ololon in Blake's garden—Blake is now
a union of Milton, Los, and Blake—the perspective on a single instant
in the mind of Blake is completely reestablished. As we would expect
from the prior rhythm of change in perspective throughout the poem,
the poem expands to include the historical and macrocosmic implications of the internal action.[12] It then returns to the confrontation between Milton and Satan in the mind of Blake, another aspect of the
struggle between Milton and Urizen introduced in Book 1.

> Satan! my Spectre! I know my power thee to annihilate
> And be a greater in thy place, & be thy Tabernacle
> A covering for thee to do thy will, till one greater comes
> And smites me as I smote thee & becomes my covering.
> Such are the Laws of thy false Heavns! but Laws of Eternity
> Are not such: know thou: I come to Self Annihilation
> Such are the Laws of Eternity that each shall mutually
> Annihilate himself for others good, as I for thee[.]
> Thy purpose & the purpose of thy Priests & of thy Churches
> Is to impress on men the fear of death; to teach
> Trembling & fear, terror, constriction; abject selfishness
> Mine is to teach Men to despise death & to go on
> In fearless majesty annihilating Self, laughing to scorn
> Thy Laws & terrors, shaking down thy Synagogues as webs
> I come to discover before Heavn & Hell the Self righteousness
> In all its Hypocritic turpitude, opening to every eye
> These wonders of Satans holiness shewing to the Earth
> The Idol Virtues of the Natural Heart, & Satans Seat
> Explore in all its Selfish Natural Virtue & put off
> In Self annihilation all that is not of God alone:
> To put off Self & all I have ever & ever Amen

(Bk. 2, pl. 38:29–49)

Blake saw the flaws in the vision of Milton as resulting from the pas-
sions and errors in his Selfhood, as all visions must be influenced by
the errors of perception in the individual poet and his age. The only

12. See bk. 2, pl. 37:4–60 and pl. 38:1–28.

way Blake could advance beyond the vision of Milton was to purge within himself the errors Milton had not overcome, to avoid tainting his imagination with the distortions of Selfhood. "In Milton himself, Blake discerned the conflict between the Selfhood seeking justification and Genius seeking Christian liberty. Milton's desire for self-justification was the expression of his Selfhood which had to be cast out before his Genius could redeem his creative work, called his emanation, from appearing to be the isolated apology for his natural existence instead of the complete expression of his human existence." [13]

After his conquest of Satan in the annihilation of Selfhood, Milton is ready for union with Ololon, the embodiment of the Six-fold Female in Milton's life. The sexual element in Milton's life had appeared to him a hindrance to the full performance of what he felt was his duty. He also, according to Blake, felt it limited or corrupted his integrity. Only when Ololon becomes for Milton what Jerusalem was to be for Albion can Milton achieve a complete human existence. The initial struggle between Milton and Urizen is still going on, yet all is now in readiness for the final step, the confrontation between Milton and Ololon. The trumpets begin to sound, heralding the complete regeneration; Albion once again stirs in anticipation. Milton addresses Ololon in the accents of "terrible majesty" appropriate to "the Inspired Man" rather than with the Urizenic majesty he affected during his lifetime to the detriment of his poetic vision.

> All that can be annihilated must be annihilated
> That the Children of Jerusalem may be saved from slavery
> There is a Negation, & there is a Contrary
> The Negation must be destroyd to redeem the Contraries
> The Negation is the Spectre; the Reasoning Power in Man
> This is a false Body; an Incrustation over my Immortal
> Spirit; a Selfhood, which must be put off & annihilated alway
> To cleanse the Face of my Spirit by Self-examination.

(Bk. 2, pl. 40:30–37)

In the presence of the purified Milton, the Virgin in Ololon divides sixfold

> with a shriek
> Dolorous that ran thro' all Creation, A Double Six-Fold Wonder

13. Fisher, *Valley of Vision*, pp. 247–248.

Away from Ololon she divided & fled into the depths
of Milton's shadow as a Dove upon the stormy Sea.

(Bk. 2, pl. 42:3–6)

Blake responds directly to the dispersal of the Six-fold Female with a
vision of Jesus entering the bosom of Albion and the now united Four
Zoas sounding their apocalyptic trumpets to the four winds. There is no
vision of the apocalypse itself, for the poem has been a prelude to the
vision that will supposedly *create* the apocalypse. The perspective of the
poem returns to Blake rising from the trance-like moment of preparation and vision to find the purified Ololon, his "Sweet Shadow of Delight" trembling by his side; and the poem opens out, for the last time,
to a vision of the world in *its* state of readiness for the vision of a poet
who will call into being the Great Harvest and the final, complete
awakening of man.

Rintrah & Palamabron view the Human Harvest beneath
Their Wine-presses & Barns stand open; the Ovens are prepar'd

The Waggons ready: terrific Lions & Tygers sport & play
All Animals upon the Earth, are prepard in all their strength

(Bk. 2, pl. 42:36–39)

In a note on the back of a sketch for the design of the last plate of
*Milton,* Blake gives a final indication of the wonderful state of awakened self-confidence that both caused and resulted from the writing
of the poem: "Father & Mother, I return from flames of fire tried &
Pure & white." [14]

If this were a more perfect world, one could point to *Jerusalem* as the
complete realization of the vision prepared for in *Milton.* However, as
magnificent and complete a poem as *Jerusalem* is, it is not the vision of
a natural world redeemed through poetic imagination that *Milton* looks
forward to. It is a more complete and cosmic vision of the condition of
man than any poet since Milton has achieved, and its very existence in
complete form indicates a greater psychological success for the prelude
*Milton* than can be claimed for the preludes of any later poets who
have attempted similar preparations for vision. The existence of *Jerusalem* leaves *Milton* in a somewhat strange position in the canon of

14. *Poetry and Prose of Blake,* p. 730, K535.

Blake's writing. Only Wordsworth, who went on after *The Prelude* to write *The Excursion*, offers a comparable example of a poet whose prelude was followed by something different from the anticipated work. *The Excursion* seems to me a work far inferior to *Jerusalem*, and an even greater disparity exists between the final poem and its prelude. Keats and Crane, like Shelley in *The Triumph of Life*, seem to have anticipated, before completing their preludes, that their final vision had to be a vision of the fallen condition of man, a vision of the world of experience they knew rather than that other, regenerated world they so much desired.

# Chapter 4
# Wordsworth: The Wavering Balance

Why wilt thou number every little fibre of my Soul,
Spreading them out before the Sun like stalks of flax to dry?
The Infant Joy is beautiful, but its anatomy
Horrible, ghast & deadly! nought shalt thou find in it
But dark despair & everlasting brooding melancholy!

—Blake, *The Four Zoas*

And is there one, the wisest and the best
Of all mankind, who does not sometimes wish
For things which cannot be, who would not give,
If so he might, to duty and to truth
The eagerness of infantine desire?

—Wordsworth, *The Prelude*

## Union That Cannot Be

During the period in which Blake was conceiving and writing *Milton*, Wordsworth had begun and already completed part of *The Prelude*.[1] Although Blake and Wordsworth held basically different attitudes toward nature, as first pointed out by Blake himself,[2] both of these poems

---

1. All quotations of *The Prelude* are from the text of 1805, ed. E. de Selincourt, rev. Helen Darbishire (London & New York: Oxford Univ. Press, 1960); citations refer to book and lines. Quotations of other Wordsworth poems are from *The Poetical Works of Wordsworth*, ed. Thomas Hutchinson, rev. E. de Selincourt (London & New York: Oxford Univ. Press, 1950); citations refer to title, book, and lines.
2. See Blake's "Annotations to 'Poems' by William Wordsworth," in *The Poetry and Prose of William Blake*, ed. David V. Erdman (Garden City, N.Y.: Doubleday & Co., 1968). Subsequent quotations of Blake are from this edition; citations refer to title and lines.

are concerned with the same problem of achieving a state of consciousness or mode of vision that would be a sustaining basis for the creation
of an epic vision of man to succeed Milton's *Paradise Lost*. Both Blake
and Wordsworth found it impossible to separate the "thing contemplated" from

> the Mind and Man
> Contemplating; and who, and what he was—
> The transitory Being that beheld
> This Vision; when and where, and how he lived;—

("Prospectus" to The Recluse: 95–98)

Both poets had intuitions of an organic universe that were strong
enough to whet desire, strong enough to stimulate hope, and almost
strong enough to establish faith in the faculties that gave them visions.
The inability to perceive a unity of being was attributed by both to an
inadequate sensibility or perceptive power, a weakness that could be
overcome only through discovery and cultivation of the proper mode of
vision—through a recovery from what was, for both, a fallen state of
consciousness, the loss of a former power. It is within this important
area of agreement that we must mention, in passing, their most basic
differences.

Blake tended to see this loss of vision in historical terms, and in *The
Four Zoas* he attempted to create his own mythic history of the fall.
Feelings of guilt, which seem to be an essential part of all theories of
fallen consciousness, are diffused throughout Blake's historical view,
and he felt that the "prophets" who achieve visions counter to the
historical movement wear, in spite of their individual weaknesses, a
certain air of righteousness.

Although Wordsworth commented occasionally on man's fallen state
of consciousness, he had a basically different concept of the fall as
something each man reexperiences individually, and for which he must
bear his own burden of guilt in direct proportion to the strength of his
memory or intuition of his own prior state of consciousness. Although
there are "natural" explanations for many of the expressions of guilt in
*The Prelude* (for stealing, destroying, idleness, etc.), there is a general
obsession with the feeling of guilt that goes beyond the psychological
function of a super ego. *The Prelude* eludes the obvious Freudian re-
duction of the poem: the repressed desires of the adult are the result

of the action of education on the unrepressed, sexual desires of the child. Like all neurotic symptoms or dreams, *The Prelude* represents a return or regression to the experiences of early childhood. Whereas psychology may thus offer a "natural" explanation of Wordsworth's emotional experience, it does not explain the poetic use he was attempting to make of the experience, as a metaphor for a recoverable mode of vision. Wordsworth returns repeatedly to early instances of guilt, remembering how he felt, to serve metaphorically as reminders of his loss of a prior mode of vision and to express the possibility, which he could never completely reject, that the fault for the loss was his own. For if nature is at all times truly accessible to man, then the failure to take advantage of nature's generosity is the fault of man.

Although the "thing contemplated" by Blake and Wordsworth was the same, in the broad sense of an "organic universe" mentioned above, they decidedly did not share—or desire—the same vision of man, or of the mind of man contemplating. Blake, desiring the minimum existence outside his own mind to relate to, was drawn to the idea of historical movement, and especially progressive development—to the vision of a line of prophecy in which he could create a place for himself through inspiration and self-discipline. He emphasized historical recovery in the apocalypse; yet he saw in the individual man's imaginative life the potential for beginning the movement toward the apocalypse.

Wordsworth found himself "left alone, / Seeking the visible world, nor knowing why," and he was also looking for something beyond his own mind to relate to, something that would maintain the integrity, the "creative" aspect of that mind. He could not believe, as Blake tried to believe, that the imagination could bring into existence or create that "other," that the human powers of vision could be teleological, or that the human imagination could usurp the relation to reality held by God in myths of the creation. Like Blake, however, he wanted to believe that the imagination, inspired and properly disciplined, could establish or recognize the existence of a relationship to something real beyond his own mind. The "other" for Wordsworth, however, was not a theory of history, but a theory of nature, and this distinction is the source of most of the obvious differences between the two poets.

"Natural objects," said Blake, "always did & now do weaken, deaden & obliterate Imagination in me" ("Annotations to 'Poems' by William Wordsworth"). For Blake, these "natural objects" interfered with the imagination's recognition of the immortal human form divine within one's self. Truth—or true perception—could only be achieved by complete independence from natural objects and the tyranny of the senses.

> Mental Things are alone Real; what is call'd Corporeal, Nobody knows of its Dwelling Place: it is in Fallacy, & its Existence an Imposture. Where is the Existence Out of Mind or Thought? Where is it but in the Mind of a Fool? I assert for My Self that I do not behold the outward Creation & that to me it is hindrance & not Action. . . . I question not my Corporeal or Vegetative Eye any more than I would question a Window concerning a Sight. I look thro' it & not with it.
>
> (A *Vision of the Last Judgment*)

Thus poetry is true, or can be true, only when it corresponds to or creates a reality transcending the world of sense; it is *the* mode of vision, and "Vision or Imagination is a Representation of what Eternally Exists, Really & Unchangeably," in a realm outside "the things of Vegetable & Generative Nature."

Wordsworth recognized the possibility of a tyranny of the senses, especially the eye, but was extremely uneasy at those few moments when he felt himself to be in a purely subjective state.

> In childhood . . . I was often unable to think of external things as having external existence, and I communed with all that I saw as something not apart from, but inherent in, my own immaterial nature. Many times while going to school have I grasped at a wall or tree to recall myself from this abyss of idealism to the reality.[3]

In his general reaction to the external world, Wordsworth was, as Abrams points out, "an honest heir to the centuries-old English tradition of empiricism."[4] In his constant concern with interpreting nature's "temperate show / Of objects that endure," and in the uneasiness that underlay his exposure of human illusion in the theatre of London in Book 7 he echoes the spirit of Bacon's cry: "God forbid that I should

3. Fenwick note to the *Immortality Ode*, in Raymond D. Havens, *The Mind of a Poet*, 2 vols. (Baltimore: Johns Hopkins Press, 1941), 2:155.
4. Meyer H. Abrams, *The Mirror and the Lamp* (London & New York: Oxford Univ. Press, 1953), p. 314.

substitute a dream of my own mind for the world." [5] His attitude is analogous to that of the early Christian theorists who expanded on Paul's Epistle to the Romans, 1:20, to justify a polysemous view of the world of sense as both a world of physical objects and a typology of the divine attributes of power, love, and glory.[6] But whereas these commentators beheld manifestations of God in both the Scriptures and in the book of nature, Wordsworth had only nature, and his own faculties regarding it, in the attempt to find his way from its literal to its typological significance.[7] Wordsworth in his reaction to nature is like the curious child he describes in Book 4 of *The Excursion*.

> I have seen
> A curious child, who dwelt upon a tract
> Of inland ground, applying to his ear
> The convolutions of a smooth-lipped shell;
> To which, in silence hushed, his very soul
> Listened intensely; and his countenance soon
> Brightened with joy; for from within were heard
> Murmurings, whereby the monitor expressed
> Mysterious union with its native sea.
> Even such a shell the universe itself
> Is to the ear of Faith; and there are times,
> I doubt not, when to you it doth impart
> Authentic tidings of invisible things;
> Of ebb and flow, and ever-during power;
> And central peace, subsisting at the heart
> Of endless agitation.

> (4:1132–1147)

In his attempts to know nature, Wordsworth was drawn toward the idea of truth as the result of a union or interaction between the perceiving eye (the "inner eye," not the physical one) and the perceived

5. This uneasiness climaxes in the image of the blind beggar and in the possibility that "in this Label was a type, / Or emblem, of the utmost that we know, / Both of ourselves and of the universe" (bk. 7:616–618). Cf. Coleridge's image in *Limbo* of the blind man who "seems to gaze at that which seems to gaze at him!"

6. "For the invisible things of Him from the creation of the world are clearly seen, being understood by the things that are made, even His eternal power and Godhead."

7. Harold Bloom (*Visionary Company* [Garden City, N.Y.: Doubleday & Co., 1961], p. 124) points out that "Blake constructs his poetry as a commentary upon Scripture; Wordsworth writes his poetry as a commentary upon Nature."

object or manifestation of nature. This differs from complete subjectivity in that a primary mode of existence is attributed to the external object.

> Of these, said I, shall be my song; of these . . .
> Will I record the praises, making verse
> Deal boldly with substantial things.
>
> (*Prelude*, 8:232–235)

Yet Wordsworth recognized that an object is known only as it is perceived; that the process of knowing is perception in which the perceptive faculty makes its own contribution. Perception for Wordsworth was ideally an active form of union with nature, and true perception, as process, became an end in itself because it could itself be a manifestation of the union it recognized. It was a desired mode of existence rather than a means of discovering static principles or abstract truths.

The problem of the exact nature and degree of the contribution to this union made by the perceptive faculty was never adequately solved by Wordsworth, in *The Prelude* or elsewhere. What he hoped was that the true union, if he could find and express it, would be reciprocal —that is, neither purely subjective nor purely passive sensory reception. The most constant feature in *The Prelude's* exploration of the possibilities of error in achieving this union is the necessity for anchoring the perception on a firm natural object or image that, Wordsworth felt, must partake of reality. It has been argued that Wordsworth's selection of the most simple forms of nature for his images reflects a disguised tendency to subjective projection in the poet. The more simple the image, the argument goes, the more open to those emotions or significances the poet wished to find expressed in nature.[8] But for Wordsworth, the concentration on these simple images was motivated by a fear of this kind of projection, and it was the best guarantee he had that his emotions were the result of recognitions rather than projections. Thus the linking of books 7 and 8 is achieved in part by the simple juxtaposition of London, where man is separated from permanent forms of nature, and the country, where man is constantly reminded of the "substantial things" that are the only clues to the reality in his existence.

8. See David Perkins, *The Quest for Permanence* (Cambridge, Mass.: Harvard Univ. Press, 1959), pp. 52ff.

The one truth Wordsworth attempts to establish in *The Prelude* is
the possibility of a reciprocal union with nature that would justify his
theory of perception.

> Paradise, and groves
> Elysian, Fortunate Fields—like those of old
> Sought in the Atlantic Main—why should they be
> A history only of departed things,
> Or a mere fiction of what never was?
> For the discerning intellect of Man,
> When wedded to this goodly universe
> In love and holy passion, shall find these
> A simple produce of the common day.
> —I, long before the blissful hour arrives,
> Would chant, in lonely peace, the spousal verse
> Of this great consummation:—and, by words
> Which speak of nothing more than what we are,
> Would I arouse the sensual from their sleep
> Of Death, and win the vacant and the vain
> To noble raptures; while my voice proclaims
> How exquisitely the individual Mind
> (And the progressive powers perhaps no less
> Of the whole species) to the external World
> Is fitted:—and how exquisitely, too—
> Theme this but little heard of among men
> The external World is fitted to the Mind;
> And the creation (by no lower name
> Can it be called) which they with blended might
> Accomplish:—this is our high argument.

> ("Prospectus" to *The Recluse*: 47–71)

The "spousal verse" is to celebrate a union of man and nature which
is, at the beginning of *The Prelude*, still a hope or theory. The "blissful
hour" has not arrived. But the "spousal verse" can in effect create the
reality it celebrates, and can "arouse the sensual from their sleep / Of
Death," cause them to live in union with nature by instructing them
how to *see* the union.[9] This begins to sound like Blake's theory of the

9. Blake was so concerned in his "Annotations" with denouncing the "Fit" and
"Fitting" relation as belonging "not to Mind, but to the Vile Body only & to
its Laws of Good & Evil & its Enmities against Mind," that he did not comment on
the parallel here with his *Jerusalem*: "Of the Sleep of Ulro! and of the passage
through / Eternal Death! and of the awaking to Eternal Life."

creative imagination, but what Blake and Wordsworth shared was not the theory of the imagination, but the fusion of (or circularity between) a desired theory of knowledge or perception and a desired theory of reality. Each poet desired a reality that holds man in a particular relationship with nature: for Blake, a relationship of complete independence; for Wordsworth, a reciprocal relationship of mutual giving that will ultimately justify particular instances of suffering and guilt in a larger context of reciprocal benignity and love. Their theories of perception presume the reality to be perceived as justification for their validity and for the validity of poetry, yet Blake always—and Wordsworth at times—suggested that the perception or vision, if it could be achieved, could create the reality. For both, then, reality exists as a potential mode of existence, one that can be achieved only through the cultivation of proper vision.

To embody this theory of reality as a reciprocal union between man and nature is thus a desired goal in *The Prelude*, and "Hope," as Coleridge so aptly pointed out, is "The Angel of the vision." As a hope or potential only, it may be "afflicted and struck down" (*To William Wordsworth*: 43, 38). It may die from pressures of circumstance, or even prove to be an illusional "union that cannot be!" (*Prelude*, 2:24).[10] Wordsworth's goal in *The Prelude* is to learn how to see the union and to substantiate this mode of vision by finding a sustaining image of the mind of man in active reciprocal union with nature, thus ending the circularity by combining in one image the reality and the mind perceiving it. The "feeling" of union, the emotional dimension of "joy" that follows the soul's recognition of union was not a major problem for Wordsworth because he experienced it metaphorically in youth and could experience it still by remembering how he felt.

> Of union or communion doth the soul
> Rejoice as in her highest joy: for there,
> There chiefly, hath she feeling whence she is,
> And, passing through all Nature rests with God.

> (8:823–835)

But the feeling and poetic expression of this "joy" is not enough to substantiate the union, even though Wordsworth could conceive of it

10. The text of 1805 has "things which cannot be," but the final version moved to the more explicit and significant "union that cannot be."

only as the result of the union. The emotion was not a constant in Wordsworth's experience, and he required an embodiment of the union that would not be dependent on uncontrollable fluctuations in his own mood. *The Prelude* shows nothing like the progressive corrosion of "joy" that Coleridge traces in himself in the *Dejection* ode, but it does reveal a distinctly cyclical and uncontrollable emotional pattern. Also, the expressions of joy (memories of "how" he felt) are strongest in connection with the period of infancy or youth, when the poet was experiencing a feeling of security and well-being in a union that was not yet reciprocal. The images of union in youth relate Wordsworth to a maternal Nature, a substitute mother, but the goal of the poem must be expressed in a conjugal image, an image of reciprocity.

The "joy" of the infant in union with its mother, and of the spouse entering the "great consummation" are more readily linked metaphorically than the roles of the infant and the spouse. One is passive and receptive, the other must be active, giving, and reciprocating; it must contribute to a "creation." One of the problems in *The Prelude* never solved is how to move from the relatively accessible maternal images of infant-mother union to the desired conjugal image of a reciprocal union. Thus the constant variations on the theme of thwarted marriages (usually with children, legitimate or otherwise) produced during the period of writing *The Prelude* are a comment on the central problem of the poem. Although I shall discuss its larger significance later, I should point out here the relevance of the Vaudracour and Julia episode in *The Prelude*, particularly the image contrasting their infant's natural relation to his mother and Vaudracour's frustrated attempts to consummate a conjugal relationship with her.

> Propping a pale and melancholy face
> Upon the Mother's bosom, resting thus
> His head upon one breast, while from the other
> The Babe was drawing in its quiet food.
>
> (9:811–814)

Behind the hope for a conjugal union between man and nature, we can often detect a sense of covenant between man and nature, which adds a certain amount of faith to the hope required for seeking the image of union. Wordsworth, like Job, was willing to undergo any amount of physical suffering or emotional despair to preserve or regain his sense of the co-responding breeze, the answering voice from nature reminding him that "Nature never did betray the Man that loved her." But in spite of his frequent legalistic language and his concern with the problems of "betrayal" related to a covenant, Wordsworth never settled on the Biblical concept for his image of the relationship between man and nature. Although the concept of betrayal suggested numerous concrete images, the concept of a fulfilled covenant, I feel, was too abstract to fully arouse an emotional response in Wordsworth. It lacks the sense of active reciprocity demanded by the consummated marriage. Also, if we take Job's covenant as our pattern, faith in a covenant eventually demands some external, definitive answering voice, assuring the covenantor that his faith is properly placed. During the writing of *The Prelude*, Wordsworth had not yet heard what was later to become for him the definitive voice of a revealed religion replacing the imaginatively sought-for nature.

> A Voice to Light gave Being;
> To Time, and Man his earth–born chronicle;
> A Voice shall finish doubt and dim forseeing
> And sweep away life's visionary stir.

> (*On the Power of Sound:* 209–212)

The Prelude is not, then, an expression of faith in a covenant, although the concept can be found frequently in the language and images. In its attempt to find an expression of the reciprocal relation between man and nature, it is perhaps more like a love poem than anything else.[11] The self-examination to discover if one is worthy of his beloved, the constant attention to all possible signs of progress or regression coming from the loved one, the emotional vacillation, the fear of a change in either party, the anticipation of a permanent state of joy and bliss in the married state, the expectation of being able to create poetry based on and legitimized by the union—all are exploratory attempts to establish the great marriage metaphor Wordsworth announces in the "Prospectus" to *The Recluse*. Although Wordsworth never approaches the explicit eroticism of *The Song of Songs*, the relation of allegorical implications to emotional correlatives of the love

11. See Geoffrey Hartman's discussion of the "dialectic of love between man and nature" in *The Unmediated Vision* (New Haven: Yale Univ. Press, 1954), ch. 1. His concern with the emotional dimension of the dialectic is an invaluable supplement to Abrams's more strictly epistemological consideration

relationship is similar to the *Song* and to the works of other religious writers who have found the sexual relationship to be the best metaphor for what is basically a spiritual union. In general, Wordsworth's poetry—especially *The Prelude*—is far more consistently erotic than many seem willing to admit.

Ideally, a love poem should lead to consummation in marriage, and *The Prelude*, to fulfill the prelude function as an enabling work, should lead to the epithalamion or "spousal verse," the achieved epic vision that was Wordsworth's avowed goal. Intruding upon the love-poem metaphor of *The Prelude*, however, with its hopeful anticipation of the conjugal consummation, is an alternative form of union with nature— one which forced itself on Wordsworth's imagination, in what may be called "latent" image content, yet one he did not fully recognize until he lost all hope in the desired conjugal union.

In the second "spot-of-time" image in *The Prelude* (11:346–389), Wordsworth remembers waiting at Christmas vacation for the horses that were to take him and his brothers home. He waits on "a crag, / An Eminence," on the "highest summit" of which he sat "half-shelter'd by a naked wall," watching "those two roads, / By each of which the expected Steeds might come, / The choice uncertain." The description of himself is of one watching and waiting, "Straining my eyes intensely, as the mist / Gave intermitting prospect of the wood / And plain beneath." This is one of those images of himself regarding nature so important and central to *The Prelude*. Coming toward the end of the poem, in the context of the spots-of-time theory, it suggests an image of the poet, surveying his life from the heights, "as the mist / Gave intermitting prospect." The poet is looking "in such anxiety of hope" that the death of his father shortly afterward "appear'd / A chastisement" by "God, who thus corrected my desires." What the "desires" or "anxiety of hope" were for, or why they deserved chastisement, is not made clear. But the image suggests, in the "uncertain choice" between the two roads, and in the excessive hope, that the poet was chastised for refusing to recognize the uncertainty and for unjustifiably placing his hope in one road over the other. What is significant in the image— although never explicitly spelled-out in the poem—is not the boy's natural enthusiasm for returning home at vacation time, nor the child's natural reaction of taking his father's death personally in recognition of the burden of guilt he carried for the usual reasons, but the possibilities Wordsworth sees in this remembered experience for finding an image relevant to the growth of his own mind.

Having already taken the image from its context, I will take one further step by suggesting what the two roads represent in the larger movement of *The Prelude*. One road, that in which the poet has placed his hope, leads uncertainly to the possibility of a reciprocal union with nature. In crossing the Alps (bk. 6), his eagerness for a direct ascent of the "lofty Mountain" led him to choose the wrong track, the upward path rather than that going "downwards, with the current of that Stream." Therefore the poet found the real crossing an anticlimax. He had to descend into a "gloomy Pass" rather than scale the heights. Only two days later, in the depths below, he was again "lost, bewilder'd among woods immense" because of his "eagerness, and by report misled / Of those Italian clocks." All of this because of his desire to "behold the scene / In its most deep repose" and his "doubting not that day was near." We know from other examples in *The Prelude* the kind of emotional experience of harmony and union the poet was seeking in the "eagerness" emphasized by these two mistakes; in both cases he finds images, not of a marriage with nature, but of a fallen world of error and illusion. Book 6 concludes with an anticipation of the French Revolution, to be presented in books 9 and 10, as an even more significant case of eagerness to find a desired natural image which leads to error and disillusionment.

All of Wordsworth's earlier misplaced hopes are suggested in the two-road image in the second spot of time, and all of his errors stemmed from the same desire to elevate man, to give him a conjugal relationship with nature and a reciprocal role in a perception that is also a creation. He consistently hoped to give man the highest role vis-à-vis nature that he could conceive for him, a role in which men would have minds that "are truly from the Deity" (13:108). Concrete embodiments of these masterful minds are not frequent in *The Prelude*. The boy of Winander from the period of Wordsworth's youth dies, adding to the many suggestions that the union with nature, though possible in some form during youth, can have no continuity or development into a mature state of consciousness. We do have the masterful shepherd who mounts "higher and higher," "*wedded* [italics added] to his life of hope," and who is

> a Power
> Or genius, under Nature, under God. . . .
> In size a giant. . . .
> A solitary object and sublime,

> Above all height! like an aerial Cross
> As it is stationed on some spiry rock
> Of the Chartreuse, for worship. . . .
> To me was like an index of delight,
> Of grace and honour, power and worthiness.[12]

$$(8:393-416)$$

After the image of chastised hope concluding Book 11, Book 12 is full of hints as to what the other "road," the alternative to the union achieved by the shepherd, might be. The possibility of nature being deceitful, exciting false hopes, is put down by Wordsworth's observation that nature "gives birth / To no impatient or fallacious hopes," and he reveals a slight shift in his attitude toward nature by emphasizing—the suggestion was, of course, present before—the endurance of "those unassuming things, that hold / A silent station in this beauteous world." He speaks of himself as "moderated" and "composed," with "The promise of the present time retired / Into its true proportion," of having gained a "More judicious knowledge of what makes / The dignity of individual Man," and of having sought

> For good in the familiar face of life
> And built thereon my hopes of good to come.

$$(12:67-68)$$

He describes his love for "a public road" and the knowledge to be gained "From mouths of lowly men," concluding the book with a reference to the "lonesome journey" he took on the plain of Sarum and the suggestion that *Guilt and Sorrow*, based on this trip, represented the true direction his poetry should take. The return to the plain after the period of illusion in France recalls the false ascent of the Alps, the following descent and confusion on the plains, and the parallel anticipated there between his Alpine crossing and his involvement in Anglo-French politics. He speaks of having discovered at this time a "new world" and a new form of union between man and nature, and without going into

---

12. Wordsworth's attempt throughout Book 8 to find epic stature in the unlikely image of the shepherd is neither so new nor so incongruous as it might seem. John S. Coolidge ("Great Things and Small: The Virgilian Progression," *Comparative Literature* 17, no. 1 [Winter 1965]:1–23) discusses the progression from a small pastoral scene to a great epic one in Vergil and Milton, which provides a useful context for understanding Wordsworth's larger strategy in Book 8.

the differences between this union and the marriage he had been seeking, he claims that it could be a source of human dignity.

> I seem'd about this period to have sight
> Of a new world, a world, too, that was fit
> To be transmitted and made visible
> To other eyes, as having for its base
> That whence our dignity originates,
> That which both gives it being and maintains
> A balance, an ennobling interchange
> Of action from within and from without,
> The excellence, pure spirit, and best power
> Both of the object seen, and eye that sees.

(12:370–379)

This book, and particularly this passage, presents one of the harder
moments for the reader attempting to grasp an overall view of the poet
trying through a poem to establish a basis for a present vision, yet
claiming, in the poem, to have found that basis before the poem was
even conceived. It is possible, however—reserving this problem for later
discussion—to find in the passage an indication of the other road, the
alternative vision that the poet has been slighting because of his eagerness to achieve a different vision.

The road that has been slighted in the poem is the "public road" of
Book 13 or "public Way" of Book 4 along which Wordsworth found
examples, not of the masterful mind in a reciprocal creative union with
nature, but of men like the Cumberland Beggar and the leech gatherer,
and images like the Thorn. It is significant for a larger perspective of
The Prelude, and of Wordsworth, that most of the images of the alternative union are not in The Prelude itself, which seeks a different
union, but in poems written during the conception and writing of The
Prelude.[13] Their exclusion indicates both the larger importance of the
two-road image and the imaginative struggle Wordsworth undertook in
order to follow the road that led to the reciprocal conjugal union. The
most important image of the second form of union in The Prelude is
that of the old soldier returning from the tropic islands. If, as de Selincourt suggests in his Introduction, the end of Book 4 was at one time a

13. The Old Cumberland Beggar (1797), The Thorn (1798), Three years she
grew (1799), A Slumber did my spirit seal (1799), Ruth (1799), Resolution and
Independence (1802), and She was a Phantom of delight (1804).

possible stopping point for *The Prelude*, this passage is even more significant, as it anticipates the concluding direction of the poem. The old soldier is a strong contrast to the independent shepherd of Book 8. The soldier is first described as an "uncouth shape," which on closer observation reveals several suggestive aspects.

> A milestone propp'd him, and his figure seem'd
> Half-sitting, and half-standing. I could mark
> That he was clad in military garb,
> Though faded, yet entire. He was alone,
> Had no attendant, neither Dog, nor Staff,
> Nor knapsack; in his very dress appear'd
> A desolation, a simplicity
> That seem'd akin to solitude.
>
> (4:412–419)

The soldier answers Wordsworth's questions, but

> in all he said
> There was a strange half-absence, and a tone
> Of weakness and indifference, as of one
> Remembering the importance of his theme
> But feeling it no longer.
>
> (4:474–478)

Wordsworth's initial reaction to the man is "a mingled sense / Of fear and sorrow," and his parting impression is of a "poor unhappy Man." The clearest indication of the relation with nature represented by this figure is his response to Wordsworth's objection to his way of life: " 'My trust is in the God of Heaven / And in the eye of him that passes me.' " In view of the other poems written during this period, it is possible to find in the soldier the outlines of a union with nature that is contrary to that hoped for in most of *The Prelude*. The soldier represents trusting, passive survival in an almost physical assimilation with nature. Leaning upon the milestone, half-sitting and half-standing, he reminds us of the leech gatherer in *Resolution and Independence*, an old man who was "not stood, not set, but 'was'—the figure presented in the most naked simplicity possible." The leech gatherer is more fully assimilated than the soldier; he is like "a huge stone" which is in turn like "a sea-beast crawled forth." The soldier's "strange half-absence," and "tone / Of weakness and indifference" approach the minimal con-sciousness of the leech gatherer, a man "not all alive nor dead, / Nor all asleep." He anticipates the parallel (almost equation) between life and death in the final lines of *The Old Cumberland Beggar*.

> As in the eye of Nature he has lived,
> So in the eye of Nature let him die!

The emphasis on figures like these cannot coexist with the ideal of a reciprocal union with nature leading to mutual creation sought by Wordsworth in *The Prelude*. Yet they have a direct relevance to *The Prelude* in that they offer an alternative to the guilt and despair of the search for a different union. Despair is impossible without false hope, and in an utterly passive union tending toward physical assimilation, man becomes incapable of betraying nature.

The tendency toward physical assimilation is clear in the posture of these figures, their reliance on staffs, and in the imagery used to describe them. It reaches a climax in *The Excursion* when the Wanderer finds the ancient "neglected veteran" who has been lost gathering winter fuel.

> We there espied the object of our search,
> Lying full three parts buried among tufts
> Of heath-plant, under and above him strewn,
> To baffle as he might the watery storm:
> And there we found him breathing peaceably,
> Snug as a child that hides itself in sport
> 'Mid a green hay-cock in a sunny field.

> (2:817–822)

Although Wordsworth's veteran approaches the degree of assimilation Shelley gives Rousseau in *The Triumph of Life*, he insists on finding in his images a recognition of human dignity and a power of consolation that contrasts strongly with Shelley's theme. The possibility of this kind of union with nature, opposed as it is to the kind of union *The Prelude* is trying to establish, is still for Wordsworth a discovery, a new world, and he attempts to end *The Prelude* on a note of complacence, or even triumph—to turn, as in the great Ode, from despair at losing the vision-ary gleam, to an attempt to consolidate some kind of gain from the memory of his former powers, something that will carry him through the ever-darkening period to come.

> I see by glimpses now; when age comes on
> May scarcely see at all.

$$(9:338-339)$$

Much of the ambiguity and uncertainty that permeates the final two books comes from Wordsworth's attempts to make the transition from one form of union with nature to the other without finally giving us a concrete image of the alternative union such as we have in *Resolution and Independence* or *The Old Cumberland Beggar*. He claims that "this history is brought / To its appointed close," and that it is, "in the end / All gratulant *if rightly understood*" [italics added]. The qualification is essential, because it is difficult to regard the direction of the conclusion as "gratulant" if we have been carried along with Wordsworth's desire for a different conclusion.

Near the end, Wordsworth himself reminds us of the mood in which the poem began.

> Call back to mind
> The mood in which this Poem was begun,
> O Friend! the termination of my course
> Is nearer now, much nearer; yet even then
> In that distraction and intense desire
> I said unto the life which I had lived,
> Where art thou?

$$(13:370-376)$$

In the thirteenth book Wordsworth sings a palinode, both for the "life which I had lived" with its visionary gleam, now admitted to be gone, and for the "distraction and intense desire" that motivated the writing of *The Prelude*.

> still to the last
> Even to the very going out of youth,
> The period which our Story now hath reach'd,
> I too exclusively esteem'd that love,
> And sought that beauty, which, as Milton sings,
> Hath terror in it. Thou didst soften down

> This over-sternness; but for thee, sweet Friend,
> My soul, too reckless of mild grace, had been
> Far longer what by Nature it was framed,
> Longer retain'd its countenance severe,
> A rock with torrents roaring, with the clouds
> Familiar, and a favourite of the Stars:
> But thou didst plant its crevices with flowers,
> Hang it with shrubs that twinkle in the breeze,
> And teach the little birds to build their nests
> And warble in its chambers.
>
> (13:221–236)

Coleridge also recognized the terror in Wordsworth's search, in those moments when the beauty of the union was felt, yet could not be held securely because of the unresolved question of its permanence. He describes *The Prelude* as a record

> of moments awful,
> Now in thy inner life, and now abroad,
> When power streamed from thee, and thy soul received
> The light reflected, as a light bestowed.
>
> (*To William Wordsworth:* 16–19)

Wordsworth's recognition that his story ends "with the very going out of youth" is perhaps the most awful moment of all, for it describes a permanent change in his soul, a resignation of the attempt to remain like a rock with torrents roaring, familiar with the clouds and a favorite with the stars. The terms in which the change is presented are significant, not only for the final resignation of youth and for the admission of error, but also for the specific delineation in his soul of the process of physical assimilation which he now sees as the right road. His soul is planted with flowers and shrubs, and it echoes with the warble of domesticated birds which, like the cuckoo in an earlier poem, can remind him of his former search without arousing him to take up the quest again.[14]

I have suggested that *The Prelude* reveals, although reluctantly, and with a somewhat forced complacency, the resignation of the attempt to find a basis for writing the great spousal verse of a reciprocal, creative

14. *To the Cuckoo* (1802). Also note the effect of the caged thrush's song on Susan in *The Reverie of Poor Susan* (1797).

union with nature. Implicit in this resignation is the loss of the creative potential which was so significant a part of the union. This is a clue, I think, to the obsession with the theme of frustrated marriages and dead children that occupied Wordsworth during the period of writing *The Prelude*. The children die before reaching maturity; and the poem that Wordsworth wished to write, or the hope for it, dies before it can be fully realized. In *The Prelude* itself, there is no final image of the alternative union which suggests ultimate physical assimilation and passivity. There is the anticipatory image of the soldier in Book IV, an image which Wordsworth finds terrible and pathetic, but which he embodies because of the intense, though undefinable, emotional reaction he has to it as a part of his remembered experience. Also, there is the image of his own soul playing host to flowers, shrubs, and nesting birds, and that of the naked, drowned man in Book 5, who for rather ambiguous reasons does not frighten the boy Wordsworth or the poet remembering the experience. But there is no image that stands out as the summation of the final movement of the poem toward a union that is "all gratulant if rightly understood." The Vaudracour and Julia episode suggests in some detail the reasons for the frustration of the marriage, the death of the child, and the isolation of the poet, but it offers no alternative union. Instead it anticipates and leads to the despair which was to find in the alternative union its only solace—the despair of Wordsworth in *Resolution and Independence,* facing what seemed inevitable madness just before he found the image of the leech gatherer, a man who could survive because, like a natural organism, he simply *was.*

Before leaving this central aspect of *The Prelude,* it is worth taking a look at *The Thorn,* a poem written about the time Wordsworth began work on *The Prelude,* and one which suggests both the beginning and the end of that poem. *The Thorn* has proved hard to take as an important part of Wordsworth's work, in spite of the serious effort that went into its composition. Wordsworth wrote a long, somewhat apologetic note to the poem, partly to explain the persona of the narrator, and partly to explain the diction and his choice of meter. The significant part of the note on the persona tells us that he was conceived as a retired sea captain, selected "to exhibit some of the general laws by which superstition acts upon the mind. Superstitious men are almost always men of slow faculties and deep feelings; their minds are not loose, but adhesive; they have a reasonable share of imagination, by which word I mean the faculty which produces impressive effects out of simple elements; but they are utterly destitute of fancy, the power by which pleasure and surprise are excited by sudden varieties of situation and by accumulated imagery. It was my wish in this poem to show the manner in which such men cleave to the same ideas." [15]

Byron left a clever parody of Wordsworth's note in his Preface to *Don Juan*,[16] and no doubt the note's claim to seriousness has made it even harder to gain a proper perspective of the poem. Wordsworth claims in the note that the sea captain is himself "utterly destitute of fancy," yet in Book 8 of *The Prelude*, he slightingly refers to his earlier poems like *The Thorn* as exhibiting a "wilfulness of fancy and conceit" in a "humour" that led him to make the "tragic super-tragic, else left short." The typical widow described here by Wordsworth, visiting and weeping at a grave the whole year through while "all the storms of Heaven must beat on her," is a Martha Ray abstract. And the solitary foxglove, under which the Vagrant sits "with her Babes," resembles the thorn.[17] Since the sea captain does not actually write the poem, but merely looks at the pond, the grave, the thorn, and Martha Ray, the question of his lack of fancy is not important, except as it reveals the amount of consideration Wordsworth gave to the imaginary mind perceiving the images of the poem. What is more important is the attitude—what Wordsworth characterizes as superstition—with which the captain regards the objects in the poem. His mind is "adhesive," he becomes obsessed with the thorn and the grave and Martha's grief without really understanding them and their significance and without making any attempt to explain them or the effect they have on him.

> 'But what's the Thorn? and what the pond?
> And what the hill of moss to her?
> And what the creeping breeze that comes
> The little pond to stir?'
> 'I cannot tell. . . .'

$$(199-203)$$

The captain is a slightly disguised projection of the poet Wordsworth, as the newly arrived observer who plans to look through his

15. *Poetical Works*, p. 701.
16. Written in 1818, but not published until 1901; reprinted in *Don Juan*, ed. Leslie A. Marchand (Boston: Houghton Mifflin Co., 1958), pp. 2–4.
17. In spite of this self-parody, *The Thorn* long remained one of Wordsworth's favorite poems. See *The Early Letters of William and Dorothy Wordsworth*, ed. E. de Selincourt (Oxford: Clarendon Press, 1935), p. 488.

telescope at "the ocean wide and bright," but instead is forced to seek shelter where he finds some entirely unanticipated natural images or objects.[18] He is shown regarding these objects in much the same way Wordsworth must have done, recognizing in them some deep significance, yet not willing or able to commit himself to any interpretation of what he sees. Even the grief of Martha Ray, with its obvious natural cause in Stephen's breach of faith and the loss of her child, is a mystery no one can explain.

The clue to Martha Ray's grief lies in the hill of moss, and what it represents or suggests in terms of *The Prelude*'s search for a union with nature. The young Martha, "blithe and gay" as Wordsworth at the beginning of *The Prelude*, had placed all her hopes in her intended marriage with Stephen, even to the point of conceiving a child by him to be born and reared after the marriage. But the wedding does not take place, and the child is born dead, or dies soon after from exposure. The only "opinion" offered by the captain in the whole poem is that Martha Ray did not kill the baby herself. Therefore, for natural reasons—the specific details are not important—the child, conceived in hope of a union that cannot be, is not able to survive and grow to maturity. Similarly, there is no specific cause given for the death of the child of Vaudracour and Julia in Book 9 of *The Prelude*. It dies "by some mistake / Or indiscretion of the Father," in what must seem a climax of absurdity unless we are aware of the larger context in which the death is inevitable. To tie the death to too specific a cause would reduce the total effect of inevitability that is being expressed. The child dies because the union fails, and the actual physical circumstances of death are irrelevant.

All that remains of the child in *The Thorn* is a memorial in the beautiful hill of moss.

> a fresh and lovely sight,
> A beauteous heap, a hill of moss,
> Just half a foot in height.
> All lovely colours there you see,

18. For a more explicit and extended use of the telescope as a metaphor for poetic perception, see *Star-Gazers* (1806), in which the telescope is fixed on the "resplendent vault" of the heavens, and for reasons that cannot be explained all the impatient viewers go away "as if dissatisfied." And cf. the attempt in *The Prelude* to behold a scene "in its most deep repose" (bk. 6:617–657) which ends with Wordsworth's becoming "lost" and "bewildered" in a wilderness of "darkness visible."

> All colours that were ever seen;
> And mossy network too is there,
> As if by hand of lady fair
> The work had woven been.
>
> (35–42)

It is almost as if nature (the "lady fair"?) were giving the memorial the highest beauty in compensation for the death of the hope that was natural but was for "things that cannot be."

The babe can be seen under special circumstances; and here the "superstition" of the persona is most useful to Wordsworth, for it allows him more plausibly to offer one of the most suggestive images of the poem.

> Some say if to the pond you go,
> And fix on it a steady view,
> The shadow of a babe you trace,
> A baby and a baby's face,
> And that it looks at you;
> Whene'er you look on it, 'tis plain
> The baby looks at you again.
>
> (214–220)

Is it really Martha Ray's baby, we wonder, or is it the "baby" in *The Prelude*, the lost infancy and youth of Wordsworth himself, which was felt to hold the clues to the death of the visionary gleam and the hoped-for possibility of its rebirth? Or is it really the poet's own face reflected back, a special case of receiving "The light reflected, as a light bestowed." These possibilities are implicit in the superstition, and it is no coincidence that Wordsworth returns to a similar image in *The Prelude* to describe the search for his own infancy.

> As one who hangs down-bending from the side
> Of a slow-moving Boat, upon the breast
> Of a still water, solacing himself
> With such discoveries as his eye can make,
> Beneath him, in the bottom of the deeps,
> Sees many beauteous sights, weeds, fishes, flowers,
> Grots, pebbles, roots of trees, and fancies more;
> Yet often is perplex'd, and cannot part

The shadow from the substance, rocks and sky,
Mountains and clouds, from that which is indeed
The region, and the things which there abide
In their true dwelling; now is cross'd by gleam
Of his own image, by a sunbeam now,
And motions that are sent he knows not whence,
Impediments that make his task more sweet;
—Such pleasant office have we long pursued
Incumbent o'er the surface of past time
With like success.

(4:247–264)

Although the baby and the pond are of equal importance, the thorn gives the poem its name, as a particular thorn he saw gave Wordsworth the stimulus to write the poem. Martha Ray buried the infant "close beside" the thorn; and it is "to this old Thorn" that she goes, and "beside the Thorn" that she sits, crying her misery to the wind. It is as if she intuitively recognized some power or significance in the thorn, some alternative to the pathetic beauty of the dead baby's grave, that would ease her grief, if only she could recognize it. But she cannot, and the captain cannot find it either. Instead we have only the thorn itself.

The thorn is so old it is without age, like the leech gatherer or the Cumberland Beggar. It is so passive that it has no leaves or "prickly points," yet it has enough stamina to endure and to resist the "heavy tufts of moss that strive / To drag it to the ground." The struggle between the thorn and the moss is personified, but the image remains a natural one; the thorn remains only a personified plant.

The step from the thorn to the leech gatherer by his pond is so small that he seems "Like one whom I had met with in a dream," yet it is a crucial step, for the leech gatherer is human and able "To give . . . human strength by apt admonishment." [19] Thus the image of the

19. These two poems should be compared with a poem Blake sent to Thomas Butts; in particular Wordsworth's distinction of seeing the leech gatherer with his "mind's eye" is comparable to Blake's seeing the thistle with his "inward Eye."

A frowning Thistle implores my stay.
What to others a trifle appears
Fills me full of smiles or tears;
For double vision is always with me.
With my inward Eye 'tis an old Man grey;
With my outward, a Thistle across my way.

The Letters of William Blake, ed. G. Keynes (Cambridge, Mass.: Harvard Univ. Press, 1968), p. 61.

leech gatherer cures the poet's despair with the life he saw heading for inevitable "despondency and madness," and the image was anticipated, though not fully realized, in *The Thorn*.[20]

My reasons for dwelling so long on a poem without conventional poetic merit should by now be obvious, for it contains much of the potential of which *The Prelude* is a realization. Whereas *The Thorn* only asks questions, *The Prelude* attempts to find the answers. The attempt to dig up "that hill of moss so fair," to discover whether or not there is indeed a dead baby under it, is abortive in *The Thorn*. But in *The Prelude*, the excavation is completed, even to "the last going out of youth," and Wordsworth discovers that a humanized thorn, therapeutic but uncreative, is the only solace for his despair.

## All Gratulant If Rightly Understood

In my approach to *The Prelude* so far, there have been several assumptions about Wordsworth's selection and use of images. The most important of these assumptions is that the images, which Wordsworth recognized and remembered primarily according to emotional criteria, have nevertheless a latent intellectual content that can be described and related to the rest of his work. At his best Wordsworth rarely intellectualizes images for us himself. When he does, as in the Simplon Pass section, or in the ascent of Snowdon, he often reveals a sense of strain, as if the attempt were made as much for self-conviction as for explanation.

It is important to remember that, for Wordsworth, there were two distinct stages of image formulation. The first was the experience itself, the original contact with the natural object or scene that contained the potential image. One of the best descriptions (or images) of this kind of experience is found in *A Night Piece*, a small poem written in 1798.

> —The sky is overcast
> With a continuous cloud of texture close,
> Heavy and wan, all whitened by the Moon,
> Which through that veil is indistinctly seen,
> A dull, contracted circle, yielding light

20. Or, the relationship could be approached from the other direction. Wordsworth points out that "This Poem ought to have been preceded by an introductory Poem, which I have been prevented from writing by never having felt myself in a mood when it was probable that I should write it well." *The Prelude* is the fullest introduction to *The Thorn* we have, for it teaches us how to see the poem's images, and to understand the despair of Martha Ray.

So feebly spread that not a shadow falls,
Chequering the ground—from rock, plant, tree or tower.
At length a pleasant instantaneous gleam
Startles the pensive traveller while he treads
His lonesome path, with unobserving eye
Bent earthwards; he looks up—the clouds are split
Asunder,—And above his head he sees
The clear Moon, and the glory of the heavens.
There in a black-blue vault she sails along,
Followed by multitudes of stars, that, small
And sharp, and bright, along the dark abyss
Drive as she drives: how fast they wheel away,
Yet vanish not!—the wind is in the tree,
But they are silent;—still they roll along
Immeasurably distant; and the vault,
Built round by those white clouds, enormous clouds,
Still deepens its unfathomable depth.
At length the Vision closes; and the mind,
Not undisturbed by the delight it feels,
Which slowly settles into peaceful calm,
Is left to muse upon the solemn scene.

It is from such a visionary and emotional experience that the mind, or inner eye, remembering "how" but not "what" it felt, constructs its poetic images. In spite of changes in himself after such moments of perceptual experience, Wordsworth hoped that in them there was "life and food / For future years." In *Tintern Abbey* we have a pure example of the whole process, where the physical return to the banks of the Wye functions primarily as a metaphor of the continued availability of the original experience.

*The Prelude* goes beyond *Tintern Abbey* in being a large collection of such images, in which the reader must not only cope with each remembered experience and its imaged memorialization, but must also look for larger patterns relating the images to each other. *The Prelude* is the history of "a mind beset / With images, and haunted by itself" (6: 179–180), and, as with any attempt to understand a poem by Wordsworth, we must begin a reading of *The Prelude* with an understanding of separate visions of natural objects or scenes. These remembered objects are not remembered simply as objects to be described, but as parts of a perception; thus the experience of perception, and what can be remembered of it and learned from it, is what is important in *The Prelude*. For in *The Prelude* these experiences are reconstructed in the context of a quest for a particular "appointed end," an image of himself seeing—and thus participating in—a reciprocal union between man and nature.

Because the meaning of *The Prelude* lies in an interpretation of its images, it is easy to pick out and discuss particular images with only cursory attention to their context in the poem.[21] Such an approach tends to result in some form of static meaning found in the poem, where different images from different parts of the poem are linked according to general type and significance. There is part of the poem missing in such discussions, as there has been part missing so far in my attempt to describe the two potential forms of union with nature that underlie many of the poem's images. What is missing is the overwhelming sense of action *in the present* that the poem gives when read as a search of the past for images that fit a predetermined pattern, images that can be hopefully interpreted, but never securely controlled and made to lead to the desired end. The poem is not merely a record of past acts of perception, or a history of former experiences. The real action is in the poet's mind at the time of writing as he recalls his experiences, trying to preserve in his recollection and selection the honesty that can be the only basis of secure self-conviction. Yet as he tries to re-create the past, he is also trying to make a poem immediately relevant to the present and, ultimately, to the future. *The Prelude* is not merely a biographical retracing of the poet's experience to a predetermined chronological point. It is Wordsworth's attempt to find, in the retracing, a secure basis for his hope that he could indeed perform the "arduous labour" of creating a "work that will endure."

Wordsworth's seeming complacent optimism is often misleading as he moves from the relatively secure confidence of the beginning, through the many present-tense comments on his progress, to the final claim that "all is gratulant if rightly understood." In his eagerness to reach "the appointed end," he often gives the impression of writing the poem after the manner of his conversations with Beaupuy.

> We summon'd up the honourable deeds
> Of ancient Story, thought of each bright spot
> That could be found in all recorded time
> Of truth preserv'd and error pass'd away

$$(9:371-374)$$

21. G. W. Knight (*Starlit Dome* [New York: Barnes & Noble, 1960]) takes an extreme form of this approach, sorting the images according to archetype and then unfairly accusing the poet of lacking a sense of action.

But *The Prelude* is not a record of bright spots only. It is a record of repeated attempts to push forward from the period of youth and outward from the pastoral realm described in Book 8 without losing the sense of relationship with nature that Wordsworth remembers having felt so strongly as a child. The degree of complacency, with which each withdrawal—or push—toward maturity is described, decreases, and the degree of relief with which he returns to the earlier time and setting increases until the final disillusionment of his hopes roused by the French Revolution.

> sentiments
> Could through my understanding's natural growth
> No longer justify themselves through faith
> Of inward consciousness, and hope that laid
> Its hand upon its object, evidence
> Safer, of universal application, such
> As could not be impeach'd, was sought elsewhere.
>
> (10:785–791)

From this loss of "inward consciousness" in the past, he returned to the Plains of Sarum; and he repeats the former movement in *The Prelude*, turning from the hope for a reciprocal union with nature and the poetry he might create on the basis of such a union, to the alternative "new world" described at the end of Book 12.

There is a fine line between complacency that is genuine, as Wordsworth's is in Book 1, and complacency that seems more an attempt at self-conviction than secure confidence. But it is a line that must be drawn when we come to Book 13 with Wordsworth's claim of "having track'd the main essential Power, / Imagination, up her way sublime." After he loses the "inward consciousness" in Book 10, he never fully recovers it, or the track or pattern he had been following. Instead, he begins to shift to an alternative union with nature which is not fully revealed in *The Prelude* alone, but can be recognized there in a potential form.

The description of the ascent of Mount Snowdon in Book 13 is a problem only if we attempt to interpret it as a successful final image of the poem, as a resolution toward which the poem constantly moves and in which Wordsworth fully realizes the hope of the poem. The scene demands comparison with the ninth Night of *The Four Zoas* and the concluding *Atlantis* part of *The Bridge*. In all three of these sections, we find a final attempt to deny all preceding ambiguities, to achieve a moment of vision so intense and inclusive that it will recover the progressive loss of confidence and control in the earlier part of the poem. It is neither accident nor coincidence that both Crane and Wordsworth fall back at this point to an earlier moment of vision, to a moment that had helped give them their intuitions of the final vision toward which their poems were meant to progress.[22] The desperation of their attempts to deny failure and to wrench a poetic rebirth from a lapse of hope and faith, must be felt at the end in the context of the whole movement of the poem. And if so felt, underneath can be seen the same desperation exhibited by Los in his terror at Non Existence.

> Terrified at Non Existence
> For such they deemd the death of the body. Los his vegetable hands
> Outstretchd his right hand branching out in fibrous Strength
> Siezd the Sun. His left hand like dark roots coverd the Moon
> And tore them down cracking the heavens across from immense to immense
> Then fell the fires of Eternity with loud & shrill
> Sound of Loud Trumpet thundering along from heaven to heaven
> A mighty sound articulate Awake ye dead & come
> To Judgment from the four winds Awake & Come away
>
> (*Four Zoas*, 9:5–13)

While there is no deceit in such attempts, nothing that could be called a failure of poetic honesty, it is all too easy to accept the affirmative aspect of such an attempt and to miss or ignore the equivocal elements.

In Book 13 Wordsworth once again sets out on a journey to a predetermined end, and once again the end is a particular desired view of nature, in this case "to see the sun / Rise from the top of Snowdon." He begins at night, as he had set out by night to see the lake in Book 6, and with a guide who is "the Shepherd, who by ancient right / Of office is the Stranger's usual guide." This particular shepherd is a "Con-

---

22. The Snowdon episode is found in MS w written in February and March, 1804. Abbie Findlay Potts (*Wordsworth's Prelude* [New York: Octagon Books, 1966], pp. 7–9) thinks the Snowdon part was written during these months and reflects a "formal advance" in the manuscript. Havens (*Mind of a Poet*, p. 610) argues that it "may well belong to the early period when the best parts of *The Prelude* were composed," because they are in a fair copy state and in a different handwriting from the rest of the manuscript. I am inclined to agree with Havens, because the way the poem works calls for a return to an earlier moment of vision.

ductor" and a "tried Pilot" in whom Wordsworth expresses complete "faith." As the idealized shepherd in Book 8 guided the boy Wordsworth to his desired vision of human dignity, this shepherd is to guide him to a sunrise, the birth of a new day, the "perfect" image of a peaceful, tranquil, inevitable renewal. We should remember at this point his earlier expression of renewed hope on hearing of the death of Robespierre.

> Great was my glee of spirit, great my joy
> In vengeance, and eternal justice, thus
> Made manifest. "Come now ye golden times,"
> Said I, forth-breathing on those open Sands
> A Hymn of triumph, "as the morning comes
> Out of the bosom of the night, come Ye:
> Thus far our trust is verified. . . ."

$$(10:540-546)$$

The similarity here is not so much that Wordsworth has used the image of a sunrise before, for in a complex sense, the later image includes the earlier one, in which the poet was attempting to find a parallel for human experience in the natural image of renewal. In Book 13 he again shows himself looking for the image of renewal, but this time he does not commit the "juvenile error" of thinking he has found it in the expected form or image. Yet he does repeat the same movement, and does once more make the same mistake: this is the significant similarity. Both times he is looking for something that will bring dawn out of "the bosom of the night," something that will, in a calm, tranquil, yet unmistakeable way turn one vision into another. In the Snowdon image he does not find the sunrise, but he does find an image from which he attempts to extract the same security and confidence that he found earlier in the death of Robespierre that was to lead to a "golden time."

> The schemes I framed more calmly, when and how
> The madding factions might be tranquillized,
> And how through hardships manifold and long
> The glorious renovation would proceed.
> Thus interrupted by uneasy bursts
> Of exultation, I pursued my way
> Along that very shore which I had skimmed

In former days, when—spurring from the Vale
Of Nightshade, and St. Mary's mouldering fane,
And the stone abbot, after circuit made
In wantonness of heart, a joyous band
Of school-boys hastening to their distant home
Along the margin of the moonlit sea—
We beat with thundering hoofs the level sand.

(10:554-567)

The false hope following the death of Robespierre took him back to the earlier illusion "that the abbey existed out of time and that he could enjoy there a kind of timeless paradise on earth." [23] In Book 13 Wordsworth does not find the sunrise, but he does find a natural image or scene in which he tries to find the same power, the power to wrest reborn light or vision out of the "night" of his despair at the poem's direction.

The Moon stood naked in the Heavens, at height
Immense above my head, and on the shore
I found myself of a huge sea of mist,
Which, meek and silent, rested at my feet:
A hundred hills their dusky backs upheaved
All over this still Ocean, and beyond,
Far, far beyond, the vapours shot themselves,
In headlands, tongues, and promontory shapes,
Into the Sea, the real Sea, that seem'd
To dwindle, and give up its majesty,
Usurp'd upon as far as sight could reach.
Meanwhile, the Moon look'd down upon this shew
In single glory, and we stood, the mist
Touching our very feet; and from the shore
At distance not the third part of a mile
Was a blue chasm; a fracture in the vapour,
A deep and gloomy breathing-place through which
Mounted the roar of waters, torrents, streams
Innumerable, roaring with one voice.
The universal spectacle throughout
Was shaped for admiration and delight,

23. David Ferry, *The Limits of Mortality* (Middleton, Conn.: Wesleyan Univ. Press, 1959), p. 153. The quotation is from Ferry's discussion of the hidden irony in bk. 10.

Grand in itself alone, but in that breach
Through which the homeless voice of waters rose,
That dark deep thoroughfare had Nature lodg'd
The Soul, the Imagination of the whole.

(13:41–65)

Impressive and suggestive as the scene is, Wordsworth does not leave
it, as he usually does, connected with only an expression of the emotions the scene waked in him. He explicates the image at some length,
even though claiming the while that it is a "perfect image" which "even
the grossest minds must see and hear" and one which "thrusts forth
upon the senses . . . the express / Resemblance" between the unity
of the visual scene and the unity the human imagination can create.
Thus the image is held up as proof that the "higher minds" can

send abroad
Like transformations, for themselves create
A like existence, and, whene'er it is
Created for them, catch it by an instinct.

(13:93–96)

The scene is left behind as Wordsworth continues his description of
the higher mind that he has been seeking to establish through the
poem.

Such minds are truly from the Deity,
For they are Powers; and hence the highest bliss
That can be known is theirs, the consciousness
Of whom they are habitually infused
Through every image, and through every thought,
And all impressions; hence religion, faith,
And endless occupation for the soul
Whether discursive or intuitive;
Hence sovereignty within and peace at will
Emotion which best foresight need not fear
Most worthy then of trust when most intense.
Hence chearfulness in every act of life
Hence truth in moral judgments and delight
That fails not in the external universe.

(13:106–119)

The vision is complete and "perfect," as it needs to be if the poem is to reach its "appointed close." But Wordsworth does not leave it without suggesting the question that motivated writing *The Prelude*, and which is still unanswered even though he has found a vision of "higher minds." Is *he* in fact a representative of those minds, or is anyone?

> Oh! who is he that hath his whole life long
> Preserv'd, enlarged, this freedom in himself?
> For this alone is genuine Liberty.

> (13:120–122)

Wordsworth's "genuine Liberty" is in the preservation and improvement of the state of "consciousness," but from the description itself there should be no question of the permanence of the state. The higher minds are *"habitually* infused / Through *every* image, and through *every* thought, / And *all* impressions" (italics added). These higher minds experience a "peace" which "best foresight need not fear," and which is "most worthy then of trust when most intense." Yet *The Prelude,* as the history of Wordsworth's mind, reveals a decidedly cyclical emotional pattern and proves nothing so much as that Wordsworth's emotion has been *least* worthy of trust when most intense. For it is the intensity of his emotional involvement that led him to error in the Simplon Pass, to "darkness visible" in his attempt to see the lake in its most peaceful moment at dawn, and to the ambiguous "anxiety of hope" and its "chastisement" in the second spot of time.

In the remainder of Book 13 it becomes increasingly clear that once more Wordsworth's "emotion," the intensity of his desire, has led him to a vision of higher minds in which he cannot find himself. His attempt to fit himself into the vision is weak and halting and begins with the disqualifying admission of a disunified mind.

> And yet, I trust, with undiminish'd powers,
> Witness, whatever falls my better mind,
> Revolving with the accidents of life,
> May have sustain'd, that, howsoe'er misled,
> I never, in the quest of right and wrong,
> Did tamper with myself from private aims;
> Nor was in any of my hopes the dupe

> Of selfish passions; nor did wilfully
> Yield ever to mean cares and low pursuits

$$(13:127-135)$$

Blake ended *Milton* with an intense moment of vision which can be compared with Wordsworth's vision on Snowdon. The structure of *Milton*, as an amplified single moment of time, and the internalized reference of all Blake's images, made that the perefect end for a prelude that sought to establish the autonomy of the human imagination. Wordsworth could not end his prelude there because his vision is, finally, of a group of minds, and the question of his own membership in the group—perhaps even the existence of the group—is left hanging, except as *The Prelude* seems to deny his claim of "having track'd the main essential Power, / Imagination, up her way sublime."

In addition to the problem of interpreting Wordsworth's tone, and the tendency to accept his complacency at face value, Wordsworth has confused the structure of the poem with his frequent suggestions that the selection of images for presentation is random. I have already discussed Wordsworth's image of himself in a "slow-moving boat," gazing at the water, "incumbent o'er the surface of past time." In an earlier image, Wordsworth claimed the same kind of random movement as the source of his earlier experiences themselves.

> Carelessly
> I gaz'd, roving as through a Cabinet
> Or wide Museum (throng'd with fishes, gems,
> Birds, crocodiles, shells) where little can be seen
> Well understood, or naturally endear'd,
> Yet still does every step bring something forth
> That quickens, pleases, stings; and here and there
> A casual rarity is singled out,
> And has its brief perusal, then gives way
> To others, all supplanted in their turn.

$$(3:651-660)$$

Wordsworth often emphasizes that he is selecting one image from many possible ones, but he does this lightly, as if any example would do as well as another.[24] There is a purpose behind this emphasis on

24. See bk. 7:148–150, 566–571, 648–649 where the repetition in close proximity almost achieves a formulaic effect.

random selection. Many of the childhood scenes are fungible in that they equally have "the charm / Of visionary things," and can all serve equally well the function of "almost" making "our Infancy itself / A visible scene, on which the sun is shining" (1:659–663). In context, of course, this is a minimal function; more important is the sense of honesty in a truly random selection that attempts to fully represent all aspects of early experience. To have ended *The Prelude* with Book 4 would have violated this sense of honesty by limiting the selection from experience. It would have meant imposing a pattern and making *The Prelude* into a work like the allegorical puppet show in Book 3—an "inferior exhibition, play'd / By wooden images" which expressed in "dwarf proportions—The limits of the great world." Even though the selection from experience is random and honestly attempts to be fully representative, Wordsworth still hoped that a pattern of growth would emerge to "fix the wavering balance of [his] mind" (1:650), that the incidents taken from his life would give the poem a structure, a movement from malady to cure, from loss of power to restoration, from fall to redemption.

*The Prelude* can profitably be compared at this point, where we are concerned with potential patterns in experience, with Book 1 of *The Excursion*, in which Wordsworth has given us a highly idealized biography of the Wanderer as a poet "sown by Nature" who achieves the "vision and the faculty divine." [25] The biography is divided into three parts: the boy (108–196); the youth (197–307); and the man (308–433). The first part reads almost like a highly selective abstract of the early parts of *The Prelude*. The Wanderer too sees the hills "Grow larger in the darkness" and with nature holds "communion, not from terror free." From the "great objects that . . . lay / Upon his mind like substances" he receives the "precious gift" of "An active power to fasten images / Upon his brain." Like Wordsworth, the Wanderer does not need books, but has been exposed to old romances. Finally, although he lacks the "pure delight of love," he has been prepared by Nature "to receive / Deeply the lesson deep of love," which one taught by nature "cannot but receive."

In the period of youth, the Wanderer learns the lesson of love from the "silent faces" of the clouds; and it is an emotional, not an intellectual lesson.

25. Begun in 1795 as *Margaret; or, The Ruined Cottage*, it later merged (probably after 1809) with *The Excursion*, bk. 1.

> Sound needed none,
> Nor any voice of joy; his spirit drank
> The spectacle: sensation, soul, and form,
> All melted into him; they swallowed up
> His animal being; in them did he live,
> And by them did he live; they were his life.
> In such access of mind, in such high hour
> Of visitation from the living God,
> Thought was not; in enjoyment it expired.
> No thanks he breathed, he proffered no request;
> Rapt into still communion that transcends
> The imperfect offices of prayer and praise,
> His mind was a thanksgiving to the power
> That made him; it was blessedness and love!
>
> (1:205–218)

Instead of watching the shepherds in their mountain glory as Words-worth did, the Wanderer himself is "A Herdsman on the lonely mountain-tops," where he learns directly the lesson that Wordsworth read into his image of the shepherd.

> But in the mountains did he *feel* his faith.
> All things, responsive to the writing, there
> Breathed immortality, revolving life,
> And greatness still revolving; infinite:
> There littleness was not; the least of things
> Seemed infinite; and there his spirit shaped
> Her prospects, nor did he believe,—he *saw*.
> What wonder if his being thus became
> Sublime and comprehensive!
>
> (1:226–234)

He reads Milton, and is intrigued as Wordsworth was, with a rudi-mentary knowledge of geometry. All this brings him almost to his eighteenth year, to a period of crisis in which

> he was o'erpowered
> By Nature; by the turbulence subdued
> Of his own mind; by mystery and hope
> And the first virgin passion of a soul
> Communing with the glorious universe.
>
> (1:282–286)

At this point the Wanderer is described as having a "fever of his heart" which he strives vainly "to mitigate." The experience is suggestive of Wordsworth's crucial period in books 10 and 11 of *The Prelude* which he attributed to a cause "That seems almost inherent in the Creature" (11:168). As Wordsworth was, the Wanderer is bothered by an obsession with what in *The Prelude* (10:848) is called "false imagination."

> From his intellect
> And from the stillness of abstracted thought
> He asked repose; and, failing oft to win
> The peace required, he scanned the laws of light
> Amid the roar of torrents, where they send
> From hollow clefts up to the clearer air
> A cloud of mist, that smitten by the sun
> Varies its rainbow hues. But vainly thus,
> And vainly by all other means, he strove
> To mitigate the fever of his heart.

> (1:291–300)

This scanning "the laws of light" suggests the attempt in *The Prelude* to find an image of perception that will illustrate a reciprocal union with nature. The failure of this image to mitigate the fever, and its similarity to the Snowdon image in Book 13 of *The Prelude,* can help us to understand the ambiguities of that image. But the main emphasis to be made here is that the "fever" rises just when the Wanderer "was summoned to select the course / Of humble industry that promised best / To yield him no unworthy maintenance." At the point of choosing his life's work, he is suffering a malaise that only the right choice can mitigate.

After a false start teaching in a village school, "a task he was unable to perform," the Wanderer elects the profession of "vagrant Merchant," and it is his devotion to this calling and to the "public roads" that alleviates—without effort—the troubling fever.

> there
> Spontaneously had his affections thriven
> Amid the bounties of the year, the peace
> And liberty of nature; there he kept
> In solitude and solitary thought
> His mind in a just equipoise of love.
> Serene it was, unclouded by the cares

Of ordinary life; unvexed, unwarped
By partial bondage.

(1:350–358)

As the absence of "painful pressure from without" leads him to "wisdom," it also purges the guilt and fear of his early life, so that "Whate'er in docile childhood or in youth, / He had imbibed of fear or darker thought / Was melted all away." Thus taught and purged, he is eventually able to become a true teacher, helping the narrator to see in "the forms of things" around the ruined cottage "an image of tranquility," and

That secret spirit of humanity
Which, 'mid the calm oblivious tendencies
Of nature, 'mid her plants, and weeds, and flowers,
And silent overgrowings, still survived.

(1:927–930)

It is the same lesson that remained implicit and unavailable to Martha Ray (and the sea captain *and* Wordsworth) in *The Thorn*, but here it is brought into the open. The narrator is both "admonished" and "comforted" by the Wanderer's tale and retires calmly with him to his "evening resting-place." This is a marked and deliberate contrast to the narrator's condition at the beginning of the poem, fighting his way forward in a state of "hope" towards a place of "Rest" and "livelier joy."

Across a bare wide Common I was toiling
With languid steps that by the slippery turf
Were baffled; nor could my weak arm disperse
The host of insects gathering round my face,
And ever with me as I paced along.

(1:21–25)

Book 1 of *The Excursion* is almost a complete abstract, or canon, of an ideal poetic career. It describes the growth and education of the poet, gives an example of his mature poetic work (469–916) and illustrates the desired emotional and educational effect on the audience in the person of the narrator. It is, in miniature, an example of the kind of framework in which *The Prelude* should fit. *The Prelude* was intended to be an embodiment in concrete biographical detail of the same kind of growth pattern attributed to the Wanderer. There is also an oblique correspondence between the Wanderer's tale, and its effect, and the kind of poetry (*Guilt and Sorrow*) Wordsworth describes in Book 12 as his own best poetic achievement.

The Wanderer, however, is not a poet in the true sense, and Wordsworth warns us, even before the biography begins, that he is never to become one; he is only one of those "Poets that are sown by Nature." Somewhere in his development was missing an essential experience that might have enabled him to become a poet in the true sense. Wordsworth suggests several possible reasons for this failure in development, important clues to Wordsworth's concept of a poet.

> Oh! many are the Poets that are sown
> By Nature; men endowed with highest gifts,
> The vision and the faculty divine;
> Yet wanting the accomplishment of verse,
> (Which, in the docile season of their youth,
> It was denied them to acquire, through lack
> Of culture and the inspiring aid of books,
> Or haply by a temper too severe,
> Or a nice backwardness afraid of shame)
> Nor having e'er, as life advanced, been led
> By circumstance to take unto the height
> The measure of themselves, these favoured Beings,
> All but a scattered few, live out their time,
> Husbanding that which they possess within,
> And go to the grave, unthought of.

$$(1:77–91)$$

The Wanderer's lack of "the accomplishment of verse," and its three possible causes, does not seem too crucial to his career. Judging from *The Prelude*, the Wanderer was exposed to an adequate amount of "culture" and to the necessary minimum of "books." And even though he seems to have a rather severe "temper," and probably a certain degree of "nice backwardness," these handicaps could be overcome by aspiration if the desire to become a poet were strong enough. Therefore more significant is the second reason with its implications that the self-conscious choice to become a poet is necessary and that the choice is somehow imposed "By circumstance" that forces the potential poet

to undergo a detailed ("unto the height") self-examination. In this
context the lack of conflict in the Wanderer's life would seem to be
relevant. After his one crisis, the inevitable "fever" accompanying "the
first virgin passion of a soul / Communing with the glorious universe,"
he is "spontaneously" cured. His life became one

> unclouded by the cares
> Of ordinary life; unvexed, unwarped
> By partial bondage.

> (1:356–358)

Although his life is a comfortable and valuable one—which is much of
the point of the whole book—he lacks both the aspiration and the
self-doubt that led Wordsworth to attempt *The Prelude*. Wordsworth's
attitude is too complex here, and the evidence too meagre, for us to
attempt a complete description of his state of mind. Yet we can detect
signs of an ambivalence that is important for an understanding of *The
Prelude* and of the more general concept of a prelude to vision. The
Wanderer's is a happy, perhaps even ideal, life with adequate financial
reward and an even more important moral reward in his ability to
teach the comforting and admonishing message of "The secret spirit
of humanity." But the Wanderer is not a poet, and the "Circumstance"
that would enable—or force—him to become a poet is missing in the
general benignity of his life. Wordsworth is clearly implying that to
become a poet, the Wanderer would have to give up his inner tranquility and the exclusively *outward* nature of his sympathy and experience.

> In his steady course,
> No piteous revolutions had he felt,
> No wild varieties of joy and grief.
> Unoccupied by sorrow of its own,
> His heart lay open; and, by nature tuned
> And constant sympathy with man, he was alive
> To all that was enjoyed where'er he went,
> And all that was endured; for, in himself
> Happy, and quiet in his cheerfulness,
> He had no painful pressure from without
> That made him turn aside from wretchedness
> With coward fears. He could *afford* to suffer

With those whom he saw suffer. Hence it came
That in our best experience he was rich,
And in the wisdom of our daily life.

(1:358–373)

His very richness in the "best experience" stands between him and the
necessity of the self-examination that might enable him to become a
poet. It seems unwise to ask if Wordsworth, given the choice, would
have changed places with the Wanderer; for the one point to be made
from comparing the life of the Wanderer to the life of the poet is that
the "choice" or self-election to poethood is one forced on some potential
poets and not on others. This is as close as Wordsworth comes to
seeing poetry as the result of a demonic urge, or curse. Hidden though
it is, the doubt implied about whether or not it is really a good thing
to attempt to become a poet, to be compelled to sacrifice personal
happiness to the search for vision, is a question of values that a poet
attempting a prelude to vision must inevitably encounter, either directly
or indirectly. Wordsworth never asked the question directly, as did
Keats in his *Fall of Hyperion*, and Crane in *The Tunnel* part of *The
Bridge*, but he became increasingly aware, as had Blake, of the difficulty
and sacrifice involved in the attempt to become a poet. It is in the later
poets that we find the strongest and most direct expressions of doubt
about the value of the struggle, coupled, however, with the same sense
of the inevitability of the struggle implied by Wordsworth when he
speaks of being "led / By circumstance." In this respect Crane's metaphor of the cruel inoculation seems as applicable to Wordsworth's
career as to his own.

O cruelly to inoculate the brinking dawn
With antennae toward worlds that glow and sink;—
To spoon us out more liquid than the dim
Locution of the eldest star, and pack
The conscience navelled in the plunging wind,
Umbilical to call—and straightway die!

(*The Tunnel*: 109–114)

*The Prelude*, like the great *Ode*, is the history of the loss of the visionary gleam which Crane calls a "song we fail to keep," a song "Our
tongues recant like beaten weather vanes." For both, the visionary

power is associated with youth, as a state of "conscience navelled in the plunging wind, / Umbilical to call," a state doomed to death. Wordsworth is forced to mourn and memorialize the death in *The Prelude*, but he is also able to find an alternative vision and to see the aspiration behind *The Prelude* as a mistake, a weakness in himself, rather than a deceit in nature or a "cruel inoculation."

Although he never came to see it as a curse, Wordsworth was clearly aware that to become a poet it is not enough to have been sown as a potential poet by nature as were both the Wanderer and Wordsworth ("fair seed time had my soul"). One must in some sense prove he is a poet, and this demands the peculiar combination of aspiration to create "a work that should endure" together with self-doubt, "the wavering balance of my mind," a combination that stimulated the writing of *The Prelude* and gives it its strong sense of urgency. It is on the success of *The Prelude* that Wordsworth felt his becoming a true poet depended; and the passage in Book 1 of *The Excursion* suggests an even broader necessity. All poets must "take unto the height / The measure of themselves" before they can realize their hope of becoming poets.

By Wordsworth's own criteria *The Prelude* is obviously a failure because it did not, in fact, enable him to go on and write the "spousal verse" of the "great consummation" of man and nature. Within *The Prelude* itself are signs of failure, in Wordsworth's recognition that the hope motivating his self-examination was mistaken: he could never find *in himself* the image he sought of man in a creative union with nature. Therefore, he could not find the image of the poet he was seeking, he could not *be* that poet, and the creation, the epic vision he hoped to accomplish, was thus one of the "things that cannot be."

The poem becomes a qualified success when we recognize that it tentatively offers an alternative union with nature and an alternative kind of poetic statement that can be achieved on the basis of such a union. Wordsworth could not be one of the "higher minds," but he could be the poet of *Guilt and Sorrow*, a poet in the limited sense of the Wanderer, reading "an image of tranquility" in "the forms of things," admonishing and comforting the reader as the narrator of *The Excursion* is admonished and comforted by the Wanderer. Wordsworth reached the public road of the Wanderer only after taking the lengthy detour of *The Prelude*, but it was a detour necessary for him as it was not necessary for the Wanderer. The nearest Wordsworth could come to writing the great work was *The Excursion*, and the state of consciousness revealed in that work is that of the Wanderer, not that of the higher mind Wordsworth had hoped to find in himself.

There is finally no specific reason we can find in *The Prelude* for Wordsworth's failure to become, in and through the process of writing it, an epic poet. Instead, we are left with a vague but strong sense of inevitability, the feeling that Wordsworth has attempted to achieve "things that cannot be." *The Prelude* begins as a song of triumph, but the attempt itself, and its failure, become in the end material for a song of experience.

The part of *The Prelude* that most clearly and fully expresses this failure is the Vaudracour and Julia episode in Book 9. The story is a condensation of much of *The Prelude* and is, in a double sense, the poem *The Prelude* prepared Wordsworth to write. First, it is an expression of the most important discovery made in the poem—the recognition that the desired union with nature cannot be. Second, because it is a tale like the Wanderer's, it is an example of the limited kind of poem the poet will finally recognize as the only work he is capable to perform. It lacks only the final part, the moral comfort to be gained from a properly perceived catastrophe; but this is supplied indirectly in the remainder of *The Prelude*.

Book 9 begins with an important observation on the movement of the poem up to that point.

> As oftentimes a River, it might seem,
> Yielding in part to old remembrances,
> Part sway'd by fear to tread on onward road
> That leads direct to the devouring sea
> Turns, and will measure back his course, far back,
> Towards the very regions which he cross'd
> In his first outset; so have we long time
> Made motions retrograde, in like pursuit
> Detain'd. But now we start afresh; I feel
> An impulse to precipitate my Verse.
> Fair greetings to this shapeless eagerness,
> Whene'er it comes, needful in work so long,
> Thrice needful to the argument which now
> Awaits us; Oh! how much unlike the past!
> One which though bright the promise, will be found

Ere far we shall advance, ungenial, hard
To treat of, and forbidding in itself.

(9:1–17)

The fear of the "devouring sea" reminds us of the dream allegory in Book 5 and the quixotic attempt to save poetry and geometry from a nature that threatens to become shapeless and chaotic, incommensurable with man's faculties. Now, no matter "how much unlike the past," he feels a "shapeless eagerness" to explore the new experience. This is not to be merely a recording of a former experience, for the "shapeless eagerness" is a reference to his present emotional state. In addition to recalling the history of a past crisis, he is entering a new crisis in the attempt to review a past experience and to fit it into the desired pattern of the growth of his own mind toward a reciprocal union with nature. He is ready for the attempt, even though he knows the experience was, and will be, "hard / To treat of, and forbidding in itself."

Although there are frequent Miltonic allusions throughout *The Prelude*, there is a particular kind of allusion, with a particular tone, which stands out with a greater degree of significance. It comes whenever Wordsworth verges on an encounter with the problem of the fall and can convey a definite tension when the reader is aware of the conflict implicit in Wordsworth's use of Milton.[26] Wordsworth's theme forces him to recognize fallen vision in his own world of experience, and Milton gives him an invaluable point of reference for suggesting the fall and describing its effects. Yet Wordsworth is hoping to recover in his own life the "Paradise" Milton saw as lost forever.

Paradise, and groves
Elysian, Fortunate Fields—like those of old
Sought in the Atlantic Main—why should they be
A history only of departed things,
Or a mere fiction of what never was?

("Prospectus" to *The Recluse*: 47–51)

He is hoping to return to the perceptual paradise described in Book 8, but his allusion to Milton at the beginning of Book 9 is a premonition

26. See bk. 7, in which Wordsworth relies heavily on Milton in treating the theme of fallen vision in the "theatre" of London; also bk. 8, in which he uses allusions to Milton's description of the garden in his presentation of the perceptual paradise in which he grew up.

that he has not found the "greater Muse, if such / Descend to earth or dwell in highest heaven!" He may be turning, as Milton turned at the beginning of Book 9 of *Paradise Lost*, from an unrecoverably lost paradise to a recognition of

> foul distrust, and breach
> Disloyal on the part of Man, revolt,
> And disobedience; on the part of Heav'n
> Now alienated, distance and distaste,
> Anger and just rebuke, and judgement giv'n.

After the introduction, Wordsworth returns in chronology to the end of Book 7 ("Residence in London"), in which he drew heavily from Milton to suggest the disorder and chaos of the city. He traces the course of his identification of the Revolution as an expression of the dignity of man with his own earlier impression of the dignity of man as described in Book 8.

> To aspirations then of our own minds
> Did we appeal; and finally beheld
> A living confirmation of the whole
> Before us in a People risen up
> Fresh as the morning Star: elate we look'd
> Upon their virtues, saw in rudest men
> Self-sacrifice the finest, generous love
> And continence of mind, and sense of right
> Uppermost in the midst of fiercest strife.

> (9:387–395)

The attempt to make the transition from a theoretical "hope in Man, / Justice and peace," achieved first in the "retirement" of "academic Groves," to a concrete embodiment of that hope in living men is recognized as a trial of nature comparable to the Revolution. Beaupuy becomes the political counterpart or projection of Wordsworth in his attempt to give hope "outwardly a shape . . . of benediction to the world."

> And when we chanc'd
> One day to meet a hunger-bitten Girl,
> Who crept along, fitting her languid self

> Unto a Heifer's motion, by a cord
> Tied to her arm, and picking thus from the lane
> Its sustenance, while the Girl with her two hands
> Was busy knitting, in a heartless mood
> Of solitude, and at the sight my Friend
> In agitation said, " 'Tis against *that*
> Which we are fighting."

(9:510–519)

It is against *that* image of man Wordsworth is fighting in the poem, and he too sees the cause of the problem as a thwarting of nature's availability for a higher union with man. The girl is given basically the same mode of existence as the leech gatherer or the Old Cumberland Beggar, except that they are old almost beyond age, and she is young. The solitude that contributed to their nobility is, for her, a "heartless mood," and her having to "fit" her motion to that of a dumb beast is degrading, whereas their passive endurance "fitting" them to the natural scene is an essential part of their message of survival in nature.

Even before this image of the girl, Wordsworth has planted a suggestion that his hope, now as then, is for "things that cannot be." Among his seemingly casual descriptions of the landscape he mentions a rural castle

> where a Lady lodg'd
> By the first Francis wooed, and bound to him
> In chains of mutual passion; from the Tower,
> As a Tradition of the Country tells,
> Practis'd to commune with her Royal Knight
> By cressets and love-beacons, intercourse
> 'Twixt her high-seated Residence and his
> Far off at Chambord on the Plain beneath.

(9:485–492)

Wordsworth did not know, or remember, or care about the outcome of the courtship. What was memorable for him was the suggestive image of the lady in the heights, Francis on the plain below, and the confinement of their passion to an awkward intercourse of signs. In it we can see an image of the poet, trying to read the signs of nature from his distant position on the plain of error and confusion, making his own overtures and signs, and hoping for an eventual consummation of his passion. The image is, in itself, of minor importance in the context of Book 9, but it serves as an important anticipation of the Vaudracour and Julia episode which concludes the book.

The transition to the tale is a bit strange, and Wordsworth does nothing on an explicit level to make it "fit" the poem. "Having touch'd this argument," he says (of Beaupuy's beliefs and hopes), "I shall not, as my purpose was, take note / Of other matters which detain'd us oft." What he does instead is "Draw from obscurity a tragic Tale / Not in its spirit singular indeed / But haply worth memorial." If the tale is indeed a stray digression, then it is remarkable that it comprises nearly half of and concludes a book beginning in a spirit of "shapeless eagerness." We must believe that the tale is, in fact, "worth memorial" for Wordsworth, even though the nature of its significance does not lie near the surface.

The "obscurity" from which the tale is drawn has had an unfortunate effect on almost all readers' reactions to the tale—and I say "reactions" deliberately, for there has been almost no attempt to interpret the tale and to find in it a significant relation to the rest of the poem. Instead, the tale is regarded as a deliberately disguised, clumsy, and poorly written biographical episode, which was wisely omitted from the later version of the poem.[27] Wordsworth is accused of hypocrisy and prudery for slighting what must have been one of the most important emotional periods of his life. Or he is commended for wisdom in having left the past in the past, except for a coded allusion that could be recognized with propriety by intimate friends and family.

I suggest that Wordsworth has condensed in the tale the true emotional crisis of the poem and has come as close as he could to giving the reasons for the crisis and his loss of hope for achieving the desired union with nature. The idea came to Wordsworth from a recognition of the parallel between his poetic quest for a union with nature and his courtship of Annette Vallon. The analogy suggested earlier, between *The Prelude* and a prolonged love poem, becomes in this tale a metaphor, so that Wordsworth, when "he beheld / A vision, and he lov'd the thing he saw," is not "viewing a woman and not Nature," but

27. According to Havens, the more one studies it, "the more amazingly inept and inexplicable it becomes" (*Mind of a Poet*, p. 512). Bloom suggests that "the story is a gap in the poem" whether it is included or left out (*Visionary Company*, p. 153). The tale is usually not discussed at all by critics who limit their attention to the later version of *The Prelude*.

viewing nature in the guise of a beloved woman.[28] The French Revolution was crucial in both sides of the parallel, for it represented the opportunity of a trial of nature for the poet, and it brought the lover to his mistress. Also, the outcome of the Revolution—circumstance external to the desired union in both cases—forced the lover Wordsworth from his Annette and thwarted forever his poetic desire to confirm the hope for a reciprocal union between man and nature. From the few certain biographical details available, we do know that Wordsworth's feeling for Annette paralleled chronologically his growing interest in the Revolution, and that Annette's being a Royalist must have created some tension in the relationship even before the enforced separation. This is as far as we can safely take the biographical detail, for Wordsworth's illegitimate child lived, Wordsworth did not retire into an "imbecile mind," and the whole elaborate paraphernalia of the tale does not fit what little we know about the relationship between Wordsworth and Annette Vallon. It does, however, fit the poem Wordsworth was writing; and details that seem inappropriate to the biography, or to a good tale of lovers, are essential for a full understanding of *The Prelude*.

The tale begins in the "happy time of youthful Lovers" with Vaudracour coming into an "inheritance of blessedness," which is to be, like the "heritage" in the great *Ode*, something that cannot survive the passing of youth. The youthful lovers, like Romeo and Juliet, live in a separate world that cannot survive contact with the older world of conventional maturity. But there is more to it than this, for they also cannot grow into that conventional maturity and preserve the reciprocal union they have established in youth.

> Each other's advocate, each other's help,
> Nor ever happy if they were apart:
> A basis this for deep and solid love,
> And endless constancy, and placid truth

$$(9:574-577)$$

Mention is made of something that might "Beneath the outside of their youth, have lain / Reserv'd for mellower years," but the lovers in their passion cannot ignore present desire for a possible union in the

28. Bloom (*Visionary Company*, p. 152) cites this as the only place Wordsworth uses such language to describe a woman, but I think it should be read as another case of woman standing, not for herself, but for the passionately desired mother-wife nature.

future. Vaudracour takes the initiative and attempts an immediate consummation, trusting to nature "for a happy end."

> Seeing so many bars betwixt himself
> And the dear haven where he wish'd to be
> In honourable wedlock with his love
> Without certain knowledge of his own,
> Was inwardly prepared to turn aside
> From law and custom, and entrust himself
> To Nature for a happy end of all.

$$(9:597-603)$$

Standing in the way of the union, however, are the inevitable unwilling parents, especially Vaudracour's father, who is most removed from youth and thus from possible sympathy, and who has the largest investment in custom. Julia's parents are, like the French populace, "Unhonour'd of Nobility," and Vaudracour's passion for her, in opposition to his father's nobility, parallels Wordsworth's interest in the French Revolution in this respect.

Vaudracour's trust in nature causes him to anticipate "honourable wedlock," and the remainder of the tale is concerned with the pair's attempts to avoid the pressure of external circumstances working against their union and the survival of their child. Vaudracour pledges that "nothing less / Than death should make him yield up hope to be / A blessed Husband of the Maid he loved," as Wordsworth expressed a willingness to perish for the Revolutionary cause. But their only recourse is to withdraw completely to a remote place where they can, if not preserve their youth, at least preserve their union and share their happiness in solitude.

So far, Vaudracour has felt completely worthy of Julia, but when an attempt is made to capture him, he commits a murder. The murder is caused by interference from without, but it is also Vaudracour's own "first impulse" of "rage" that causes him to kill rather than submit. The shadow of guilt complicates still further the problem of achieving a union, for it suggests an internal failure, such as Wordsworth is concerned with in the first two books of *The Prelude*. After the murder, the only way Vaudracour can regain his freedom is to promise "to sit down / Quietly in his Father's House." The father, like the force of custom in the *Ode*, is intent on seeing the "Shades of the prison-house begin to close / Upon the growing Boy." But Vaudracour rebels after only eight days and flees to Julia with his new burden of guilt.

> "All right is gone,
> Gone from me. Thou no longer now art mine,
> I thine; a Murderer, Julia, cannot love
> An innocent Woman; I behold thy face
> I see thee and my misery is complete"

$$(9:706-710)$$

To this Julia "could not give him answer," and though they are reunited the time is now one of "dejection, sorrow and remorse" for Vaudracour. There is a marked contrast between Vaudracour's apparent lack of remorse for his relations with Julia and his extreme regret at having violated a different convention in his desire to join Julia.

Still another mandate is issued for Vaudracour's arrest, and he hides to avoid the searchers; but when he returns, thinking them gone, he is taken again, and forced in solitude to contemplate his prospects.

> and what
> Through dark and shapeless fear of things to come,
> And what through strong compunction for the past
> He suffer'd breaking down in heart and mind.

$$(9:747-750)$$

He lives for a while under guard in the same city with Julia, until once more he obtains his liberty "upon condition / That to his Father's house he should return." Although his father's house is a kind of prison, it has become the only place where Vaudracour can achieve something like liberty. Conformity to custom, suggested by enforced residence in his father's house, is the only way he can avoid the error of giving way to his impulses and to the guilt and suffering to which they lead him.

Their child is finally born, to a prayer "that he might never be / As wretched as his Father," and at times Vaudracour is able to hope that the child itself may be the answer to his problems. Perhaps through the child he can be reunited with his love, even though the union seemed doomed before the child was conceived.

> With ornaments the prettiest you shall dress
> Your Boy, as soon as he can run about,
> And when he thus is at his play my Father
> Will see him from the window, and the Child
> Will by his beauty move his Grandsire's heart,
> So that it shall be soften'd, and our loves
> End happily, as they began.
>
> (9:803–809)

The union seemed impossible or difficult from the first, yet Vaudracour trusted in nature and fathered the child. Now the child itself might be the means to achieving the marriage, the union that is the only basis for its continued survival. The situation parallels exactly the poet's attempt to write a prelude. The only sound basis for a genuine imaginative creation, a work that will endure, is the reciprocal union with nature that the poet desires, but has not yet found through his poetry. So Wordsworth begins *The Prelude* in anticipation of the union, knowing that if found or achieved the union will in a sense be retroactive, providing a basis for both *The Prelude* and for a great work that will then follow.

Vaudracour, however, is "but seldom" able to see the possibility of achieving his union through the child and is totally unable to follow through with any concerted effort.

> These gleams
> Appeared but seldom; oftener was he seen
> Propping a pale and melancholy face
> Upon the Mother's bosom, resting thus
> His head upon one breast, while from the other
> The Babe was drawing in its quiet food.
>
> (9:809–814)

The relationships at this point in the poem are complicated, but extremely significant. After the birth of the child, Julia is both a mother and a lover. In both roles she continues to suggest the nature with which the poet (as Vaudracour) is seeking a form of reciprocal union. In this image, Wordsworth has combined the two functions of nature (lover and mother) and has divided himself, simultaneously seeing himself as past infant and present man. As infant he is like the babe he recalls in Book 2 of *The Prelude*.

> Bless'd the infant Babe,
> (For with my best conjectures I would trace
> The progress of our being) blest the Babe,
> Nurs'd in his Mother's arms, the Babe who sleeps
> Upon his Mother's breast, who, when his soul
> Claim's manifest kindred with an earthly soul,
> Doth gather passion from his Mother's eye!

$$(9:237-243)$$

This is a recalled union only, however, one forever past, but one that should be succeeded by a new union in a different relationship. Nature should change from mother to spouse, and the poet from infant to spouse, keeping only the "passion" kindled in the mother/wife's eye.

> "Julia, how much thine eyes
> Have cost me!"

$$(9:817-818)$$

Yet the change cannot be accomplished. The poet retains the happy memory of himself as a child, but now he can only prop a "pale and melancholy face" upon the "Mother's bosom," which gives him neither maternal nor marital comfort. He can be neither the child he once was, nor the spouse he desires to be.

When the unavoidable decision is made, that Julia must "retire / Into a Convent, and be there immured," Vaudracour receives the news "in calm despondency, / Composed and silent, without outward sign / Of even the least emotion." The reason for his surprising resignation soon becomes clear: he has transferred his entire concern to the child, the only thing remaining to him that he has a chance of keeping.

> His eyes he scarcely took,
> Through all that journey, from the Chair in which
> The Babe was carried; and at every Inn
> Or place at which they halted or reposed
> Laid him upon his knees, nor would permit
> The hands of any but himself to dress
> The Infant or undress.

$$(9:879-885)$$

The concern for the child now is not for the "creation" that was to thrive on the basis of the reciprocal union with nature. The significance of the child has changed from the symbol of such a creation to a reminder of the poet's youth, when he too lay upon nature as upon a "Mother's bosom." If he cannot achieve the marriage, perhaps he can at least keep alive the memory of the former maternal union.

But this too is denied to him, for after his journey he "reach'd / His Father's House, where to the innocent Child / Admittance was denied." As in the *Ode*, the conditions of residence in the father's house, or the "prison-house," are that the visionary gleam of youth be given up: "At length the Man perceives it die away, / And fade into the light of common day." Vaudracour cannot enter the house with the child, and he will not leave it behind, so he retires "with leave given" to a "lodge that stood / Deep in a Forest . . . at the age / Of four and twenty summers."

> It consoled him here
> To attend upon the Orphan and perform
> The office of a Nurse to his young Child
> Which after a short time by some mistake
> Or indiscretion of the Father, died.
> The Tale I follow to its last recess
> Of suffering or of peace, I know not which;
> Theirs be the blame who caused the woe, not mine.

> (9:903–910)

This is indeed a climax of absurdity, if we insist on reading the whole episode only as an inserted tale of lovers. But details that seem meaningless or absurd in such a context become highly significant when the tale is read as an integral part of *The Prelude*. Wordsworth goes on, despite having claimed not to know whether Vaudracour's "last recess" was one of "suffering or of peace," to say that "in those solitary shades / His days he wasted, an imbecile mind." So far as the tale parallels his own development, as he was exploring that development in *The Prelude*, he cannot yet say whether his is to be a fate of continued suffering or peace. At the end of Book 11, in the second spot of time, Wordsworth does return to his father's house, and he returns to a chastisement and correction of desire. In Book 13 he has carried the work "Even to the very going out of youth, / The period which our Story now hath reached." Thus he has not made Vaudracour's mistake of refusing to reenter his father's house in order to keep alive his youth, and Vaudracour's fate remains a memory of something that "had been escaped."

> Behold me then
> Once more in Nature's presence, thus restored
> Or otherwise, and strengthened once again
> (With memory left of what had been escaped)
> To habits of devoutest sympathy.

(11:393-397)

This is basically a negative conclusion, resignation of a wrong desire and escape from the ultimate consequences of that desire. At this stage, the positive outcome is still tentative—he is "restored / Or otherwise"— and we must turn, as I have already suggested, to other poems written during the period for a full understanding of the final resolution, the alternative union toward which *The Prelude* leads.

In *Resolution and Independence,* we have a description of the "escape" which is fuller than that in *The Prelude;* it goes beyond the "memory left of what had been escaped" to suggest in the image of the leech gatherer what Wordsworth has escaped to. In this poem Wordsworth considers Chatterton and Burns, poets who, like Vaudracour, refused to give up their youth. "We poets in our youth begin in gladness; / But thereof come in the end despondency and madness." Wordsworth escapes this particular madness and the isolated "imbecile mind" of Vaudracour and the eternal despair of Martha Ray. At the point where *he* is "Perplexed, and longing to be comforted," he finds his image of "human strength" in the leech gatherer, realizing the opportunity (unrecognized by Martha Ray and the sea captain) for finding human significance in the image of the thorn.

In the final book of *The Prelude* Wordsworth identifies "The period which our Story now hath reached" as "the very going out of youth." This is the period of the Snowdon ascent, which is introduced as "one of those excursions" he had been recalling at the very end of Book 12.

> Nor is it, Friend, unknown to thee, at least
> Thyself delighted, who for my delight
> Hast said, perusing some imperfect verse
> Which in that lonesome journey was composed,
> That also then I must have exercised

> Upon the vulgar forms of present things
> And actual world of our familiar days,
> A higher power, have caught from them a tone,
> An image, and a character, by books
> Not hitherto reflected. . . .
>              and I remember well
> That in life's every-day appearances
> I seem'd about this period to have sight
> Of a new world, a world, too, that was fit
> To be transmitted and made visible
> To other eyes

(12:356–373)

It seems clear that the "imperfect verse" referred to here is *The Female Vagrant,* which later became *Guilt and Sorrow: Or Incidents Upon Salisbury Plain.* Although this poem was composed in 1791/1792, 1793/1794, 1795, 1798, and was revised frequently up to 1845, Wordsworth associated the poem with "the latter part of the summer of 1793" in his "Advertisement, Prefixed to the First Edition of this Poem, Published in 1842." Thus the chronological terminus of *The Prelude* is Wordsworth's twenty-fourth year, the very going out of his youth, and we have in the "Advertisement" an important version of his state at that time.

> During the latter part of the summer of 1793, having passed a month in the Isle of Wight, in view of the fleet which was then preparing for sea off Portsmouth at the commencement of the war, I left the place with melancholy forebodings. The American war was still fresh in memory. The struggle which was beginning and which many thought would be brought to a speedy close by the irresistible arms of Great Britain being added to those of the Allies, I was assured in my own mind would be of long continuance, and productive of distress and misery beyond all possible calculation. This conviction was pressed upon me by having been a witness, during a long residence in revolutionary France, of the spirit which prevailed in that country. After leaving the Isle of Wight, I spent two days in wandering on foot over Salisbury Plain, which, though cultivation was then widely spread through parts of it, had upon the whole a still more impressive appearance than it now retains.
> The monuments and traces of antiquity, scattered in abun-

dance over that region, led me unavoidably to compare what we know or guess of those remote times with certain aspects of modern society, and with calamities, principally those consequent upon war, to which, more than other classes of men, the poor are subject.

It is more than coincidence that Vaudracour retires with his child "at the age / Of four and twenty summers" only to have it die "by some mistake / Or indiscretion of the Father." This is the same age Wordsworth associates with the going out of his youth, with his finding a "new world," and his finding a new poetic mode in the form of a moralistic narrative or tale. Thus the period of writing *The Prelude* may be seen as a digression from that poetic mode, and *The Excursion* a return to it—with a premonition of the return strongly expressed at the end of Book 12. The form of the Vaudracour and Julia episode, a tale with a potential but ambiguous and hidden message, is a crucial factor in understanding its function within the larger scope of *The Prelude*. The "shapeless eagerness" of the beginning of Book 9 is fulfilled in a surprising but not entirely unanticipated way. The tale reflects both Wordsworth's loss of the hope of returning to his youth and finding in it the basis for a spousal union with nature, and the poetic mode appropriate to the alternative union with nature. The many recalled experiences of over-eager journeys, thwarted attempts at elevated communion with nature, and the mistaken hope that the French Revolution would be a successful trial of nature, are prefigurations of the total structure of *The Prelude*.

In *Guilt and Sorrow* the "Traveller on the skirt of Sarum's Plain," wandering lost and buffeted by the storm, catches a brief glimpse of a guide-post that seems to indicate a split in the road.

> Once did the lightning's faint disastrous gleam
> Disclose a naked guide-post's double head,
> Sight which, tho' lost at once, a gleam of pleasure shed.

(133–135)

Similarly, when he wrote *Guilt and Sorrow*, Wordsworth had caught briefly the "sight / Of a new world." But he lost it and had to retrace his development in and through *The Prelude* up to that point again, where he could at last see that there were two roads and that his anxiety of hope had led him to desire the wrong alternative. The traveller in *Guilt and Sorrow,* his "hope returned" after a long period at sea away from his wife and children, tries to return home.

> By Fancy's aid
> The happy husband flies, his arms to throw
> Round his wife's neck; the prize of victory laid
> In her full lap, he sees such sweet tears flow
> As if thenceforth nor pain nor trouble she could know.
>
> (59–63)

But he failed, for a motiveless crime—attributed to "a mood" only— laid on him a burden of guilt that forced him to flee and become a vagrant. His "fancy" and "hope" misled him, and his mood betrayed him. The story is another premonition of the course Wordsworth was to follow in his attempt to write *The Prelude.*

The Wanderer finds his road at the proper age, eighteen, after a brief mistaken attempt to teach public school, "a task he was unable to perform." Wordsworth missed this road in his own eighteenth year, and in the following six years, he accumulated the experiences the Wanderer avoids, the "circumstance" that leads poets "to take unto the height / The measure of themselves." In writing *The Prelude,* Wordsworth took another six years to retrace his development, to take measure of himself up to the very going out of youth and to his own final discovery that writing the spousal verse of man and nature was a task he was unable to perform. After this discovery he turned, like the Wanderer, to the public road of *The Excursion* and the images it still held of

> That secret spirit of humanity
> Which, 'mid the calm oblivious tendencies
> Of nature, 'mid her plants, and weeds, and flowers,
> And silent overgrowings, still survived.
>
> (1:927–930)

Keats, who was forced to condense most of a whole life's experience into the span of a few intense years, was to follow the same pattern of developing self-recognition that Wordsworth followed. Keats did not live long enough to find the moral lessons of human catastrophe that finally admonished and comforted the despair of Wordsworth's vision. He died still in the midst of the struggle. Wordsworth finally gave up the attempt to achieve the *segno lieto* (joyous mark) that Dante finally reached only through divine grace and the guidance of Beatrice. But "gave up" perhaps implies more deliberate power of the will than Wordsworth actually exercised in the resignation of his attempt to write a prelude to vision. The best description of this resignation is given by Beatrice to Dante in the first canto of the *Paradiso*; and the description here can serve as the last of the images I shall bring to bear upon Wordsworth's collection of images in *The Prelude*.

> It is true that, as a shape often does not accord with the art's intention because the material is deaf and unresponsive, so sometimes the creature, having the power, thus impelled, to turn aside another way, deviates from this course, and, as fire may be seen to fall from a cloud, so the primal impulse, diverted by false pleasure, is turned to the earth.[29]

29. *The Divine Comedy*, trans. J. D. Sinclair, vol. 3 *Paradiso*, canto 1 (London & New York: Oxford Univ. Press, 1961), pp. 127–135.

# Chapter 5

# Keats: In the Interval

I am ambitious of doing the world some good: if
I should be spared that may be the work of ma-
turer years—in the interval I will assay to reach
to as high a summit in Poetry as the nerve bestowed upon me will suffer. The faint conceptions
I have of Poems to come brings the blood frequently into my forehead.

—Keats

And I am merely a shadow hunched

Above the arrowy, still strings,
The maker of a thing yet to be made.

—Wallace Stevens, *The Man
With the Blue Guitar*

For Keats almost the whole problem of writing the "great poem" lay
in maintaining the aspiration that Wordsworth pointed to as distinguishing the true poet from the poet sown by nature. The problem for
him, even more than for Wordsworth, was a question of will, of achieving confidence in poetic vision as a valid and useful mode of perceiving
reality and in the finished poem as an embodiment of truth. His attempt to move from the lyric to the epic was an attempt to sustain
and expand the intense "happiness" experienced in the "moment" of
of inspired vision.

Wherein lies happiness? In that which becks
Our ready minds to fellowship divine,
A fellowship with essence; till we shine,

> Full alchemiz'd, and free of space . . .
>       —that moment have we stept
> Into a sort of oneness, and our state
> Is like a flowing spirit's.[1]

(*Endymion*: 777–797)

Of this particular passage Keats later said, "My having written that [Passage] Argument will perhaps be of the greatest Service to me of any thing I ever did." Yet he could also say, three months later, that he was "sometimes so very sceptical as to think Poetry itself a mere Jack a lanthern to amuse whoever may chance to be struck with its brilliance." The contradiction, and Keats's awareness of it, is essential for our understanding of what he was attempting in *The Fall of Hyperion* and for our interpretation of the results of his attempt. If "every mental pursuit takes its reality and worth from the ardour of the pursuer," then the maintenance of the "ardour" in its fullest intensity will be essential for the completion of any "mental pursuit." [2]

The inward history we can trace in all of Keats's writings, and especially in *The Fall*, lacks the more theoretical concern with vision found in Blake and Wordsworth. Their attempts to explore the epistemological basis of poetry are not of central relevance to Keats, although when he did make epistemological claims he tended to echo their spirit.

> What the imagination seizes as Beauty must be truth—whether it existed before or not—for I have the same Idea of all our Passions as of Love they are all in their sublime, creative of essential Beauty. . . . The imagination may be compared to Adam's dream—he awoke and found it truth. I am the more zealous in this affair, because I have never yet been able to perceive how any thing can be known for truth by consequitive reasoning—and yet it must be—Can it be that even the greatest Philosopher ever [when] arrived at his goal without putting aside numerous objections—However it may be, O for a Life of Sensations rather than of Thoughts! It is "a Vision in the form of Youth" a Shadow of reality to come—and this consideration has

---

1. All quotations of Keats's poetry are from *The Poems*, ed. E. de Selincourt, 5th ed. (London: Methuen & Co., 1926). Quotations of Keats's letters are from *The Letters of John Keats*, ed. Hyder E. Rollins, 2 vols. (Cambridge, Mass: Harvard Univ. Press, 1958).
2. Keats to John Taylor (Jan. 30, 1818), *Letters of Keats* 1:218; Keats to Benjamin Bailey (Mar. 13, 1818), *ibid.*, 1:242.

further conv[i]nced me for it has come as auxiliary to another favorite Speculation of mine, that we shall enjoy ourselves here after by having what we called happiness on Earth repeated in a finer tone and so repeated—And yet such a fate can only befall those who delight in Sensation rather than hunger as you do after Truth—Adam's dream will do here and seems to be a conviction that Imagination and its empyreal reflection is the same as human Life and its spiritual repetition.[3]

In Adam's dream, Keats found a perfect, condensed metaphor for the teleological imagination, but it was to prove a metaphor which had a logic and necessity of its own, a "silent Working" like that of the human imagination it illuminated for Keats. Adam's dream came from desire, as did Keats's urge to write an epic poem. But the realization of the dream for Adam led to knowledge of good and evil, to despair, and to the fall. In using the metaphor Keats was tempting fate, as Wordsworth had before in his use of Milton to describe a fall he hoped would be reversible.

Blake and Wordsworth did not slight the agony and despair necessary for achieving a comprehensive poetic vision of life. But they were as much concerned with the problem of *how* loss becomes profit as they were with the question of *whether* loss becomes profit. Keats went beyond them in his urge to question the spiritual rewards of poetry for the poet in this life, and in making this question a test of whether poetry can ultimately serve man. Even when Wordsworth resigned the hope of making paradise "a simple produce of the common day," he still was able to look for and find a spiritual benefit in the power of poetry to admonish and comfort man in his fallen state.

Few poets have been so concerned as Keats with turning their attention inward on the emotional aspects of the process of creation. In one of his earliest ambitious poems, *Sleep and Poetry*, he considered problems of poetic creation and value and produced some remarkable prophetic insights into the cause of his future development as an artist. In his last major work, *The Fall of Hyperion*, he turned again to the poet and the poetic process. In this difficult, incomplete yet somehow "finished" poem, we have his last poetic consideration of how a poet is made and what his poetry is worth to the world.

Before looking at the later poem, it is necessary to begin with an

3. Keats to Benjamin Bailey (Nov. 22, 1817), *Letters of Keats*, 1:184–185.

understanding of Keats's earlier views expressed in *Sleep and Poetry*, written when the poet was at the very beginning of his career.

> O Poesy! for thee I hold my pen
> That am not yet a glorious denizen
> Of thy wide heaven

(47–49)

Although he is a confessed tyro, the poet has a vision of his poetic development as decreed by the inner working of his own soul. He agrees with Blake and Wordsworth in seeing the first stage he must pass through as that of a sensuous, pleasurable kind of poetry.

> First the realm I'll pass
> Of Flora, and old Pan: sleep in the grass,
> Feed upon apples red, and strawberries,
> And choose each pleasure that my fancy sees

(101–104)

This stage of development is delightful, but it must give way to a nobler and more difficult one inspired by a vision of Apollo.

> And can I ever bid these joys farewell?
> Yes, I must pass them for a nobler life,
> Where I may find the agonies, the strife
> Of human hearts: for lo! I see afar,
> O'er sailing the blue cragginess, a car
> And steeds with streamy mains

(122–127)

The difference between this realm and the former is made in terms of perception. Life is no longer to be "a lovely tale," for it is seen to contain "the agonies, the strife / Of human hearts." The poem goes on to censure various schools of poetry, including the followers of Boileau. For a long time now, the poet confidently asserts, the "potency of song" has been misused by those who forget "the great end / Of Poesy, that it should be a friend / To sooth the cares, and lift the thoughts of man" (245–247). Although admittedly lacking wisdom, the poet claims to have a "vast idea" of "The end and aim of Poesy," by which he apparently means the ends stated above in lines 245–247. The end is not to be achieved without difficulty, for in the "nobler life" the poet must face the agonies of human existence; and in spite of all his self-confidence he sees his ultimate task as one of almost insurmountable difficulties.

> An ocean dim, sprinkled with many an isle,
> Spreads awfully before me. How much toil!
> How many days! What desperate turmoil!
> Ere I can have explored its widenesses.
> Ah, what a task! upon my bended knees,
> I could unsay those—no, impossible!
> Impossible!
>
> (306–312)

When the time comes, the poet thinks, it will be impossible to renounce this ultimate goal; but for the time being he must remain in the lower realm of Flora and Pan, the realm of "The hearty grasp that sends a pleasant sonnet / Into the brain ere one can think upon it" (319–320). To signify that he is indeed in this realm, the poet closes with a few "peaceful images" from his "store of luxuries," and the glib facility of these reads almost like satire after the vivid intensity of lines 306–312. If we accept these lines on the poem's own terms, however, they are the consequences of being in the first realm of poetry where life is still "a lovely tale." After pointing out the course he must eventually follow, the poet comes to rest on the initial step toward his goal.

This cursory treatment of *Sleep and Poetry* will indicate the general tenor of Keats's early thought about what it meant to become a poet of the highest sort. Compared with *The Fall*, this is a very simple poem, yet there are incipient ideas in it which find fuller expression later; it is well to keep these in mind while attempting to read *The Fall*. Byron said of *Sleep and Poetry* that it was written by "a young person learning to write poetry, and beginning by teaching the art." [4] For Keats, as for Blake and Wordsworth, the beginning and end of poetry was teaching the art. But art was for them primarily the art of seeing rather than composing. The ultimate value of poetry lay in its potential for achieving, and teaching others to achieve, a mode of

4. *Blackwood's Magazine* (August, 1819), quoted by de Selincourt in *The Poems*, p. 403.

vision. The "teaching" in Keats's poetry is primarily self-teaching, with the assumption that what Keats can learn about vision will be communicable and have value for all men.

One of the thorniest problems in reading *The Fall* is partly textual, partly interpretive. Normally, before beginning a careful reading of any poem one tries to assure himself that he has the best text available. For *The Fall*, however, there are two texts, both supported by scholarly authority, and differing in the acceptance or rejection of lines 187–210. The existence of these lines gives the critic a predetermined focus for any attempt to read the poem, for it cannot be proved conclusively from external evidence whether the lines should be excluded or included. Therefore an argument for rejecting the lines must be supported by an interpretation of the poem that depends for its validity on their absence; and vice versa. The problem would be of little significance if the presence or absence of the lines did not seem to have some bearing on the general quality or meaning of the poem. My own view of these lines differs from both the two main schools of reading, represented by de Selincourt and Murray, but I shall try to do justice to their views when I reach these lines in my interpretation.[5]

Although this study is not directly concerned with the first *Hyperion*, it should be noted that there too Keats was concerned with the problem of the existence of two kinds of poetry. It is clear that Hyperion, representing the old order, is also representing a kind of poetry or poet that is to be replaced by the new poet Apollo. As in *Sleep and Poetry*, Keats carries us to the opposition of two kinds of poetry, but this time he stops before reaching a conclusion. When he gave up *Hyperion*, Keats was not giving up the attempt to cope with his problem; he was giving up a mode that had proved inadequate to the experience he sought to explore. According to Murry: "He did not abandon it because he had abandoned the thought it contains, but because he knew that the thought could not be uttered 'in an artful or rather artist's humour'; the knowledge he was trying to reveal, he knew he must reveal in another way and in another mood." [6]

This sounds as if Keats had reached a definite conclusion and was trying to find the right form or "mood" to cast it in. Such a view, however, is incompatible with the meaning of *The Fall*, which shows us a

5. E. de Selincourt in *The Poems*, pp. 515–519; J. M. Murry, *Keats and Shakespeare* (London & New York: Oxford Univ. Press, 1925), pp. 177–179; idem, *Studies in Keats New and Old*, 2d ed. (London: Oxford Univ. Press, 1939), pp. 98–106.
6. Murry, *Keats and Shakespeare*, p. 169.

poet trying valiantly to work out his thought in and through his poetry. In *Hyperion* the contrast between the two types of poetry was to be made by comparing the allegorical figures of Apollo and Hyperion. It was perhaps some preconception of this scheme that led him to associate Apollo with the poetry of the "nobler life" in *Sleep and Poetry*. As Keats began to create Apollo's dying into life, he realized that the significant action of the poem was there, and that the experience he wished to express took place within a single mind. Furthermore, he saw the contrast as a development from one state to another within the single mind. Apollo had to be Hyperion before he could be Apollo. The difference between the two poetic states, or modes of vision, could not be shown in a static contrast between two mythic gods, nor could the transition clearly be shown in the displacement of one god by the other.

On a highly general level, the movement is similar in kind to the shift Blake made from *The Four Zoas* to *Milton*. Blake's allegory is much more complex than Keats's, especially in *The Four Zoas*, in which he was still expressing his internal argument in terms of an historical myth. But in spite of numerous differences, the shift they made in their conceptions of the poem they were ready to write, and had to write, is the same. It is a shift from a basically external poetic argument, with subjective or internal implications, to a basically private exploration of inner consciousness and the problem of becoming a poet. Both Keats and Blake maintained the assumption, or hope, that this exploration would necessarily have a significant relation to the external world, and both reflected the same shift in mode of vision of the external world. The external world was to be seen *with*, not *through* the inner consciousness; and that inner consciousness itself had somehow to be established before any vision of the world could be achieved. Of course, what I am discussing as two visions (of the inner self and of the external world) were ultimately to be identical, once a complete vision of the inner self was achieved.

Thus there were two reasons for Keats's rejection of the first *Hyperion*. First, there should be no resistance to the transition from one state to another, but the epic opposition between the two figures called for resistance from Hyperion (unless, like Oceanus, he simply acknowledges the higher order). Second, the allegorization of a revolt was too distant from the phenomenon that Keats wished to express, which was a development within, not an overthrow from without. For these reasons, when he transformed *Hyperion* into *The Fall*, Keats began directly with an allegory of the stages in a poet's development. The device of a vision—or dream—enabled him to be openly subjective and lyrical, whereas the demands of a more objective epic form had delayed and complicated treatment of the poetic consciousness.

Although the first eighteen lines of *The Fall* may at first seem un-related to what follows, they are an introduction to the thought of the poem and serve to distinguish two elements of poetry, the first of which is a dream or vision that may be had by "fanatics," "the savage," and "every man whose soul is not a clod." The second element is "the fine spell of words" that makes the visionary a poet, earns the laurel, and distinguishes him from the fanatic.[7] Lines 16–18 express doubt as to Keats's own position in this system.

> Whether the dream now purposed to rehearse
> Be poet's or fanatic's will be known
> When this warm scribe, my hand, is in the grave.

These lines introduce the atmosphere of doubt that is to permeate the rest of the fragment, and they indicate the importance of a vision in Keats's conception of poetry. All who have visions are not poets, but all who are poets have had their visionary perception of life.

> For Poesy alone can tell her dreams,—
> With the fine spell of words alone can save
> Imagination from the sable chain
> And dumb enchantment.

                              (8–11)

After the induction, the poem does not begin immediately with the poet's vision, as might have been expected. The first part is devoted to the poet's preparation for the vision he is to receive under Moneta's guidance. The preparation is described in three allegorical stages of development through which the would–be poet passes as if in a dream. The first stage is an exotic arbour, where he finds an indiscriminate

7. Cf. *The Excursion*, bk. 1:77–106 (*The Poetical Works of Wordsworth*, ed. Thomas Hutchinson, rev. E. de Selincourt [London & New York: Oxford Univ. Press, 1950]) in which Wordsworth claims that poets "sown by nature" are not true poets until their natural gifts of perception are supplemented by "the accomplishments of verse."

mixture of sensory stimuli of all kinds. There are "trees of every clime," the noise of fountains, the scent of flowers, and the "refuse of a meal / By angel tasted or our Mother Eve." This is the sensual heritage of fallen man, and although delightful in the usual sense of physical pleasure, there is something incomplete and unsatisfying about this paradise. The disorder and irregularity of the landscape is echoed by the disarray of the meal which (though of "more plenty than the fabled horn") consists of remnants, shells scattered on the grass, and half bare grape stalks. The arbour seems to have no ordering principle save abundance and variety. Although the poet eats "deliciously," the result is not satisfaction, but the stimulation of a new appetite.

To satisfy this new appetite the poet turns to "a cool vessel of trans-parent juice" and drinks, "pledging all the mortals of the world, / And all the dead whose names are in our lips." The pledge to his fellow mortals is given on the threshold of the poet's entrance into the realms of art, signifying the awareness of others which is to become an issue in line 154.[8] The poet struggles against the influence of the draught, but its power is too great; almost against his will he is taken from the irregular realm of sensuous pleasure "among the fragrant husks and berries crush'd / Upon the grass" into a world of artifice, where beauty exists in the form of unchanging works of art. The draught seems to resemble the "sweet draught" that Dante takes at the end of the *Purgatorio* (canto 33); but whereas Dante's draught could never have sated him, the poet here "struggled hard against / The domineering potion, but in vain." One explanation for the struggle is Keats's intui-tion that the draught will lead to the marble steps and the agony of experiencing "What 'tis to die and live again before / Thy fated hour." [9] Keats was familiar enough with medicine to know that some poisons, if taken properly, could heal instead of kill. His hope in taking the draught of poesy was that it might prove to be a healing poison and that he might find the secret of its dosage. "I have the choice as it were of two Poisons (yet I ought not to call this a Poison) the one is voyaging to and fro from India for a few years; the other is leading a fevrous life

8. Cf. *Sleep and Poetry*: 245–247: "the great end / Of Poesy, that it should be a friend / To sooth the cares, and lift the thoughts of man."

9. The marble steps are also from Dante's *Purgatorio* (canto 9), as is the concep-tion of his guide Moneta. The Dantesque influence throughout *The Fall* is more crucial than the indication of occasional borrowings might suggest. The pattern of *The Fall* is purgatorial, and it can be seen as a prelude to vision in the sense that the *Purgatorio* is. *The Fall* is a self-accusing work in a more radical way than *Milton* or *The Prelude*, although these works too have their purgatorial dimensions.

alone with Poetry—This latter will suit me best—for I cannot resolve
to give up my Studies. . . . I must take my stand upon some vantage
ground and begin to fight—I must choose between despair & Energy—
I choose the latter." [10]

The transformation effected by the draught in *The Fall* is apparent
even before the poet awakes, for he sinks down "like a Silenus on an
antique vase." Upon awakening,[11] he finds the irregular world of the
senses replaced by the "carved" sides of "an old sanctuary," an "eternal
domed monument" which is a storehouse of many beautiful religious
artifacts.

> Store of strange vessels, and large draperies,
> Which needs had been of dyed asbestos wove,
> Or in that place the moth could not corrupt,
> So white the linen, so, in some, distinct
> Ran imageries from a sombre loom.
> All in a mingled heap confus'd there lay
> Robes, golden tongs, censer and chafing-dish,
> Girdles, and chains, and holy jewelries.
>
> (73–80)

The temple represents the art of the past. It is necessary for the
poet to be exposed to, and to appreciate such beauty before he will be
able to create things of beauty himself; but this too is only a stage in
his development. In the temple he tries "to fathom the space every
way," but there is only one way for him to progress. In the east the
"black gates / were shut against the sunrise evermore," even though
from Wordsworth and the earlier Keats we might expect hope for an
"answer" from a new dawn in the east, bringing Apollo "O'er sailing
the blue cragginess." To the north and south he finds "mist / Of
nothing" and so is forced to "step westward" with Wordsworth, and
"To Find the Western path / Right thro' the Gates of Wrath" with
Blake and Crane. The poet must submit to the fall before he can overcome it, and so here he turns west to find the purgatorial stairs, ac-

---

10. Keats to Sarah Jeffrey (May 31, 1819), *Letters of Keats*, 2:112–113.
11. The awakening (58–59), "I started up / As if with wings," demands comparison with Wordsworth's image of the beginning of his prelude: "Anon I rose / As
if on wings, and saw beneath me stretch'd / Vast prospect of the world which I
had been / And was; and hence this Song" (*Prelude*, bk. 13:377–380).

knowledging the inevitable ending of the day and the consummation of
man's life in death.

The poet turns from the treasures with awe to begin the final stage
which will equip him for his vision. The earlier development was relatively easy and painless; now the difficulties begin, for the altar is

> To be approach'd on either side by steps
> And marble balustrade, and patient travail
> To count with toil the innumerable degrees.
>
> (90–92)

After finally reaching the foot of the altar, a challenge and a dual threat
are announced to the poet's "two senses both at once." One threat is
that if he cannot ascend the "immortal steps," his flesh will parch for
lack of nutriment, and he will quickly experience physical death. The
other threat is that if he fails he will be so totally annihilated, no one
will know he ever existed, and this goes beyond the threat of physical
death in suggesting a negative answer to the question asked in lines
16–18. Knowing he must die immediately and without fame unless he
mounts the steps, the poet wages a tremendous struggle and, at the
very point of death, reaches the first stair, which seems to pour life in
through his toes. The dying into life here is like Apollo's transformation
at the end of the fragment of *Hyperion* (bk. 3:124–135), including even
the shriek just before the crucial moment.

The poet's first response to his change is to ask Moneta for an explanation of what he is and why he should have been saved from death.
Her answer is one of the key passages of the poem; it declares the essential nature of the change the poet has experienced.

> "Thou hast felt
> What 'tis to die and live again before
> Thy fated hour; that thou hadst power to do so
> Is thy own safety; thou hast dated on
> Thy doom." "High Prophetess," said I, "purge off,
> Benign, if so it please thee, my mind's film."
> "None can usurp this height," returned that shade,
> "But those to whom the miseries of the world
> Are misery, and will not let them rest.
> All else who find a haven in the world,

> Where they may thoughtless sleep away their days,
> If by a chance into this fane they come,
> Rot on the pavement where thou rotted'st half."

(141–153)

This answer is still not enough for the poet, who wants to know not only the nature of his experience, but also what the consequences of that experience will be for him and his fellow men. Why, he asks, are there not others with him, who also have experienced "the giant agony of the world, / And more, like slaves to poor humanity, / Labour for mortal good?" Moneta's reply seems almost to deny the value of the poet's previous development, for she tells him that the others are different from him, and better for humanity, because they are not visionaries or dreamers and are content with the human face and voice as sources of wonder.

> They come not here, they have no thought to come—
> And thou art here, for thou art less than they.
> What benefit canst thou [do], or all thy tribe,
> To the great world? Thou art a dreaming thing,
> A fever of thyself; think of the earth;
> What bliss, even in hope, is there for thee?
> What haven? every creature hath its home,
> Every sole man hath days of joy and pain,
> Whether his labours be sublime or low—
> The pain alone, the joy alone, distinct:
> Only the dreamer venoms all his days,
> Bearing more woe than all his sins deserve.

(165–176)

The meaning of the poem at this stage is overwhelmingly negative. After all his suffering, the poet seems denied the opportunity to help his fellow men or to achieve happiness himself. His dreaming has even brought on him more suffering "than all his sins deserve," for he has sacrificed his sensual pleasure without gaining the prospect of a redeeming vision. It is at this point that the crucial lines 187–210 appear.

> "Majestic shadow, tell me: sure not all
> Those melodies sung into the world's ear
> Are useless: sure a poet is a sage;

A humanist, physician to all men.
That I am none I feel, as vultures feel
They are no birds when eagles are abroad.
What am I then: thou spakest of my tribe:
What tribe?" The tall shade veil'd in drooping white
Then spake, so much more earnest, that the breath
Moved the thin linen folds that drooping hung
About a golden censer from the hand
Pendent—"Art thou not of the dreamer tribe?
The poet and the dreamer are distinct
Diverse, sheer opposite, antipodes.
The one pours out a balm upon the world
The other vexes it." Then shouted I
Spite of myself, and with a Pythia's spleen
"Apollo! faded! O far-flown Apollo!
Where is thy misty pestilence to creep
Into the dwellings, through the door crannies
Of all mock lyrists, large self-worshippers
And carelesss Hectorers in proud bad verse?
Though I breathe death with them it will be life
To see them sprawl before me into graves"

Obviously Keats could not be happy with a view of his art and his future life that denied their validity; yet the poem, as it was developing in his mind, was pointing that way. The poetic force of *The Fall* rests primarily on Keats's efforts to convince himself that his vision of "the giant agony of the world" was a privilege rather than a curse. According to Professor de Selincourt, we must accept lines 187–210 as Keats's answer to the self-doubts expressed earlier in the poem. They are "a bald expression of an idea which would be glorified in such a revision of the poem as *Hyperion* underwent between the first and second drafts, and such as this poem would surely have undergone had it not been thrown aside in sickness and despair." The value of these lines, according to de Selincourt, is that they give the affirmative statement demanded by the context of the poem and provide a "valuable commentary upon Keats's conception of the poetic art."

The object of the singer, he tells us, is to pour out a balm upon the world, not by luring men away from it to a fanciful land of dreams, but by seeing things as they are, and by concentrating his imaginative powers upon reality. Only then, after the character of the true poet has been made clear in its relation both with the man of action and with the mere dreamer, does Moneta unfold to him the Vision which contains within it the lesson of all the ages, as Oceanus revealed it to his fallen brethren; and from this Keats catches a glimpse of that last stage in his development after which he is striving, wherein his strenuous devotion to Beauty will have raised him above the limitations of ordinary life, and he will have gained that sublime serenity by which he will be able "to bear all naked truths / And to envisage circumstance, all calm." [12]

This is an inspiring theory, elegantly stated, but it does not fit the poem as we have it in its fragmentary state. Keats does indeed *attempt* to make an affirmative statement in the doubtful lines. He admits his own unworthiness and asks Moneta if there are not some poets who benefit their fellow men; in the same double question he asks once more what he is, since he feels he is not a poet. Moneta answers, "Art thou not of the dreamer tribe?" Of those who view the agony of the world, some are dreamers and some are not. The dreamer is one, like Keats, who can only question and vex the world. He has no balm, no comfort or solace to offer. Wordsworth's *Excursion* is lurking behind the positive pole of this contrast, but the antithesis rests uneasily in its context in the poem. What good does it do to hypothesize the ideal poet who "pours out a balm" if Keats's problem is not whether such ideal poets exist, but what he himself is, and what good he can do. Keats has reached the position of Wordsworth, conceiving the existence of "higher minds" yet not being able to find his own identity among them. His constant questioning of Moneta is an attempt to find his identity, which is obviously not that of the ideal poet. The possible existence of the ideal poet was extremely important for Keats, and he still finds it difficult to reject the possibility, even though he feels at the moment that the goal is beyond his powers. Murry feels that Keats rejected the distinction between the dreamer and the poet because he doubted that such a poet par excellence could really exist.[13] Keats did doubt he could be the ideal poet, and perhaps doubted the ideal could exist; but the distinction itself remains centrally important, because for Keats the only thing that could justify the struggle in *The Fall* was the reality of the ideal poet and the possibility he might become that poet.

12. *The Poems*, p. 519.
13. J. M. Murry, *Keats* (New York: Noonday Press, 1955), p. 246.

Moneta's mention of the ideal poet prompts an outburst against "all mock lyrists, large self-worshippers / And careless Hectorers in proud bad verse," with whose fate he seems to identify himself, although wishing for their destruction.

> Though I breathe death with them it will be life
> To see them sprawl before me into graves.

> (209–210)

At this point the poem has clearly left the problem of the dreamer's usefulness and the poet's identity for the opportunity to renew an old attack upon Byron, first begun in *Sleep and Poetry*. Keats apparently realized that such an attack had no place at all in such a poem as *The Fall*, for the lines are marked either for deletion or revision.

It would be a mistake to disregard completely the lines simply because they are in conflict with other parts of the poem and are "bad" poetry. Their presence, and their futility, indicate the intensity of Keats's problem of identity and his desire to find a hopeful solution to the problem. Even if the lines had not survived in any form, the problem they point to would still be the basis of the poem Keats was attempting to write. Murry argues that the lines are "not of vital importance to the argument of the poem": "In fact, they conflict with the real argument of the poem, . . . Keats, when he wrote those lines, was saying something which he did not really mean, and . . . he pulled himself up and began again at the point where he was conscious that he had 'gone off the rails.'" Murry's argument is too simple, as is his question: "Did he not know that he was a true poet? Was he not proving it at the very moment that he wrote?" [14]

Both Murry and de Selincourt confuse, though in completely different ways, their concepts of the "real" meaning of the poem with the meaning Keats wanted and hoped to achieve. They agree in seeing as "modesty" the poet's refusal to identify himself with the ideal poet, but de Selincourt passes over the modesty as if it were mere form, assuming that Keats identified himself indirectly with the ideal poet. Murry rejects the concept of the ideal poet and the modesty ("There was no time and no place for false modesty"), assuming that the writing itself was proof enough to Keats that he was a poet. The going "off the

14. Murry, *Keats*, p. 241; p. 242 (quotation from his earlier *Keats and Shakespeare*).

rails" analogy is disturbing to one who tries to follow this argument, for Keats was writing, or trying to write, *as* he went off the rails. And the direction he took in his derailment was more serious than a mere slip. How could Keats have forgotten the "real argument" of the poem to the extent of explicitly denying the real argument, when denial would have demanded cognizance of what was being denied? It is clear that, whether or not the lines are desired for inclusion in a reading text, the force of the lines remains in the poem as the main question Keats was attempting to answer. Professor de Selincourt himself, in spite of the argument quoted above, points out that the poem was "thrown aside in sickness and despair." No small part of the despair was due to Keats's inability to decide what value his imaginative powers, as they were developing, might have for him and his fellow men.

In *Sleep and Poetry* Keats considered the problem of how the poet becomes a poet through the development of consciousness that gives him full power. He knew the difference between the two kinds of poets, and he knew what the former were good for—sensuous pleasure. The problem he was attempting to answer in *The Fall* was what good was the fully-developed poet, the kind of poet Keats himself hoped to become. Did he "pour out a balm" on humanity? Did he "vex" them? Was he any good to others? Was he himself in a fortunate position or merely making the best of the consequences of an inescapable vision?

> —think of the Earth;
> What bliss even in hope is there for thee?

> (169–170)

In the lines in question Keats seems to make the assertion that the poet's knowledge can be useful to man, but that he could not become a poet in this sense. But for reasons made clear in the remainder of the poem, he wished either to reject these lines or to rewrite them.

The very existence of the remainder of the poem suggests that Keats realized it was too soon to make a conclusive statement of the kind attempted in these lines. They are not a mistake in Murry's sense, but a mistake in timing. The poet has not yet made the attempt to achieve a vision of any kind, but has only undergone the preparatory experience demanded by any attempt to achieve a vision. The poem thus far is a brave attempt to create a secular version of the *Purgatorio*, to find an allegorical pattern for the preparation for a poetic vision independent of revealed religion. Both the poet and the dreamer (to accept the distinction) must pass from a realm of innocence to a recognition of the "giant agony of the world," and Keats has made this transition. But how, before he achieves his vision, is he to decide whether that vision will vex or sooth humanity?

In the remainder of the poem the poet attempts to go beyond the allegorical preparation, engaging in the very act of creating poetry or achieving his poetic vision of man. It is a kind of trial, as *Jerusalem* was a trial of the preparation Blake had undergone in *Milton*. His questions of Moneta shift from who he is to where he is, what the faceless image represents, and who Moneta is. He has not given up the question of whether he is a poet, but he has given up the attempt to answer it a priori, which in a sense had been his approach to the problem since *Sleep and Poetry*.

The change of direction in the poet's questioning stimulates a "much more earnest" response from Moneta, and she cannot reply without shedding "long-treasured tears."

> "This temple, sad and lone,
> Is all spar'd from the thunder of a war
> Foughten long since by giant hierarchy
> Against rebellion: this old image here,
> Whose carved features wrinkled as he fell,
> Is Saturn's; I, Moneta, left supreme,
> Sole priestess of his desolation."
>
> (221–227)

Saturn lies in an "icy trance" (canto 2:45), like Blake's Albion, an image of man's "fallen divinity" (316). Moneta has the power and the "curse" of immortal vision; she must behold the fallen divinity through eternity. Keats earlier called her a "High Prophetess," and she now brings the poet himself into the line of prophecy, but with the promise that in him the power will not become a curse.

> "My power, which to me is still a curse,
> Shall be to thee a wonder; for the scenes
> Still swooning vivid through my globed brain,
> With an electral changing misery,
> Thou shalt with these dull mortal eyes behold
> Free from all pain, if wonder pain thee not."
>
> (243–248)

It is a promise that is to prove a "deadly lie" (449), for the poet's vision is not to be through "dull mortal eyes"; he too is being led toward the curse of eternal vision. Moneta parts her veils so the poet may read on her face the cruel lines of the curse.

> Then saw I a wan face,
> Not pined by human sorrows, but bright-blanch'd
> By an immortal sickness which kills not;
> It works a constant change, which happy death
> Can put no end to; deathwards progressing
> To no death was that visage; it had past
> The lily and the snow; and beyond these
> I must not think now, though I saw that face.
> But for her eyes I should have fled away.
> They held me back with a benignant light,
> Soft mitigated by divinest lids
> Half closed, and visionless entire they seem'd
> Of all external things—they saw me not,
> But, in blank splendour, beam'd like the mild moon,
> Who comforts those she sees not, who knows not
> What eyes are upward cast.
>
> (256-271)

The eyes are "visionless entire . . . / Of all external things," suggesting that the horror of vision, whatever it is, is within her "hollow brain." She is in an eternal Limbo of vision, like the blind statue in Coleridge's poem, who "seems to gaze at that which seems to gaze on him." The poet is trapped by the "blank splendour" of Moneta's eyes, and asks to receive the powers of vision she promised.

> I ached to see what things the hollow brain
> Behind enwombed: what high tragedy
> In the dark secret chambers of her skull
> Was acting, that could give so dread a stress
> To her cold lips, and fill with such a light
> Her planetary eyes, and touch her voice
> With such a sorrow.
>
> (276-282)

The power of vision forces itself on the poet as a god-like power, and he echoes Apollo's cry in the earlier version ("Knowledge enormous makes a God of me.") :

> A power within me of enormous ken,
> To see as a god sees, and take the depth
> Of things as nimbly as the outward eye
> Can size and shape pervade.

(303–306)

The ambiguity here is complex, but we must recognize it before we can understand the significance of his subsequent vision and the surprising confession that he bore the vision without stay or prop but his own weak mortality (388–389). Saturn, like Albion, represents the fallen divinity of man, and the fall is again a loss of vision as Saturn's speech (418–438) makes clear. His vision is that of a god, but a fallen god, and he represents the internal state of fallen vision in all men. Thus Moneta can see him without looking on "external things," and the poet too in seeing him is looking into himself. If the poet's vision is to be god-like, as human vision was before the fall, something must awaken Saturn from his icy trance within the poet. Otherwise, the vision will be god-like only in the sense of fallen divinity.

The first attempt to awaken Saturn is made by Thea, but she gives up when she realizes that his sleep is more comforting than the vision he would awaken to.

> "Saturn, look up! and for what, poor lost king?
> I have no comfort for thee; no—not one;
> I cannot cry, *wherefore thus sleepest thou?*
> For Heaven is parted from thee, and the Earth
> Knows thee not, so afflicted, for a God. . . .
> Saturn! sleep on:—me thoughtless, why should I
> Thus violate thy slumberous solitude?
> Why should I ope thy melancholy eyes?
> Saturn! sleep on, while at thy feet I weep."

(354–371)

The poet holds the vision of "the frozen God . . . and the sad Goddess weeping at his feet" for a "long awful time." He prays for death, "gasping with despair / Of change," for his vision is limited to the fallen divinity within himself, and his hopes for a change are dependent upon the fallen Saturn. He is in the position in which Blake found himself earlier, but he lacks the inspiration of the Bard's song which began the process of awakening the Divine Vision in Blake. Instead, the fallen god himself speaks, like "some old man of the earth / Bewailing earthly loss." In a magnificent speech, he voices the despair and the plea of the poet.

> "Moan, brethren, moan, for we are swallow'd up
> And buried from all godlike exercise
> Of influence benign on planets pale,
> And peaceful sway above man's harvesting,
> And all those acts which Deity supreme
> Doth ease its heart of love in. Moan and wail;
> Moan, brethren, moan; for lo, the rebel spheres
> Spin round; the stars their antient courses keep;
> Clouds still with shadowy moisture haunt the earth,
> Still suck their fill of light from sun and moon;
> Still buds the tree, and still the seashores murmur;
> There is no death in all the universe,
> No smell of death.—There shall be death. Moan, moan;
> Moan, Cybele, moan; for thy pernicious babes
> Have changed a god into a shaking palsy.
> Moan, brethren, moan, for I have no strength left;
> Weak as the reed—weak—feeble as my voice—
> Oh! Oh! the pain, the pain of feebleness.
> Moan, moan, for still I thaw—or give me help;
> Throw down those imps, and give me victory.
> Let me hear other groans, and trumpets blown
> Of triumph calm, and hymns of festival,
> From the gold peaks of heaven's high-piled clouds;
> Voices of soft proclaim, and silver stir
> Of strings in hollow shells; and let there be
> Beautiful things made new, for the surprise
> Of the sky-children."

$$(412-438)$$

At this point, Keats has written himself into a mythical corner from which there is no escape. Saturn is at the very end of his power, and although he has not yet died, "there shall be death," and it will be a death without the promise of continuity in a rebirth. He is loosing his power without hope of regaining it and without knowledge of what is to replace him. He can only wish that "there be / Beautiful things made new, for the surprise / Of the sky–children," but there is no sign of the power that can accomplish his wish. The "awful presence" of the fallen divinity "there" (that ambiguous region within the poet's own mind) gives the lie to the promise the poet had, that his vision would be a thing of wonder but not a curse.

> his awful presence there
> (Now all was silent) gave a deadly lie
> To what I erewhile heard: only his lips
> Trembled amid the white curls of his beard;
> They told the truth, though, round, the snowy locks
> Hung nobly, as upon the face of heaven
> A mid-day fleece of clouds.

$$(448-454)$$

After his lament, Saturn and Thea rise and depart, "speeding to the families of grief, / Where, roof'd in by black rocks, they waste in pain / And darkness, for no hope." The canto concludes with the premonition that their loss of hope may be the poet's loss too.

> And she spake on,
> As ye may read who can unwearied pass
> Onward from the antechamber of this dream,
> Where, even at the open doors, awhile
> I must delay, and glean my memory
> Of her high phrase:—perhaps no further dare.

$$(463-468)$$

In the few lines that Keats wrote of the second canto there is no significant progress in the vision. Hyperion is pictured slumbering in the arms of melody, and pacing through the pleasant hours of ease. There is no promise of the Apollo who is to depose him, for the poet himself was to be that Apollo, as promised by the change from the first *Hyperion* to *The Fall*, the transference of the dying into life of the god to the crucial step of the poet's preparation for his vision. If the poet *is* the new Apollo, then we have indeed come back full circle to Saturn, for the poet is trapped by the limited vision of the fallen divinity. There is promise neither in the East nor in the West, as "Hyperion, leaving twilight in the rear, / Is sloping to the threshold of the West" (47–48).

The logic of the change in titles, from *Hyperion* to *The Fall of Hyperion, A Dream,* becomes clear at this point, as the analogy between the biblical fall and the Titans' fall forces itself upon us. Eve, in eating the forbidden fruit of the apple, was promised by the serpent, "Your eyes shall be opened, and ye shall be as gods, knowing good and evil." The poet begins his dream by eating the refuse of a meal "By angel tasted or our Mother Eve." It would perhaps be reading too curiously to suggest that the "or" is a strong enough disjunction to point to two alternatives for the course of the poet's dream, but the poet does go on to receive the same promise of god-like vision given to Eve, only to achieve a vision of death and fallen divinity. The promise of a god-like vision is an illusion, as the physical promise of Lamia and the song of "La Belle Dame Sans Merci" were illusions leading to disappointment and despair. In "La Belle Dame Sans Merci," the knight has a pre-figurative dream of the reality to which he must awaken after having been lulled to sleep by the Dame. For him it is "The latest dream I ever dreamt / On the cold hill side." Knowing Keats's use of the dream as a metaphor for the prefigurative imagination, it is no accident that *The Fall* is subtitled *A Dream*, for in it Keats expected to find, for better or worse, the reality to which he would have to awaken. And in this latest dream he ever dreamt he found not the god-like vision he hoped for, but a vision of fallen divinity which he had to bear with only the powers of his "own weak mortality." The result of the vision is the prayer "Intense, that death would take me from the vale / And all its burthens."

If the result of the poet's vision is to wish for death, it is difficult to answer the question of what possible good the poet's vision may have for humanity. If he leads them to his vision of the world, their happiness will be destroyed, for it will, like this, be hereafter inextricably mingled with their past and future sorrows; they will be forced to pluck the poison fruit of sorrow even in the moment of laughter, as Keats himself did. "While we are laughing the seed of some trouble is put into the wide arable land of events—while we are laughing it sprouts it grows and suddenly bears a poison fruit which we must pluck." [15] Yet his vision is a vision of the truth, and the happy ones without it, though they "find a haven in the world," find it only through their inability to "feel the giant agony of the world." Their happiness is a childlike state that depends for its being on ignorance of pain and sorrow. Professor de Selincourt has suggested that "the pains which are the inevitable accompaniment of the sensitive poetic temperament" are rewarded by

15. Keats to the George Keatses (Mar. 19, 1819), *Letters of Keats*, 2:79.

"those ideal emotions which are its ample compensation." In this he does not differ significantly from Murry, who claims that "the great poet vexes the world, and himself; but in the selfless quality of his vexation is the balm." [16] They find their answers, however, in their own scale of values, and not in the poem itself. We can sense the agony of Keats's vision only from a distance, through the medium of his poetry; although the poem forcefully conveys his experience, our knowledge of that experience must remain vicarious. Otherwise, we would be poets ourselves, and the best comment we could make would be a poem expressing our own experience, not a prose critique of what we have gleaned from Keats's poem. Therefore it seems a little glib to me to say that ideal emotions are ample compensation for the pain of Keats's vision, or that the "selfless quality" of his vexation is itself the balm sought by the poet. Keats certainly does not say this, and until we ourselves have had the vision, we should not make an evaluation that he was unable to reach. Having asked the unanswerable question, he was unable to finish the poem; or, if you will, the poem *was* finished, because there was no answer.

One is tempted to follow this poetic problem into Keats's private life, to turn to biographical evidence to see if and how he solved it. It is difficult not to believe *The Fall* is the poetic embodiment of a real problem; the problem's oppressing reality demands that there be some reflection of it in the author's life.

On Tuesday, September 21, 1819, Keats wrote to John Reynolds: "I have given up Hyperion—there were too many Miltonic inversions in it—Miltonic verse can not be written but in an artful or rather artist's humour. I wish to give myself up to other sensations. . . . It strikes me to night that I have led a very odd sort of life for the two or three last years" (2:167). From the letters Keats wrote during the next few days, the kind of "other sensations" he had in mind becomes apparent. These letters indicate that Keats was almost ready to give up his poetry for some pursuit with more immediate returns.

In a letter dated the following day he told Charles Dilke, "I have no trust whatever on Poetry." He planned to go to London to do something for his "immediate welfare." "I will settle myself and fag till I can afford to buy Pleasure—which if [I] never can afford I must go without. Talking of Pleasure, this moment I was writing with one hand, and with the other holding to my Mouth a Nectarine—good god how

16. *The Poems*, p. 516; Murry, *Keats*, p. 249.

fine—It went down soft pulpy, slushy, oozy—all its delicious embon-point melted down my throat like a large beatified Strawberry. I shall certainly breed" (2:179). Keats wrote to Charles Brown the following day still in the same vein. "It is quite time I should set myself doing something, and live no longer upon hopes. . . . I purpose living in town in a cheap lodging, and endeavouring, for a beginning, to get the theatricals of some paper. When I can afford to compose deliberate poems, I will. . . . At the end of another year, you shall applaud me,—not for verses, but for conduct. . . . While I have some immediate cash, I had better settle myself quietly, and fag on as others do. . . . I shall not suffer my pride to hinder me. . . . I look forward, with a good hope, that we shall one day be passing free, untrammelled, un-anxious time together. That can never be if I continue a dead lump" (2:176–177). In a letter to Brown on the following day he wrote: "I assure you, I am as far from being unhappy as possible. Imaginary griev-ances have always been more my torment than real ones. . . . Real ones will never have any other effect upon me than to stimulate me to get out of or avoid them" (2:181).

From this time on, Keats was so oppressed by ill health, and so in-volved with Fanny Brawne and the impossibility of their marriage, that it would be unwise to take any statement from any letter as a definitive world view. The total import of these letters, however, written toward the end of September apparently after he had given up *The Fall* for the last time, seems to be that Keats was retreating from the agony of his vision for a while.[17] When anticipating his career in *Sleep and Poetry*, he had realized the difficulties inherent in following his course of de-velopment. In *The Fall* Keats was still considering an aspect of the same problem: whether the exploration of the dim ocean of the poet's consciousness would benefit either the poet or his fellow men. The pain of such an exploration was so great that Keats sought some reason for continuing it. Had he lived in health, he might have found compensa-tion, as Professor de Selincourt suggests, in the ideal emotions of the sensitive poetic temperament. The fact that at this stage of his life he had not found the compensation, or expressed it fully in his poetry, is no more an indication of surrender than the early recognition in *Sleep and Poetry* that the poet was not yet ready for his vision. In *The Fall* the poet has had his vision, but is unable yet to live with it or to put it

17. There is some evidence that Keats was still working on *The Fall* as late as De-cember, 1819. See *The Poems*, p. 515.

to use. The solution to this final problem could only have been found in a poem Keats did not live to write. "The Genius of Poetry must work out its own salvation in a man: It cannot be matured by law & precept, but by sensation & watchfulness in itself—That which is creative must create itself." [18]

Like *Milton* and *The Prelude*, as well as many other poems of the Romantic period, Keats's *Fall* is incomplete by standards that look in poetry for a structure determined by the requirements of conventional form or the pattern of a story. But it shares, in its autobiographical dimension, an even more important incompleteness with the preludes of Blake and Wordsworth as an exploration of the poet's outlook and development in the attempt to establish a satisfactory visionary state of consciousness. Blake deliberately ended *Milton* at a high point of his development, but the poem is still part of a larger pattern and is not truly complete in itself except as a prelude to what is to follow. Wordsworth went beyond the stopping point that would have corresponded to the triumphant ending of Blake's *Milton*. For Keats's *Fall* there was no end except the end of human life itself.

18. Keats to J. A. Hessey (Oct. 8, 1818), *Letters of Keats*, 1:374.

# Chapter 6

# Crane: A Myth to God

Did I tell you of that thrilling experience this last
winter in the dentist's chair when under the influence of aether and *amnesia* my mind spiraled
to a kind of seventh heaven of consciousness and
egoistic dance among the seven spheres—and
something like an objective voice kept saying to
me—"you have the higher consciousness. . . ."
A happiness, ecstatic such as I have known only
twice in "inspirations" came over me.

—Crane

And if in some bar a tart,
As she strokes your hair, should say
"This is Atlantis, dearie,"
Listen with attentiveness
To her life-story: unless
You become acquainted now
With each refuge that tries to
Counterfeit Atlantis, how
Will you recognize the true?

—Auden, *Atlantis*

The opinion of Hart Crane's *Bridge* most commonly held by respectable
critics is that it is a magnificent failure—magnificent in its lyrical evoca-
tions of mood, but a failure in its attempt to provide an epic or mythic
expression of the movement of American history. This opinion has
gained widespread acceptance only after a number of carefully reasoned
and sensitive examinations of the poem by critics well equipped for the
task. These critics are for the most part favorably disposed toward what

they see as Crane's intention in writing the poem. And they are in general agreement on the basic reasons for considering the poem a failure, even though they do have different points of emphasis and different terms for expressing their conclusions.

R. P. Blackmur, for example, approaches the poem on what he calls the "rational plane, . . . the plane of competent technical appreciation." His method is to determine "how and to what degree the effects intended were attained." Blackmur first determines "Crane's announced purpose" and then analyzes the reasons for Crane's failure in terms of his poetic language.

> He wrote in a language of which it was the virtue to accrete, modify, and interrelate moments of emotional vision—moments at which the sense of being gains its greatest access—moments at which, by the felt nature of knowledge, the revealed thing is its own meaning; and he attempted to apply his language, in his major effort, to a theme that required a sweeping, discrete, indicative, anecdotal language, a language in which, by the force of movement, mere cataloguing can replace and often surpass representation. He used the private lyric to write the cultural epic; used the mode of intensive contemplation, which secures ends, to present the mind's actions, which have no ends. The confusion of tool and purpose not only led him astray in conceiving his themes; it obscured at crucial moments the exact character of the work he was actually doing.[1]

Brom Weber, in a critical-biographical approach, similarly concludes that Crane failed because of a disparity between his purpose and his tools. The weakness he finds, however, is not the poet's language, but his inability to sustain faith in his vision of the continuity between the past and present, and in his lack of historical knowledge and technique.

> Because Crane made no effort to grasp the meaning of American history, *The Bridge* does not fulfil its assigned task of organic assimilation, of relating the historical past and present in emotional terms; it could not be expected to do so, because Crane did not attempt to arrive at any mastery over the subject. . . . Crane not only demonstrated his uncertainty before the materials of history when the problem of selection arose, but also

1. R. P. Blackmur, "New Thresholds, New Anatomies," in *Form and Value in Modern Poetry* (Garden City, N.Y.: Doubleday & Co., 1957), pp. 273–274.

revealed how intrinsically unimportant the materials of history were to him. Under these circumstances, it would have been impossible, as *The Bridge* shows it to have been, for Crane to demonstrate convincingly that the past with all its glory and its ideals lives in the present. . . . It must be recognized that Crane, despite his ambition, was unqualified by virtue of his aesthetics, his life, and his lack of knowledge to handle a didactic poem or a poem of faith.[2]

Yvor Winters finds Crane's failure built into the theme of the poem because of its connection with the morally unacceptable (to Winters) Romantic ethic. "The incomprehensibility and the looseness of construction are the natural result of the theme, which is inherited from Whitman and Emerson. The style is at worst careless and pretentious, at second-best skillfully obscure; and in these respects it is religiously of its school; and although it is both sound and powerful at its best, it is seldom at its best." [3] Winters finds biographical reasons for the poem's failure similar to those adduced by Weber, and he criticizes the language in somewhat the same terms as those used by Blackmur. His final verdict is that "the work as a whole is a failure."

Allen Tate begins his criticism with the familiar idea that "*The Bridge* is presumably an epic," and he goes on to show that "the style lacks an objective pattern of ideas elaborate enough to carry it through an epic or heroic work." [4] This argument is somewhat different from Blackmur's, but the main point, that Crane's style or poetic language did not fit his subject, seems to be the same. Tate goes beyond Blackmur, however, in examining the structure of the poem and in showing that what coherence the poem does have is "in the personal quality of the writing—in mood, feeling, and tone," rather than in the kind of objective ordering of ideas needed in a poem aimed at clarifying experience. Like Weber and Winters, Tate goes to the poet's life to support and expand his interpretation of the poem's failure; like Winters, he finds the root of Crane's inability to achieve his poetic goal to be his commitment to the Romantic ethic.

I have risked overly quoting the arguments and conclusions of these critics in hopes of illustrating the remarkable consistency of their ap-

2. Brom Weber, *Hart Crane* (New York: Bodley Press, 1948), pp. 324–328 passim.
3. Yvor Winters, "The Significance of *The Bridge*, by Hart Crane," in *On Modern Poets* (New York: Meridian Books, 1959), p. 139.
4. Allen Tate, "Hart Crane," in *The Man of Letters in the Modern World* (New York: Meridian Books, 1955), p. 286.

proach to *The Bridge*. In each case the critical investigation is based on an alleged understanding of Crane's purpose in writing the poem, and in each case the poem is classified as a failure because, for a variety of reasons, the poet failed to achieve his purpose. The two aspects of the poem most frequently objected to are those which, for me, give the poem its significance and make the question of its "success" impossible to answer by reference to already accepted epic poems. The attempt to move from an initial moment of inspired lyric vision to a sustained and comprehensive vision that retains the original intensity cannot be passed off as a mistaken strategy or a confusion of "tool and purpose." It cannot be passed off, that is, unless we also reject the similar attempts made by Blake, Wordsworth, and Keats, and declare a moratorium on the epic until our culture solves for its poets the problems they attempt to solve through their poetry. The other reason often given for the poem's failure, Crane's lack of faith, also reveals a false emphasis in critical approach. Crane's lack of faith was the beginning point and the motivating force behind the attempt to write the poem, its *raison d'être* rather than its cause of failure. The central emotional element in Crane's *Bridge*, as it was in Blake, Wordsworth, and Keats, is the hope that motivated the uncertain pilgrim in his quest for a vision to be the basis of a faith.

The mistake of overly emphasizing the question of Crane's faith is illustrated by L. S. Dembo, who paradoxically exaggerates the firmness of that faith. Dembo argues that "the poet keeps his faith and concludes the poem with a hymn celebrating the Bridge as a modern embodiment of the Word." Since Crane's faith was secure, the problem of the poet in *The Bridge* was to find "some evidence that this society was capable of a psychological experience essentially identical with the poet's ecstatic apprehension of the Ideal as Beauty." [5] Impossible as it is to measure imponderables like "hope" and "faith" in poetry, it nevertheless seems that the reading of *The Bridge* suggested by Dembo is ultimately distorted by his too-ready acceptance of Crane's hope as evidence of his faith. The vision of ecstatic affirmation that he finds by reading the poem as an expression of the Nietzschean tragic spirit is indeed the "tragic argument" or vision that Crane hoped he had achieved. But it is not the motivating vision throughout the greater

5. L. S. Dembo, *Hart Crane's Sanskrit Charge* (Ithaca, N.Y.: Cornell Univ. Press, 1960), pp. 10–11. Dembo's view is shared by R. W. B. Lewis, *The Poetry of Hart Crane* (Princeton Univ. Press, 1967).

part of the poem, and it is not a vision so securely held as Dembo suggests. The real loss in Dembo's approach is his rejection of Crane's intuitive attempts to develop an historical sense and to achieve a vision of epic rather than tragic scope.

It is not surprising that the critics I have quoted above have all, except for Dembo, reached essentially the same evaluation of *The Bridge*. For in terms of Crane's expressed intentions the poem is a failure, and Crane's life and letters after 1929 fully illustrate both the consequences and the nature of the failure. What is surprising, however, is that so few attempts have been made to approach the poem from a different point of view. Criticism should aim at setting a poem in as many illuminating contexts as possible; the context of the poet's intentions is only one of many possible contexts, and one of the more suspect contexts at that. Poets are notoriously poor critics of their own work, and instances of poets writing "better than they knew" are almost commonplace. The fact that Crane did not achieve his purpose does not mean, as everyone has agreed, that he did not write magnificent poetry here and there in *The Bridge*. It does mean, however, that any reading of the poem in the way Crane hoped it could be read is doomed to be disappointing—unless, like Dembo and Lewis, we pass over the expressions of doubt in the poem and accept as achievement the attempt to find a vision. It seems inherently valuable to find a way of reading a poem so that it becomes, as nearly as possible, unified in structure and coherent as a whole, even if the meaning of the whole is not what the poet intended or thought he was achieving. By including *The Bridge* in a study with Blake, Wordsworth, and Keats, I wish to suggest an approach to reading *The Bridge* fundamentally different from that commonly taken; one that ignores or suspends judgment on the "success" of the poem, makes it more interesting to read, and makes it much more valuable for anyone interested in the problem of the poetic consciousness as a means for organizing and expressing experience.

If one approaches *The Bridge* without a precommitment to Crane's own statements, it is possible to find in it a theme that provides a high degree of organic unity. This theme may be described roughly as a search or quest for a mythic vision, not the fixed, symbolic expression of a vision firmly held in the poet's mind. The vision sought is one that would assure a hopeful future in the face of a sorry present; one that would be based on knowledge of a glorious past and provide a bridge from that past to the hopeful future in spite of the dearth of hopeful signs in the actual present. The kind of knowledge Crane had of the past was quite different from that which Weber means when he speaks of Crane's "lack of knowledge." For Crane, knowledge of the past was like Plato's theory of knowledge as a mode of memory in the *Meno*. "All inquiry and all learning is but recollection," says Socrates, and "he who does not know may still have true notions of that which he does not know." A certain amount of historical research was necessary for Crane's "knowledge" of the past, but (as Socrates stimulated the slave boy) the research was primarily a stimulus to the poet's memory, his intuitive and empathetic identification with history and the actors in it. "Then you shall see her truly—your blood remembering," the poet tells us in "The Dance." Similarly, the future is "known" as Walt Whitman knew the future enthrallment of his readers (*Cape Hatteras:* 17) and the continuity of the soul's existence after death. The nature of the poet's knowledge is made clear throughout *The Bridge*, and at no point does it make pretense of being scientifically historical.

The poem is highly subjective in language and content, and understandably so, because the quest is a personal quest, the search of the poet for a vision that will satisfy his own needs. But like Blake, Wordsworth, and Keats, Crane saw the problem of the poet as reflecting the central problem of the society in which he lived, and the poet's solution to the problem—if he could achieve one—as having consequences far beyond the poet's private life.

> It is a terrific problem that faces the poet today—a world that is so in transition from a decayed culture toward a reorganization of human evaluations that there are few common terms, general denominators of speech that are solid enough or that ring with any vibration of spiritual conviction. The great mythologies of the past (including the Church) are deprived of enough facade to even launch good raillery against. Yet much of their traditions are operative still—in millions of chance combinations of related and unrelated detail, psychological references, figures of speech, precepts, etc. These are all a part of our common experience and the *terms*, at least partially, of that very experience when it defines or extends itself.[6]

Against the background of the poet's daily cycle from Brooklyn to Manhattan and back, essentially a closed, hopeless, and discouraging routine, the poet carries on his quest, ranging into the glorious aspects

6. Philip Horton, "General Aims and Theories," appendix to *Hart Crane* (New York: Viking Press, 1937), p. 324.

of the past for clues to the nature of historical progression. He recalls his own past and searches everywhere, even in the present, for signs of hope on which to base an optimistic vision of the future. *The Bridge* is thus a continuation, on a much larger scale, of the attempt in *For the Marriage of Faustus and Helen* to find a visionary basis from which to "affirm certain things."

> There is no one writing in English who can command so much respect, to my mind, as Eliot. However, I take Eliot as a point of departure towards an almost complete reverse of direction. His pessimism is amply justified, in his own case. But I would apply as much of his erudition and technique as I can absorb and assemble towards a more positive, or (if I must put it in so sceptical an age) ecstatic goal. I should not think of this if a kind of rhythm and ecstasy were not (at moments odd and rare!) a very real thing to me. I feel that Eliot ignores certain spiritual events and possibilities as real and powerful now as, say, in the time of Blake. Certainly the man has dug the ground and buried hope as deep and direfully as it can ever be done. . . . All I know through very much suffering and dullness (somehow I seem to twinge more all the time) is that it interests me to still affirm certain things.[7]

It is not by accident that rainbow images appear throughout the poem; Noah's voyage to the future, after God's flood had destroyed all evil in the present, symbolized for Crane both the omnipotence and the benignity of some kind of force controlling destiny. The rainbow is thus a visual image for a concretely visualized, though symbolic, bridge and a symbol of hope for men who are beset by present peril. Nor is the Job quotation on the title page a casual thing, for Crane saw himself, like Job, suffering the agonies of present doubt and despair, attempting to nourish a faith that could finally be confirmed only by the "Word" of a voice out of the whirlwind. It is Satan who comes to God, "From going to and fro in the earth, And from walking up and down in it," and Crane is like Satan too, tempting himself to the verge of renouncing his vision yet hoping that the vision, like Job's prayer, is pure.

*The Bridge* is introduced by a "Proem: To Brooklyn Bridge." The "Proem" begins with the dawn of the poet-officeworker's day and is set

---

7. All quotations of Crane's letters are from *The Letters of Hart Crane*, ed. Brom Weber (New York: Hermitage House, 1952). Crane to Gorham Munson (Jan. 5, 1923), pp. 114–115.

against the background of the bridge, which suggests to the poet the feeling of controlled, unspent motion and freedom.[8] In contrast with the vague impression of freedom glimpsed in the seagull's flight, an impression of intolerably oppressive routine builds up in the next two stanzas, and the two moods are alternated in a violently contrapuntal arrangement. The seagull disappears with its "apparitional" curve, leaving the poet deceived by a panoramic sleight like the viewer of a cinema. He turns to the bridge, which is more free, and hence more stable ("Implicitly thy freedom staying thee!"). The contrast suggests that the freedom of the bridge will not prove apparitional, like the gull's flight, but it is only a suggestion; the deception of the first image hovers behind the second as an unrealized possibility.

In the fifth stanza a suicide suggests both the oppression of "subway scuttle, cell or loft" and one way at least of finding in the bridge a path to freedom. Another way is indicated, however, by the identification of the bridge with the accoutrements of religion and with the "Terrific threshold of the prophet's pledge." The last stanza seeks to realize this second way of escape by addressing the bridge directly, seeking its aid in finding a myth to God. It becomes increasingly clear throughout the poem that the myth to God is an attitude of mind rather than an allegoric organization of symbols. The bridge, as symbol, is not to help Crane discover the attitude, but to support and confirm the "rhythm and ecstasy" which until now he has had only "at odd moments and rare." The main function of the "Proem," in terms of the whole, is to set the background mood of the poem: despair with the present, a longing for freedom, the possibility the vision will prove as "apparitional" as a panoramic sleight, and the desire to find a hopeful organization of experience, a "myth to God" that will enable the poet to avoid the bedlamite's end.

## Ave Maria

The *Ave Maria* is presumably a dream the poet has at dawn just before awakening. I say presumably, for the fluidity of the links between the various parts of the poem does not demand a rigorous time scheme; the entire poem takes place in the poet's mind during the course of a single day, against the background of his past thoughts and experiences.

---

8. All quotations of Crane's poetry are from *The Complete Poems and Selected Letters and Prose of Hart Crane*, ed. Brom Weber (New York: Liveright Publishing Corp., 1966). Reprinted by permission of the publisher.

In the *Ave Maria* Columbus is seen just before arriving in Spain after discovering America. The poet has identified himself with Columbus, described Columbus as engaged in a quest, and located him at a very precise moment. Columbus is returning successfully from a quest that depended on faith as much as anything else; he is bringing "word" of a "dim frontier"—a new world and a new era of history—to the old world, the past. Crane picks the return stage of the voyage for a definite reason: he sees his own attempt to sustain a vision as a return to the world of the present after a timeless moment of vision. It is in this return that the vision, and the poet's hope in it, will receive the true test, as the true test of Columbus is his return to Spain. The metaphor will be repeated throughout the poem in the many examples of attempts to return from somewhere with something of value. Even though Aeneas was not returning in the literal sense that Columbus was, the voyage of the *Aeneid* and Aeneas's goal lie behind the structure of the poem and the voyage metaphors as a basic analogy for Crane's conception of his own quest. Directed by a vision of his destiny, Aeneas was returning to the mainstream of history after the debacle of Troy.

The Columbus dream image is prefigurative, in Keats's sense, and provides a pattern into which the poet will try to fit his attempt to find and sustain a vision. Like Columbus, the poet must discover the new world for himself; and like Columbus, the Indians he finds there may not be the ones he expects. The history of the new world may not fit the pattern Crane hopes to find by returning to its beginnings, as the history of Wordsworth's imagination did not fit the pattern he hoped to find by returning to his beginnings. Knowing that dreams may issue from the gate of ivory as well as the gate of horn, Crane nevertheless begins his quest with "the mistletoe of dreams," hoping that the tests to come will determine favorably the origin of this particular dream.

Columbus can say, after having reached America, that he has "seen now what no perjured breath / Of clown nor sage can riddle or gainsay." Yet in spite of the conviction of his vision, it is "lost, all, let this keel one instant yield." Columbus, like the poet, is hovering between the future and the past, in a present that hinders and tests the power of the word.

> For here between two worlds, another, harsh,

> This third, of water, tests the word; lo, here
> Bewilderment and mutiny heap whelming

> Laughter, and shadow cuts sleep from the heart [9]
> Almost as though the Moor's flung scimitar
> Found more than flesh to fathom in its fall.
> Yet under tempest-lash and surfeitings
> Some inmost sob, half-heard, dissuades the abyss,
> Merges the wind in measure to the waves,
>
> Series on series, infinite,—till eyes
> Starved wide on blackened tides, accrete—enclose
> This turning rondure whole, this crescent ring
> Sun-cusped and zoned with modulated fire
> Like pearls that whisper through the Doge's hands

The image of a bridge of light is suggested, in the last few lines, as a symbol of hope for eyes starved on the blackened tides of the harsh sea, the unpleasant present. The controlled, ordered "series on series, infinite," is both an image of the sea and of time which God can make into an infinite series connecting the past, present, and future. Another image suggests prophecy come true: "—Rush down the plenitude, and you shall see / Isaiah counting famine on this lee." And in the next stanza signs are given Columbus that he is near land.

There are two things that save Columbus on his return voyage, and they are worth spelling out at some length because so much of the rest of the poem is an expression of Crane's attempt to find those two things in his own life. The first is Mary of the title, to whom Columbus appeals for protection at the height of the storm.

> O Madre María, still
> One ship of these thou grantest safe returning;
> Assure us through thy mantle's ageless blue!

Mary answers this plea with "Some inmost sob, half-heard," which "dissuades the abyss" and "merges the wind in measure to the waves." The appeal here is not to the Mary of Eliot's Ash-Wednesday, but to a more abstract, or secular, concept of a "giving" female figure, an answering maternal voice that will reassure him in his moment of crisis. He is like Aeneas in these moments, and needs some equivalent for the

9. This echo of Eliot (The Hollow Men) is the first of many that Crane uses— as Wordsworth used Milton—to suggest his competition with Eliot and the hopefully contrary direction of his vision. He confessed to Gorham Munson in 1923 (Letters of Crane, p. 114) that his work had been "more influenced by Eliot than any other modern," and I shall try to point out in passing a few of the direct echoes and allusions that confirm this statement.

promise of Venus—a mother and guide—to accompany him and keep him safe. The voice answers Columbus, Venus appears to Aeneas, but Crane is to look in vain for "the Sabbatical, unconscious smile / My mother almost brought me once from church / And once only, as I recall" ("Van Winkle"). At this stage, he does not yet know that he is doomed forever to "shoulder the curse of sundered parenthood" (*Quaker Hill*), but it is the search for his own Mary that gives point to this realization later and helps us recognize the significance of Pocahontus, the *Three Songs*, and *Quaker Hill*.

The other dimension of Columbus's salvation seems almost to contradict the first, but can perhaps be seen as complementary. This is Columbus's ability to see behind his suffering another figure, one who sleeps on himself, apart, but who can be seen as working out a higher, incognizable "parable of man" through the voyager's suffering.

> O Thou who sleepest on Thyself, apart
> Like ocean athwart lanes of death and birth,
> And all the eddying breath between dost search
> Cruelly with love thy parable of man,—
> Inquisitor! incognizable Word
> Of Eden and the enchained Sepulchre,
> Into thy steep savannahs, burning blue,
> Utter to loneliness the sail is true.

For Columbus (and for Crane who momentarily identifies with Columbus) this "Thou" is the Elohim, "Who grindest oar, and arguing the mast / Subscribest holocaust of ships." God is apart from man, omnipotent and cruel in his love for man, subscribing "holocaust of ships" yet "urging through night our passage to the Chan." God is here the fierce Elohim of the Hebrew Scriptures; he is a Hand of Fire, and to him Columbus gives thanks for the "teeming span" which was at the same time the source of all his hardships and his bridge to the word, to the new land and the future. In this figure of the Elohim, Crane comes close to the conclusion of Eliot's "Fire Sermon."

> Burning burning burning burning
> O Lord Thou pluckest me out
> O Lord Thou pluckest
>
> burning

It is a deliberate contrast, however, for Crane attempts to deny the ambiguity of Eliot's "burning" with a triumphant "Te Deum laudamus." The effort will be repeated at the end of the poem in the juxtaposition of *Atlantis*, as *Te Deum*, with the "Kiss of our agony" that Crane feels in *The Tunnel*. A large part of the desperation of this last attempt will come from the poet's failure, in this earlier part of the poem, to find his equivalent of Columbus's Mary.

At this first stage of the quest, however, the poet's identification with Columbus is complete, for all the terms of his quest are symbolically interchangeable with those of Columbus's quest. Like Columbus, the poet must cross a "teeming span," the sorry present, and return with his "word" or vision of the future. The poet must leave the dream and return to the midst of his own teeming span, to his own search for stray branches among salty teeth; but he hopes to have found in Columbus's voyage such a branch, a symbol of hope and token of success.

### Powhatan's Daughter

In "The Harbor Dawn" section of *Powhatan's Daughter*, the poet begins his secular, historical quest for the equivalent of Columbus's Mary. In a "waking dream" in a "wavering slumber," he has a vision of a sexual union with Powhatan's daughter.

> *your hands within my hands are deeds;*
> *my tongue upon your throat—singing*
> *arms close; eyes wide, undoubtful*
> > *dark*
> > > *drink the dawn—*
> *a forest shudders in your hair!*

The vision is still only a dream, although a "waking dream," but it is hopefully a prefigurative dream for which the poet can find some embodiment in his waking day. The dream anticipates a prothalamion to follow in the poem and suggests an obvious continuation of the search through New York for Helen begun in *For the Marriage of Faustus and Helen*. The dream-dimension of this symbolic fertilization of the seed that Columbus brought to the new world has its negative aspect too, and Crane does not hesitate to emphasize it: the union occurs "while sirens / Sing to us, stealthily weave us into day." In the vision to come the poet must overcome the possibility that his union is apparitional.

As in Wordsworth, although for less important reasons, there is a shift here from the mother, Columbus's "Madre Maria," to the bride—someone with whom the poet can merge his seed, someone with "eyes wide, undoubtful" whose singing arms can close about and comfort him. Although he has a clear impression of his bride's function, and of the similarity between that function and the comfort Mary gave Columbus, he still has no concrete image or vision of her identity. He must wake from the dream to find his bride in time (*"Time recalls you to your love"*) and to discover her identity. *"Who is the woman with us in the dawn? . . . whose is the flesh our feet have moved upon?"* His state is comparable to Orc's confrontation with the "shadowy Daughter of Urthona—the nameless female" in the "Preludium" to *America: A Prophecy*. But Blake has Orc seize "the panting, struggling womb" with immediate results. "She put aside her clouds & smiled her first-born smile."

The transition from dream prefiguration of the vision, to the actual search for the vision, is a slow one in the poem. Crane moves from the dream in *Ave Maria*, to the waking dream in "The Harbor Dawn," to the Sleepy Hollow region of consciousness in "Van Winkle," before he finally touches firmly on the 20th Century in "The River." In the last stanza of "The Harbor Dawn" he emphasizes once more that in this stage of his quest he is still "under the mistletoe of dreams," while a star "As though to join us at some distant hill— / Turns in the waking west and goes to sleep." The "mistletoe of dreams" phrase may indicate only a vague state of wishfulness or hope that is understandably associated with this initial stage of the quest. But the phrase also has a broader range of reference within the poem, and although it is impossible to decide how much of the range Crane grasped in the moment of writing the image, we should be aware of it as we follow our own search for the meaning of the poem.

In the sixth book of the *Aeneid*, Aeneas undertakes his journey-within-a-journey to Avernus, the birdless place. Before he begins, he is warned by the Sybil.

> Night and day lie open the gates of death's dark kingdom:
> But to retrace your steps, to find the way back to daylight—
> That is the task, the hard thing. A few, because of Jove's
> Just love, or exalted to heaven by their own flame of goodness,

> Men born from gods, have done it. Between, there lies a forest,
> And darkly winds the river Cocytus around the place.[10]

(6:126–132)

The secondary similarities here, in the river and the forest ("a forest shudders in your hair!") are not so important as the similarity in the need—and difficulty—of returning to daylight, as Columbus had to return to Spain, and the poet must return from his dream. Later, when the poet must return to the "brinking dawn" from his own birdless place in *The Tunnel*, the analogy will be more significant. Here, although the poet is in one sense "returning" from his dream and the world of sleep, or prefigurative imagination, he is also making a beginning. And it is this aspect of "The Harbor Dawn" to which the mistletoe is most directly relevant. Before Aeneas can make the descent into Avernus, he must pluck the golden bough and present it to Proserpine as a tribute.

> There is a golden bough—gold the leaves and the tough stem—
> Held sacred to Proserpine: the whole wood hides this bough
> And a dell walls it round as it were in a vault of shadow.
> Yet none is allowed to enter the land which earth conceals
> Save and until he has plucked that gold–foil bough from the tree.

(6:137–141)

Aeneas is told further that the branch will come away quite easily if he is meant by destiny to go, but that otherwise no amount of brute force will separate it from the tree. The connection between the golden bough and the mistletoe is made later, when Aeneas actually finds the bough on its tree

> Amid whose branches there gleamed a bright haze, a different colour—
> Gold. Just as in depth of winter the mistletoe blooms
> In the woods with its strange leafage, a parasite on the tree,
> Hanging its yellow-green berries about the smooth round boles:
> So looked the bough of gold leaves upon that ilex dark.

(6:204–208)

10. *The Aeneid of Virgil*, trans. C. Day Lewis (Garden City, N.Y.: Doubleday & Co., 1952).

The connection between the bough and the mistletoe, and the comparable guiding functions of the bough and the dream, help us to understand the function of "The Harbor Dawn" dream in the initial stages of Crane's quest. Crane may even have been thinking of J. G. Frazer's discussion of the golden bough, in which he identifies it firmly with the mistletoe (citing the *Aeneid* as example) and mentions the practice of placing mistletoe dust under one's pillow in order to see one's future husband appear in a dream. Frazer also mentions the more general practice of placing mistletoe under the pillow to produce "prophetic dreams." [11] On some level he may also have known of the ancient belief that dreams coming just before dawn were prophetic.[12]

Although there is something inherently awkward and pretentious in tracing a single word so far in a prose critique, Crane's use of the mistletoe is one of the better examples of his attempts to emulate Eliot's "erudition and technique." [13] The phrase fits naturally into its context, without overt academic pretense, and can be followed through its range of reference as far as the reader chooses to go, always with the increasing sense of richness that underlies Crane's poetry at its best.

In the "Van Winkle" section Crane makes a tentative beginning of his complicated chronological-geographical exploration of the continent in search of his myth to God. Time is seen passing in different ways; the poet's day passes, for the section begins with his waking and taking the subway to work, and the next part of the poem, *Cutty Sark*, finds him almost at the end of the day; the poet's own history is seen passing in glimpses, loosely identified with the passing of the history of the continent.

The first two lines encompass the whole of the continent, from "Far Rockaway to Golden Gate," and the history of the continent is identified with the poet's personal history as the transition to the past is made in terms of the poet's childhood. Except for the identification of his own past with that of the continent, Crane's use of his past is quite similar to Wordsworth's. "What I am after is an assimilation of this

---

11. J. G. Frazer, *The Golden Bough*, 3d ed., pt. 7, vol. 2, *Balder the Beautiful: The Fire-Festivals of Europe and the Doctrine of the External Soul* (London & New York: Oxford Univ. Press, 1955), pp. 284ff., 292ff.

12. Dante mentions this in *Inferno*, bk. 26, canto 7, and uses it in *Purgatorio*, bk. 9 (Lucia's dream of the golden eagle) in a way structurally similar to the poet's waking dream in *The Bridge*.

13. Less fortunate examples can be found in some of Crane's awkward spellings (e.g., "casque" for cask in *Ave Maria*) and in the dubious *Panis Angelicus* (heavenly loaf?) in *Cape Hatteras*, by which Crane may mean something like "Holy Pan."

experience [history], a more organic panorama, showing the continuous and living evidence of the past in the inmost vital substance of the present." [14] For both, the need to establish a continuity between two states was crucial, and the use of childhood experience the only means available.

It was in Crane's childhood that he, like the land, first felt the influence of Pizarro and Cortez, Priscilla and Captain Smith. The land itself, symbolized by Pocahontus, is to be his equivalent of Columbus's Mary.

> *Like Memory, she is time's truant, shall take*
> *you by the hand . . .*
>
> *to those whose addresses are never near*
>
> *but who have touched her, knowing her without name*
>
> *nor the myths of her fathers . . .* [15]

The poet must first discover "those whose addresses are never near," who know "her without name," before he finds Maquokeeta in "The Dance," who will hopefully help him to "see her truly." But before he finds "those," in the figures of the hoboes of his childhood, he touches still another intermediate state of consciousness in the Sleepy Hollow figure of Rip Van Winkle.

In the third stanza, the youth of the continent and the poet's youth are suddenly contrasted with the maturity of the poet and his twentieth-century environment.

> *And Rip forgot the office hours,*
> > *and he forgot the pay;*
> > *Van Winkle sweeps a tenement*
> > > *way down on Avenue A,—*

But the grind-organ's insistence forces the poet into his childhood again, only to be interrupted by another contrasting view of the awakened Rip.

---

14. Crane to Otto H. Kahn (Sept. 12, 1927), *Letters of Crane*, p. 305.
15. Marginal notes in "Van Winkle" and "The River."

> And Rip was slowly made aware
>    that he, Van Winkle, was not here
>    nor there. He woke and swore he'd seen Broadway
>       a Catskill daisy chain in May—

The subsection ends with an explicit identification of the poet with the awakened Rip as he starts his subway ride to work.

> Keep hold of that nickle for car-change, Rip,—
> Have you got your *"Times"*—?
> And hurry along, Van Winkle—it's getting late!

It is impossible not to compare this identification with the poet's earlier use of Columbus. Columbus was successful in bridging the gap between the past and the future, and the identification with him was strongly affirmative and optimistic. Van Winkle, however, is memorable precisely because he lacked an adequate link between the past and the future. He woke to find himself out of time, in a world incommensurable with his past, and he was a pathetic rather than a triumphant figure. He awoke from his sleep of death not to a rebirth but, like Keats's Saturn, to decrepitude in an older world and to death.[16]

These limitations are clearly not what Crane wished to emphasize in his use of Van Winkle, but he does not ignore them. He emphasizes the incongruity as something he must overcome by finding in the figure of Van Winkle still another prefiguration, this time the reversal of time he is attempting. The poet is like Rip in that he, also, is more aware of earlier time although living in the present. He has waked into a world he cannot understand and has lost his *"Times,"* for the link between the past and present is a state "not here / nor there." [17] But like Van Winkle, the poet has his memory.

> The grind-organ says . . . Remember, remember
> The cinder pile at the end of the backyard
> Where we stoned the family of young

16. A look at Irving's *Rip Van Winkle* will readily turn up more points of relevance than I can point out separately here. The problems of Rip's credibility, his becoming a "chronicle of the old times," and his problems with "petticoat despotism" are all suggestive. The information in the "Postscript" is heavily drawn on later, particularly in "The Dance."

17. Cf. Eliot's contrast between "To be conscious is not to be in time" and "Only through time, time is conquered" (*Burnt Norton*, sect. 2). Crane is electing the second view, attempting to grasp his *"Times"* as he starts out.

> Garter snakes under . . . And the monoplanes
> We launched—with paper wings and twisted
> Rubber bands . . . Recall—recall
>
>    the rapid tongues
> That flittered from under the ash heap day
> After day whenever your stick discovered
> Some sunning inch of unsuspecting fibre—
> It flashed back at your thrust, as clean as fire.

And as the grind-organ of almost automatic recall turns over in the poet's mind, it revives what are to be the two most important memories in the whole poem:

> Is it the whip stripped from the lilac tree
> One day in spring my father took to me,
> Or is the Sabbatical, unconscious smile
> My mother almost brought me once from church
> And once only, as I recall—?
>
> It flickered through the snow screen, blindly
> It forsook her at the doorway, it was gone
> Before I had left the window. It
> Did not return with the kiss in the hall.

There are two memories here, one of Crane's father in the act of punishing him, and one of his mother *almost* bringing him a smile from church. These memories, unlike the others, are put as questions, preceded by "Is it . . . ," and we cannot understand this section, or the poem, without realizing what the "it" refers to in both cases. In the image of his father, he is asking if *this* is his equivalent to the Elohim of Columbus; he may even be asking the psychological question whether this is the source of his need to find now, in his adult life, some means of assimilating this early experience into a pattern of benignity.

With the mother's smile, Crane is asking the same two-part question: Is this the best he can find for his own Mary, or is this the real source of his need for such a figure? With the mother, there is much more a feeling of hesitancy and doubt than with the father. At the beginning of his search for the real (not anonymous) Pocahontas, he is forced to recall a failure of love in his own life and to express the failure in terms that anticipate a similar failure in the poem. The mother almost brought the smile. The union was almost achieved, as the smile "flick-ered through the snow screen, blindly," but it proved illusional. In "The Harbor Dawn," his dream union was glimpsed, in a similar hazy perception, "while myriad snowy hands are clustering at the panes," and the section ended with the poet still at the window. His mother's smile was gone "Before I had left the window," so the possibility is driven home that the dream-vision of mingled seed in "The Harbor Dawn" may prove to be as illusional as his mother's smile.

The doubts here help explain the urgency ("It's getting late!") of the final stanza, and the importance of the "nickel for car-change" that Rip must keep as he begins his trip. It is the same nickel that will play the "nickle-in-the-slot piano" in *Cutty Sark*, and it is the coin pressed into the slot in *The Tunnel*. It is the nickel of his memories and expe-rience, which is all he has to pay his way on his journey through time.

The first twenty-three lines of "The River" section are a burlesque on the confusion and tawdriness of the poet's twentieth-century environ-ment. In this world only an express train "makes time" (the sexual pun is deliberately degrading) over the land which Crane hopes to see as Pocahontas, the giving female lover. So the Twentieth Century Limited (another pun) whizzes by, leaving "three men, still hungry on the tracks" for a different knowledge of time and the land. The poet is actually on the subway, but the confusion is expressed in terms of cross-country trains; associations with trains bring the poet to memories of his own past and, by extension, the past of the continent.

The tramps he remembers from his childhood are "Time's rendings, time's blendings" who have been left behind, like Van Winkle, and are unsatisfied by the passing of time. They have deliberately chosen their way of life as an escape from the pressures of contemporary life. The poet is able to identify himself as a child with them, but rejects their way out as too passive and lacking faith in a higher vision.

> Each seemed a child, like me, on a loose perch,
> Holding to childhood like some termless play.
> John, Jake or Charley, hopping the slow freight
> —Memphis to Tallahassee—riding the rods,
> Blind fists of nothing, humpty-dumpty clods.

There are two virtues of the tramps' mode of existence, as there were of the poet's childhood. In spite of their inadequate grasp of time (they do not have their *"Times"*), they do know the body of the land under the wide rain, as the poet knew it in his youth: "O Nights that brought me to her body bare!" This is still "knowing her without name," without the full recognition the poet hopes to achieve, but it is a start.

The second virtue is the tramps' complicated relationship to time. They do not fully grasp time, so as to accept it, but they do have a "Strange bird-wit, like the elemental gist / Of unwalled winds" which enables them to "count / The river's minute by the far brook's year." They know the passage of the seasons, the cyclical time of the "far brook's year," in which the melting snows feed the brook which eventually becomes the River. Thus the tramps are in an ambiguous, intermediary position in terms of the poet's quest. Their "Strange bird-wit," or mythic sense, enables them to know "her," although anonymously, and to know time in a cyclical, seasonal sense. But they lack the more imaginative vision of time as the River, time moving forward bearing everything with it toward a final end.

> The River, spreading, flows—and spends your dream.
> What are you, lost within this tideless spell?
> You are your father's father, and the stream
> A liquid theme that floating niggers swell.

The hoboes are "blind clods" because they have no sense of time as either a running out of life, or as going on in an upward flight to an ultimate consummation. The only use the poet can make of the tramps in his search for a myth is their love of the past and their mobility which taught them the body of the land. Their rejection of the present and future he does not accept. By their very isolation from the flow of time, they illustrate the flow's inevitability. They too "feed the River timelessly. / And few evade full measure of their fate." They were "born pioneers in time's despite," too late to find an adequate sense of time in their "Strange bird-wit." Thus "They win no frontier by their wayward plight, / But drift in stillness, as from Jordan's brow," becoming "tributaries" to the "ancient flow" of time which they have tried to ignore.

The remainder of the section is an elaboration of the force of time, identified with the River which carries with it all the "Damp tonnage and alluvial march of days," as it flows over Desoto's bones, past the whole history of the continent, to the sea. And again, the sea is the sea of the poet-as-Columbus, the sea over which the poet's vision or myth must find a bridge to link the past with the future.

> All fades but one thin skyline 'round . . . Ahead
> No embrace opens but the stinging sea;
> The River lifts itself from its long bed,
>
> Poised wholly on its dream, a mustard glow
> Tortured with history, its one will—flow!

In "The Dance" section the reason for the emphasis on the hoboes' knowledge of the land and the seasons, and their ignorance of time as represented by the River, becomes clear. The poet, after finding in the River a symbol of the progression of time, must now reverse that flow, must return up the River and back in time to the consciousness of the Indian with "Mythical brows" who "knew" his gods directly as part of the natural physical world.[18] The attempt to return is necessary, for it is "Then you shall see her truly—your blood remembering its first invasion of her secrecy." The reversal of time in "The Dance" is not a rejection of the sense of time expressed in "The River," but an attempt to return to the source of time, to achieve the primitive mythic state of consciousness, and then to rejoin time and return to the present, equipped to cross it in safety with both the mythic recognition of the female figure and the fully developed sense of time as the River. This is the significance of the name "Maquokeeta," for the Indian is an embodiment of the mythic sense, and the name literally means "Big River."

The section begins with an evocation of seasonal myths of the American Indians. These myths themselves reflect an attitude toward cyclical time, as the seasons are linked organically with the (female) land in an expression of its benignity. But ironically the myths have become separated from the poet by the noncyclical time of the River's inexorable flow: "Now lie incorrigibly what years between." The poet, in search of his myth, must therefore go back in history; his canoe trip up the Hudson represents a direct attempt to overcome momentarily the force of time as it was expressed in the preceding section.

The return up the river is accompanied by signs of the most favorable sort.

18. Wordsworth's attempt to return to the immediacy and "felt presence" of nature experienced as a child is repeated by Crane, but with an added historical dimension.

There was a bed of leaves, and broken play;
There was a veil upon you, Pocahontas, bride—
O Princess whose brown lap was virgin May;
And bridal flanks and eyes hid tawny pride.

I left the village for dogwood. By the canoe
Tugging below the mill-race, I could see
Your hair's keen crescent running, and the blue
First moth of evening take wing stealthily.

What laughing chains the water wove and threw!
I learned to catch the trout's moon whisper; I
Drifted how many hours I never knew,
But, watching, saw that fleet young crescent die,—

And one star, swinging, take its place, alone,
Cupped in the larches of the mountain pass—
Until, immortally, it bled into the dawn.

As he returns upstream, he "learns" the mythic mode of consciousness. He is able to see Pocahontus, dressed as a bride and accompanied by the sign of blue that Columbus associated with Mary. As Mary calmed and linked the waves in the Ave Maria, so the poet's vision of Pocahontus turns the waves of the River into "laughing chains the water wove and threw!" He finds the star that left him "as though to join us at some distant hill" in "Harbor Dawn," and as the star bleeds immortally into the dawn, he touches his feet to the ground in union with the land represented by Pocahontas.

At the end of his geographical-temporal journey, he is confronted with the ritualistic execution by fire of Maquokeeta, the tribal king. Maquokeeta represents for Crane what the savage and pagan represented for Keats and Wordsworth respectively. He is one of those "ancient poets" Blake saw as animating "all sensible objects with Gods or Geniuses, calling them by the names and adorning them with the properties of woods, rivers, mountains, lakes, cities, nations, and whatever their enlarged & numerous senses could perceive." [19] The experience that Maquokeeta is undergoing, and that Crane attempts to share with him, is simultaneously a wedding dance of union with Pocahontus and a ceremonial dance of death for the execution.

19. "The Marriage of Heaven and Hell," pl. 11, in The Poetry and Prose of William Blake, ed. David V. Erdman (Garden City, N.Y.: Doubleday & Co., 1968), p. 153.

The long moan of a dance is in the sky.
Dance, Maquokeeta: Pocahontus grieves . . .

And every tendon scurries toward the twangs
Of lightning deltaed down your saber hair.
Now snaps the flint in every tooth; red fangs
And splay tongues thinly busy the blue air . . .

Dance, Maquokeeta! snake that lives before,
That casts his pelt, and lives beyond! Sprout, horn!
Spark, tooth! Medicine-man, relent, restore—
Lie to us,—dance us back the tribal morn!

The air is blue, as it should be for the union, and Maquokeeta is identified with the sphinxlike immortality of the snake, becoming like one of
the snakes in "Van Winkle" that "flittered from under the ash heap
day / After day" and "flashed back at your thrust, as clean as fire." In
the death of Maquokeeta, Crane sees for the first time that his own
experience is to be a dying into life before he can achieve a poetic
image of the rebirth of America. His hope is that in Maquokeeta he
has found an image that will carry him through the experience; and
for the time, he feels that he has found it.

I, too, was liege
To rainbows currying each pulsant bone:
Surpassed the circumstance, danced out the siege!

And buzzard-circleted, screamed from the stake;
I could not pick the arrows from my side.

The identification with the death is complete, but a final stage has not
been reached.

I saw thy change begun!

And saw thee dive to kiss that destiny
Like one white meteor, sacrosanct and blent
At last with all that's consummate and free
There, where the first and last gods keep thy tent.

Crane has seen Maquokeeta embrace his destiny by accepting his death,
but this is only the beginning of the change. Crane's hope is that the

freedom of the Indian's spirit, his most desirable attribute, can survive the passing of time to be reborn as a gift to a later generation.

> Though other calendars now stack the sky,
> Thy freedom is her largesse, Prince, and hid
> On paths thou knewest best to claim her by.

Crane has returned to the "tribal morn" of the country, and experienced a simultaneous union with the land (Pocahontus) and with death. His problem now is to return, to establish a continuity of the Indian's spirit through history, and to find the pattern of his own rebirth after his visionary death with Maquokeeta. The last stanza is a summation of the section, and a "strong prayer" that he can return with his vision to the present.

> We danced, O Brave, we danced beyond their farms,
> In cobalt desert closures made our vows . . .
> Now is the strong prayer folded in thine arms,
> The serpent with the eagle in the boughs.

What the "Indiana" section attempts to do is reasonably clear after we have grasped the significance of Maquokeeta and the spirit of freedom in "The Dance." The spirit is symbolically transferred from the Indian to the pioneer boy Larry, for the Indian was doomed to extinction as he was pushed out by the white man. The doom can be read in the Indian mother's eyes, which "were not black / But sharp with pain," as she passes the pioneer mother who is returning east. Crane, as the pioneer mother, holds up the infant to receive the spirit from the Indian mother.

> I held you up—I suddenly the bolder,
>     Knew that mere words could not have brought us nearer.
> She nodded—and that smile across her shoulder
>         Will still endear her

The spirit passes to the boy, not the mother, for she already represents the decline of the pioneers, which the boy must overcome through his heritage of freedom received from the Indian.

Crane's identification with the mother rather than the boy is significant, for it identifies him with the pioneer's decline, left with only the hope that Larry will

> Come back to Indiana—not too late!
>     (Or will you be a ranger to the end?)
> Good-bye . . . Good–bye . . . oh, I shall always wait
>     You, Larry, traveller—
>                 stranger,
>                     son,
>                         —my friend—

Crane, as the mother, is "standing still," "old," and "half of stone." He pleads with the boy, "Oh, hold me in those eyes' engaging blue," for "There's where the stubborn years gleam and atone,— / Where gold is true!" The mother is first seen on "The long trail back" from the pursuit of a false vision in the "dream called Eldorado," and the error in that earlier deception is presented as an error in the grasp of time.

> But we,—too late, too early, howsoever—
>     Won nothing out of fifty-nine—those years—
> But gilded promise, yielded to us never,
>     And barren tears . . .

Once again, Crane has contrasted a vision he hopes is true with one that has proven false. The ambiguity of the contrast at once emphasizes the truth of the alternative vision ("There's where the stubborn years gleam and atone,— / Where gold is true!"), while suggesting that it too may prove illusional, as the first had. There is a note of desperation in Crane's voice as the mother bids farewell to her son, hoping that he will preserve his freedom and return with it. "You'll keep your pledge; / I know your word," she says. But in the next section there is to be a loss of the "word" that Crane has attempted to find in the continuity of the Indian's heritage of freedom.

### Cutty Sark

In *Cutty Sark* the poet, at the end of his day, meets a sailor lost in time. Like the last of the Kentuckians, whom he represents, the sailor is unable to remain on the body of the continent ("No—I can't live on land—!") and has thus lost the union with Pocahontus that Crane had tried to establish. His eyes have changed from the "engaging blue" of the "Indiana" section; they are now green, or made to appear green by the bar lights shining on them. The loss of the "blue" and the loss of the ability to stay on the land represent Crane's final resignation of the attempt to find an equivalent to Columbus's Mary in *Ave Maria*. The

best the poet can do with the nickel he kept "for car-change" is to play
"*O Stamboul Rose—dreams weave the rose!*" which degenerates into

> ATLANTIS ROSE *drums wreathe the rose,*
> *the star floats burning in a gulf of tears*
> *and sleep another thousand—*

>                              interminably
>           long since somebody's nickel—stopped—
>           playing—

The sense in which the River "spends your dream" ("The River")
seems clear now. Time has conquered the vision, the nickel has run out;
the star that was to join him ("Harbor Dawn") now floats burning in
a gulf of tears, and he is ready to give up time "and sleep another
thousand" years.

> "I'm not much good at time any more keep
> weakeyed watches sometimes snooze—" his bony hands
> got to beating time. . . "A whaler once—
> I ought to keep time and get over it—I'm a
> Democrat—I know what time it is—No
> I don't want to know what time it is—that
> damned white Arctic killed my time. . ."

*Cutty Sark* seems to be a final abandonment of the attempt to build
a myth inspired by the spirit of freedom found in America's early years,
when frontier life had an exaltation that the poet has been unable to
sustain—though he can identify with it—in the face of his present
existence. "I saw the frontiers gleaming of his mind; / Or are there
frontiers—running sands sometimes / running sands—somewhere—
sands running. . . ." Although he has been able to find, in the past,
inspiring instances of the free spirit and a mythical union with the land,
he finds that the spirit is inexorably dead as far as the present is concerned. The dawn that he sees coming is "putting the Statue of Liberty
out—that torch of hers you know—" and the liberty being extinguished
is the "chained bay waters Liberty" of the poem's first stanza. With the
last of the pioneers has gone its last glimmer. The identification of the
extinction of the country's most important symbol of freedom with
the poet's loss of his vision of freedom is complete, and *Cutty Sark*
ends one of the main movements of the poem right where it started, in

the sorry present. The poet's historical excursion has succeeded only in reaffirming the spiritual poverty of his own existence, while setting it against earlier generations whose freedom makes his lack of it all the more oppressive. In searching for his vision the poet has only succeeded in weakening the subjective attitude of faith with which he began the quest.

With this recognition, the poet "started walking home across the Bridge," but he does not complete the trip, for he has found nothing to sustain his return. Instead, he turns to a catalog of clipper ships seen as "savage sea-girls / that bloomed in the spring." There seems to be a moment of hope, as he finds a combination of three symbolic strands —female, blue, and parabola (bridge).

> Pennants, parabolas—
> clipper dreams indelible and ranging,
> baronial white on lucky blue!

> Perennial-*Cutty*-trophied-*Sark!*

But the parabola of the clipper ship's path is as apparitional as the path of the gull's flight in the first stanza of the poem, for the clippers "turned and left us on the lee." If the sailors were in union with the sea, as the Indians were with the body of the land, then this too is a vanished possibility.

> O, the navies old and oaken,
> O, the Temeraire no more!

The record voyage of the "Buntlines tusseling (91 days, 20 hours and anchored!)" is a thing of the past, as are the other clippers and the symbols Crane had attempted to hold.

> *Rainbow, Leander*
> (last trip a tragedy)—where can you be
> *Nimbus?* and you rivals two—

> a long tack keeping—

> *Taeping?*
> *Ariel?* [20]

20. The names *"Rainbow"* and *"Leander"* have fairly obvious significance here. With *"Nimbus"* Crane is recalling Whitman: "This is the female form, / A divine

At this point Crane has reached an important recognition that can be grasped fully only by a close reading of the rest of the poem, which I must anticipate briefly here. The recognition is that the loss of the vision is *itself* the mark of the "sounding heel" of the Elohim on him. Accepting the failure of his vision, as part of the "incognizable word," can be the means of transcending that failure, as his acceptance and participation in the death of Maquokeeta was an attempt to transcend it by seeing it as preparation for a rebirth. The complete expression of his failure to find and unite with a Mary figure, which comes in the *Three Songs*, is anticipated here by the reference to the "*Leander* (last trip a tragedy)*." Crane does not abandon the entire vision of Columbus's voyage, but does abandon the attempt to find his own Madre Maria, and he turns to the attempt to read his experience of lost vision as a "parable of man." Only at this point does he come close to the concept of fallen vision as a state that must be overcome by the poet, a concept we have traced in Blake, Wordsworth, and Keats. Crane is to repeat their attempts to make fallen vision the subject of a poem that will achieve, if not a reversal of the fall, a mode of vision that will transcend it. This is a step beyond the attempt to go backward in time to an earlier mythic vision, for in that attempt he did not accept the fall but thought, like Wordsworth, to find a continuity of perceptual power that had somehow not participated in the fall. Crane is now ready to write the poem Keats might have written had he lived longer, a poem beginning with the failure of his dream and attempting to transcend the failure by achieving a vision that can accept it. We could call this a "tragic argument," as Dembo suggests, but there is still the problem of how and whether the poet will in fact be able to achieve the transcendent vision. The poet must prepare for this vision, and test it too, and this is the function served by *Cape Hatteras, Quaker Hill,* and *The Tunnel.* In *Cape Hatteras* the poet attempts to prepare himself for the abandonment of his vision in *Three Songs* by identifying with Walt Whitman's "rebound seed" and his inexhaustible "love" for and acceptance of all aspects of human experience. In *Quaker Hill* the poet attempts to adjust himself to "the curse of sundered parenthood" that separates him from the Madre Maria and from the god who sleeps "apart" but whose "incognizable word" must nevertheless be accepted.

nimbus exhales from it from head to foot" (*Children of Adam* #5). Frederick Hoffmann (*The Twenties* [New York: Viking Press, 1955], p. 235) suggests that "Ariel?" is an appeal to the Ariel of Shakespeare's *The Tempest* to calm the waters and to guide him back. "*Taeping*" is the Chinese name for the Pacific Ocean.

The shift of vision to "the worm's eye view" in that part of the poem is necessary before Crane can embody in *The Tunnel* all the worst aspects of his present existence seen through his fallen vision; before he can attempt the final return to the "brinking dawn" in the East and his vision of Atlantis.

## Cape Hatteras

Crane called *Cape Hatteras* "the 'center' of the book, both physically and symbolically," and in many ways it was the most difficult section for him to write. In it he hoped "to marshal the notes and agonies of the last two years' effort into a rather arresting synthesis." [21] The kind of "agonies" referred to here are the result of the doubts and ambiguities we have traced previously in the poem. Crane found a focus in "the Spengler thesis" for these doubts, but it is a mistake to assume that Spengler was in any sense a "cause" of elements that appeared in the poem long before Crane actually read Spengler. Writing from the Isle of Pines, while reading Spengler, Crane summed up the state of his mind in a formulation that also fit the progress of *The Bridge* at the end of *Cutty Sark*.

> Emotionally I should like to write *The Bridge;* intellectually judged the whole theme and project seems more and more absurd. A fear of personal impotence in this matter wouldn't affect me half so much as the convictions that arise from other sources. . . . I had what I thought were authentic materials that would have been a pleasurable-agony of wrestling, eventuating or not in perfection—at least being worthy of the most supreme efforts I could muster.
>
> These "materials" were valid to me to the extent that I presumed them to be (articulate or not) at least organic and active factors in the experience and perceptions of our common race, time and belief. The very idea of a bridge, of course, is a form peculiarly dependent on such spiritual convictions. It is an act of faith besides being a communication. The symbols of reality necessary to articulate the span—may not exist where you expected them, however. By which I mean that however great their subjective significance to me is concerned—these forms, materials, dynamics are simply non-existent in the world. I may amuse and delight and flatter myself as much as I please—but I am only

21. Crane to Caresse Crosby (Dec. 26, 1929), *Letters of Crane*, p. 347; (Sept. 17, 1929), p. 346.

evading a recognition and playing Don Quixote in an immorally
conscious way.[22]

During this period Crane came to the conviction that "the validity
of a work of art is situated in contemporary reality to the extent that
the artist must honestly anticipate the realization of his vision in 'action'
(as an actively operating principle of communal works and faith)"; and
it is precisely this sense of "action" that he had failed to secure so far
in his attempts to write *The Bridge*. Without requiring "bona fide
evidences directly and personally signalled," the artist must nevertheless
feel that his "intuitions were salutary and that his vision either sowed
or epitomized 'experience.'" Still in the same letter, he anticipated his
use of Whitman in *Cape Hatteras*, although at that time he showed
doubts about his ability to achieve the "confidence" that for him was
Whitman's essential virtue as a poet. "If only America were half as
worthy today to be spoken of as Whitman spoke of it fifty years ago
there might be something for me to say—not that Whitman received
or required any tangible proof of his intimations, but that time has
shown how increasingly lonely and ineffectual his confidence stands."

In *Cape Hatteras*, Crane attempts to revive the confidence of Whitman in the only sense that it can be meaningful for him, by focusing his
vision on "contemporary reality." And in doing this he deliberately
picks the one aspect of contemporary reality that was most difficult for
him to accept in his former state of mind. The conquest of space
through the airplane was a perfect metaphor for the kind of "conquest"
(over time *and* space) Crane was attempting in his earlier attempts to
achieve a vision. In the beginning, *Cape Hatteras* seems to be a continuation of this attempt, an exploration of new materials (metaphors
of air flight) with which to identify his vision. But Crane knows that
the airplane flew only to crash, that the physical conquest of space was
doomed to fail as a metaphor for the poetic vision, as his earlier attempt to use Columbus had failed. Knowing this, he deliberately
pursues the metaphor, in his earlier mode, to the point where he must
admit its failure; and at that point he turns to Whitman in an attempt
to revive Whitman's confidence, to achieve an acceptance of his failure
comparable to Whitman's acceptance of the historical failure of America in the Civil War.

The dominant movement of this part of the poem is a vertical rise

22. Crane to Waldo Frank (June 20, 1926), *Letters of Crane*, pp. 260–262.

in space, beginning at the earth's "astral core," which is analogous to
Crane's earlier attempt to find a chronological beginning for his conquest of time in the "tribal morn" of the continent. Until now Crane
has not been aware of this possibility, for he has been involved in a
different kind of movement.

> But we, who round the capes, the promontories
> Where strange tongues vary messages of surf
> Below grey citadels, repeating to the stars
> The ancient names—return home to our own
> Hearths, there to eat an apple and recall
> The songs that gypsies dealt us at Marseille
> Or how the priests walked—slowly through Bombay—

He has been attempting to decipher varying "messages of surf" and re-
peating the ancient names "to the stars," but now he must "return
home," must "eat an apple" in recognition of the failure of his vision
and his fallen state. And he must read Whitman, who knows (in the
sense already described) that he is in thrall.

> To that deep wonderment, our native clay
> Whose depth of red, eternal flesh of Pocahontus—
> Those continental folded aeons, surcharged
> With sweetness below derricks, chimneys, tunnels—
> Is veined by all that time has really pledged us . . .
> And from above, thin squeaks of radio static,
> The captured fume of space foams in our ears—
> What whisperings of far watches on the main
> Relapsing into silence, while time clears
> Our lenses, lifts a focus, resurrects
> A periscope to glimpse what joys or pain
> Our eyes can share or answer—then deflects
> Us, shunting to a labyrinth submersed
> Where each sees only his dim past reversed. . .

The "sweetness" of the subcontinent is below, as the glories of the past
are behind, the derricks, chimneys, and tunnels which are the "material"
the poet must face in his present experience. The "whisperings of far
watches on the main" which he has listened to so far must lapse "into
silence," and he knows from this in advance that the new vision based
on the airplane will be deflected and shunted "to a labyrinth sub-
mersed."

This passage reflects the basic movement of the whole poem, in its faith that the continental aeons are "surcharged with sweetness" and in its relapse into pain and doubt when faced with the labyrinthine present. The periscope image represents the technique the poet has been using to find inspiration in the past, glimpsing pains and joys that he can admire and identify with.[23] But, as we saw in *Powhatan's Daughter* and *Cutty Sark*, identification with the past could not support faith in the future when faced with the absence of any kind of greatness in the poet's own realm of experience. The passage also begins the transition to space, the "new universe," as a new dimension for the poet to explore in his attempt to support his faith.

> Now the eagle dominates our days, is jurist
> Of the ambiguous cloud. We know the strident rule
> Of wings imperious. . . . Space, instantaneous,
> Flickers a moment, consumes us in its smile

He is consumed in the "smile" of space for the moment, as he had been consumed earlier by the deceptive smile of the Madre Maria. "Dream cancels dream in this new realm of act," and this smile too will flicker and go out. The use of the "eagle" image and the "Falcon–Ace," and later the "hawk's far–stemming view" in *Quaker Hill*, is an ironic repetition of the "Strange bird–wit, like the elemental gist / Of unwalled winds" offered by the tramps in "The River."

One of Crane's seemingly inevitable ambiguities, in which a false vision both supports and sheds doubt on the alternative, enters *Cape Hatteras* with the fourth stanza. Before accepting the airplane's conquest of space as a basis for his faith in the future, the poet turns in an aside to Walt Whitman, the "Meistersinger" who "set breath in steel," whose intense faith in the future and in science and the machine is directly relevant to the poem at this point. Crane wants to be another Walt Whitman, but is unsure of himself and unsure of the basis of his faith in the "new universe."

> "—Recorders ages hence"—ah, syllables of faith!
> Walt, tell me, Walt Whitman, if infinity
> Be still the same as when you walked the beach

23. The general situation of the poem at this point is comparable to Wordsworth's interlude with Beaupuy (*Prelude*, bk. 9:293–436), with the impending crisis of war and the need for companionship and models to survive the crisis.

Near Paumanok—your lone patrol—and heard the wraith
Through surf, its *bird note* there a long time falling . . .

(Italics added)

Ironically, Crane is turning to Whitman for support of a vision he knows must collapse, and when it does he will turn to Whitman *again*, and in a different sense, for the confidence he needs to overcome the collapse. Crane is distinguishing between Whitman's confidence in industry and the machine (which he is using here) and Whitman's transcendent acceptance of "Time absolutely" (to be used later) which he hopes will overcome the misuse of the machine in Time.

Endless unfolding of words of ages!
And mine a word of the modern, the word En-Masse.

A word of the faith that never balks,
Here or henceforward it is all the same to me, I accept Time absolutely.

It alone is without flaw, it alone rounds and completes all,
That mystic baffling wonder alone completes all.[24]

It is the acceptance of Time "alone" that is without flaw, transcending the more specific acceptance of the machine of materialism as an immediate good, as opposed to an ultimate good in Time. The ambiguity lies in the failure of one attempt, and the presumed success of the other, for it is impossible to ignore the fact that the second may fail too.

At this first stage the poet finds himself in a labyrinth (a synonym for "the present" used frequently in the poem) and seeks to use the eyes of Whitman, "sea eyes and tidal, undenying, bright with myth"—like the "mythic brows" of the Indian—to navigate through and out of his "prison crypt of canyoned traffic." Only then does Crane begin to explore the possibilities of the airplane's conquest of space as material on which to ground his faith.

Against the magnificent potential of the airplane, whose pilot bears a "Sanskrit charge / To conjugate infinity's dim marge— / Anew . . . !" (like the "pledge" left with Larry by his mother in the "Indiana" section), the poet must contrast the World War, the "dim past reversed"

24. Whitman, "Song of Myself" #23, *Complete Poetry and Selected Prose*, ed. James E. Miller (Boston: Houghton Mifflin Co., 1959), pp. 40–41.

which has for the time being shunted the means of conquering space into a means of destruction. Crane then attempts to identify "man's perversity" exhibited in the World War with that in the Civil War, the example Whitman had to face in his experience. This is not an appeal to the "Strange bird-wit" of Whitman, to the Whitman who shared the "open road" with the tramps in "The River," for that Whitmanesque vision has failed him so far in the poem. He now needs the Whitman who will enable him to see "Easters of speeding light" in the airplane's plunge to destruction, to achieve a vision of "the rainbow's arch—how shimmeringly stands / Above the Cape's ghoul-mound." This is the Whitman who confidently wrote:

> The smallest sprout shows there is really no death,
> And if ever there was it led forward life . . .
> All goes onward and outward, nothing collapses,
> And to die is different from what anyone supposed, and luckier.[25]

And it is to this Whitman that the second apostrophe is addressed.

> But who has held the heights more sure than thou,
> O Walt!—Ascensions of thee hover in me now
> As thou at junctions elegiac, there, of speed
> With vast eternity, dost wield the rebound seed!
> The competent loam, the probable grass,—travail
> Of tides awash the pedestal of Everest, fail
> Not less than thou in pure impulse inbred
> To answer deepest soundings! O, upward from the dead
> Thou bringest tally, and a pact, new bound
> Of living brotherhood! [26]

Even though he does not know "toward what capes" the "Years of the Modern" are headed, the poet plunges into a reaffirmation of Whitman's acceptance of "Time absolutely." "Thy vision is reclaimed! / What heritage thou'st signalled to our hands!" The rainbow is again invoked as a symbol of faith, and the poet concludes still in a dependent relationship with Whitman.

25. Whitman, "Song of Myself" #6, *Complete Poetry and Selected Prose*, p. 29.
26. That there are two apostrophes to Whitman is of great importance structurally. The first was to the Whitman who heard the "bird note" of the "wraith . . . through surf." By introducing a new apostrophe here, Crane is emphasizing the different aspect of Whitman ("the rebound seed") to which he is now turning.

                                                      Yes, Walt,
          Afoot again, and onward without halt,—
          Not soon, nor suddenly,—No, never to let go
              My hand
                      in yours,
                                      Walt Whitman—
                                                      so—

The final "so—" seems hesitant, or at least questioning, as if the
strained overwriting of much of the apostrophe to Whitman shows
more desire to believe than actual belief in the vision offered. This
weakness, at what was to be "the 'center' of the book, both physically
and symbolically," eats away at the final affirmative power of the poem
and forces us to keep in mind the ambiguity inherent in contrasting a
presently accepted vision with a formerly accepted, but now rejected
vision. Crane could not have avoided taking note of Whitman's warning
to those who would follow him.

          Whoever you are holding me now in hand,
          Without one thing all will be useless,
          I give you fair warning before you attempt me further,
          I am not what you supposed, but far different.

          Who is he that would become my follower?
          Who would sign himself a candidate for my affections?
          The way is suspicious, the result uncertain, perhaps destructive.[27]

Crane was willing to take the chance, for he had to become that fol-
lower, if he could. Whitman's equanimity in the face of death and
catastrophe is what he needed at this stage of his quest, and what he
would need even more in the final transition from *The Tunnel* to
*Atlantis.*

                              *Three Songs*
              Das Ewig-weibliche zieht uns hinan.

                                      —Goethe, *Faust*

              Woman, what have I to do with thee?

                                      —Jesus, in the Temple

27. Whitman, "Whoever you are holding me now in hand" (*Leaves of Grass,*
"Calamus" section), *Complete Poetry and Selected Prose,* pp. 85–86.

*Three Songs* begins with a quotation from Marlowe's *Hero and Leander* which is meant to recall the lost clipper ship in *Cutty Sark*. The function of the songs within the structure of the poem is complex, but I have already indicated the general nature of their function. The songs are a summation, or synecdoche of the quest begun at the first of the poem for a Madre Maria in Crane's life and in the history of the country. They recall and reemphasize the intense desire that motivated the quest and suggest more clearly the reasons for the failure of that quest. Crane's use of three songs recalls Eliot's "Song of the three Thames Daughters" in *The Waste Land*, and this comparison is as significant as that which we should also make between Crane's sailor in *Cutty Sark* and Eliot's drowned Phoenician sailor. Eliot contrasts the glory of earlier lovers with the sordid sexual life of the present, and his singer in the third song concludes, "I can connect / Nothing with nothing." Crane has failed to find a name for the nameless woman of his dream vision, and his *Three Songs* are an admission that he too can connect nothing with nothing.

The marriage metaphor is basic to the tradition in which Crane hoped to find his myth, except that Crane deliberately sought a secular equivalent of the sacred marriage, and he failed in the attempt. Religious or secular, the sexual element is inevitable in visionary poetry of the kind Crane was consciously trying to write. The idea of a fulfilled vision, as consummated union and harmony, inevitably calls forth the sexual symbol or metaphor. But *Three Songs* quite deliberately begins with an expression of *past* desire. The songs are to be the inverse of the usual sexual fulfillment, an expression of frustrated desire, of protracted and painful longing.

The first song, "Southern Cross," begins with an expression of the poet's desire, in the past tense. He "wanted" the "nameless Woman of the South / No wraith, but utterly." The woman is nameless, for the dream-vision of "Harbor Dawn" did not identify her. And the poet wants her "utterly" in the sense that implies reciprocity, some answering sign such as that given Columbus by Mary in *Ave Maria*. But the consummation the poet desires is doomed, even before he considers the problem of naming the woman, for she is apart, "High, cool, / wide from the slowly smoldering fire / Of lower heavens,—." The distance, and the high coolness, can imply the separation between fallen man and Eve in the garden. It can suggest the distance between a man and a prostitute or unreciprocating wife as they participate in the lust of a "flagrant, sweating cinch." Or it can suggest the separation between man and the idea of an immaculate Virgin Mary, even though she is a "Saturday Mary" rather than the Sunday Mary of Christianity. These possibilities—"Eve! Magdalene! / or Mary, you?"—are the ones the poet considers and rejects in *Three Songs*. For "Whatever call" the poet makes "falls vainly on the wave." There is no "sob" as in *Ave Maria* to merge the wind in measure with the waves and to "dissuade the abyss," to bridge the separation between the poet and his "nameless Woman."

Eve, the first possibility the poet considers, is now "homeless Eve, / Unwedded, stumbling gardenless to grieve." There is nothing left of the beauty of natural motherhood that the original mother, Eve, might have had before she was forced from the garden. The thought of the beauty motherhood might have had before the fall is enough to "grieve / Windswept guitars on lonely decks forever" and to reduce the poet's mind to churning spittle.

> And this long wake of phosphor,
>                          iridescent
> Furrow of all our travel—trailed derision!
> Eyes crumble at its kiss. Its long-drawn spell
> Incites a yell. Slid on that backward vision
> The mind is churned to spittle, whispering hell.

The "long wake of phosphor" is a deliberate echo of the poet's confident belief, expressed in "The Dance," that "I could see / Your hair's keen crescent running," and enforces the contrast between the poet's voyage to the dawn of history in that section and his voyage to the dawn in this song. The memory of how great his desire was in the "waking dream" comes back to the poet, and the memory is almost more than he can bear.

> I wanted you . . . The embers of the Cross
> Climbed by aslant and huddling aromatically.
> It is blood to remember; it is fire
> To stammer back . . . It is
> God—your namelessness. And the wash—

But the poet does remember, and he goes beyond that memory to recall the deceit the "nameless Woman" practised on him in his dream.

> All night the water combed you with black
> Insolence. You crept out simmering, accomplished.
> Water rattled that stinging coil, your
> Rehearsed hair—docile, alas, from many arms.
> Yes, Eve—wraith of my unloved seed!

The poet's image of a mother was a deception "Rehearsed" and passed on to him "from many arms." He has confused memory and assimilated conventions with a direct visionary perception. The "seed" are most likely the seed that were to *become* the poet, the seed of his conception rather than his own symbolic sperm. The ideal mother, the "nameless Woman," who could have conceived and borne him as Eve might have conceived and borne in the garden, is a wraith; his seed are "unloved" for he can find no mother, no "Madre Maria" who will give him the smile of recognition he desires. It is only with the coming of daylight, the waking from the dream, that he can discover his Eve was a wraith, a "phantom," who must drop below the dawn.

> The Cross, a phantom, buckled—dropped below the dawn.
> Light drowned the lithic trillions of your spawn.

The "National Winter Garden" song shows the failure of the poet's attempt to approach his "nameless Woman" as a bride rather than a mother. His inability to find any dimension but the sexual, where he had hoped to find a metaphor for a spiritual state of consciousness, leads him to a vicious sexual parody of his spiritual quest. He begins with the only "word" he is to receive from the Magdalene: "Outspoken buttocks" that invite him to join "the necessary cloudy clinch" of "The world's one flagrant, sweating cinch." In the second stanza the "salads in the brain" emphasize the confusion that the presence of lust in the poet's brain causes in his search for the "nameless Woman" as bride. Even though his sensually practiced eye can pick a "blonde out neatly through the smoke," he is always waiting for "someone else" to satisfy his other desire. The moment before the consummation is the most confusing of all.

> Always and last, before the final ring
> When all the fireworks blare, begins
> A tom-tom scrimmage with a somewhere violin,
> Some cheapest echo of them all—begins.

The sacredness of the marital consummation is destroyed, reduced to the jargon and perspective of sex that is characteristic of a cheap novel: "the final ring / When all the fireworks blare." And the poet is forced to the destruction, because always, before he can cross the threshold to his vision of spiritual union, he is forced to recognize "some cheapest echo" of the union in his physical lust. The line, "A tom-tom scrimmage with a somewhere violin," burlesques his "mythic" dance in "The Dance" section by using, again, the language of a cheap novel.[28] Considering the general tone of this section, the emphasis of "cheapest echo of them all" may be read as a reference to Crane's homosexuality. This would change the stanza to a pattern of double contrasts; as lust for a prostitute hinders his vision of an ideal bride, so the "cheapest echo," homosexual desire, hinders the consummation of the "final ring" even with the prostitute. Another possibility, of course, is that the phrase is Crane's way of acknowledging his heavy use of Eliot's *Portrait of a Lady*. Even though this song is a night song, as was "Southern Cross," the poet can't reach the same degree of self-deception; the contrast between the ideal of the desired vision and the reality is too great.

> And shall we call her whiter than the snow?
> Sprayed first with ruby, then with emerald sheen—
> Least tearful and least glad (who knows her smile?)
> A caught slide shows her sandstone grey between.
>
> Her eyes exist in swivellings of her teats,
> Pearls whip her hips, a drench of whirling strands.
> Her silly snake rings begin to mount, surmount
> Each other—turquoise fakes on tinselled hands.

The Magdalene is beyond expression of emotion, either through tears or through the "smile" that was so important an anticipation in Crane's earlier search.[29] The immortality symbol, the snake, is seen as nothing

---

28. There are strong echoes of Eliot's *Portrait of a Lady* in this song: "Inside my brain a dull tom-tom begins / Absurdly hammering a prelude of its own, / Capricious monotone." Also the general situation and even the structure draw heavily on Eliot's poem, where the Lady is visited again and again but not taken, not possessed. She presents a romantic facade which does not deceive the cynical speaker, but she may have "the advantage, after all."

29. Part of the reference in this song is to *Faustus and Helen*, in which Crane thought he had found Helen, performing in an artificial winter garden, and "still so young, / We cannot frown upon her as she smiles." In this later winter garden the poet is unable to find the smile on the Magdalene's lips.

but a string of beads, "turquoise fakes on tinselled hands"; and the
poet waits "that writhing pool in vain" for the sign that will calm and
order the waters. The discrepancy between his desired vision and the
physical fact is finally so extreme that the poet must "flee her spasm
through a fleshless door." But if he has lost his vision of the "nameless
Woman," he has gained something in perspective; he has recognized
lust as a necessary part of his experience, a fact he will have to accept in
whatever affirmation he is finally to reach. The last stanza extends the
rejection of the "silly snake rings," a false symbol of immortality, to
include the procreation that was so significant a metaphor for Wordsworth.

> Yet, to the empty trapeze of your flesh,
> O Magdalene, each comes back to die alone.
> Then you, the burlesque of our lust—and faith,
> Lug us back lifeward—bone by infant bone.

Though Crane recognizes the necessity of physical love, or lust, and the
consequence of reproduction, he rejects reproduction as an available
metaphor for the resurrection he is now seeking. Each must "die alone"
(the Elizabethan pun on "to die" meaning to consummate the sex act)
on the "empty trapeze" of flesh, only to be faced with a physical
"burlesque" of the desired resurrection of a state of consciousness. Here
again is one of those implicit ambiguities in which the poem is so rich.
If "National Winter Garden" is basically directed toward expressing the
impossibility of achieving a spiritual vision of union based on physical
analogue, the sex act, then the same principle may apply to the vision
of a spiritual resurrection. Resurrection may also be reducible to a
merely physical continuity. The last stanza strongly implies that we
must return to the life from which we have hoped to escape.

The last song, "Virginia," considers the possibility of finding a secular
equivalent for the religious figure of the Virgin Mary. In one sense, this
is of course what Crane has been doing all along, but here he makes the
comparison explicit. If the vision of a union with his "nameless
Woman" as bride is destroyed because the experience of the poet can
produce only a "burlesque" of the union, then the identification of
the woman as a "Saturday Mary" is even more difficult, for the poet is
"still waiting" for the experience that will give him the vision. He can
call to her, as Columbus called to his Madre Maria, "O blue-eyed Mary

with the claret scarf, / Saturday Mary, mine!" But Mary remains in her "high wheat tower," inaccessible to the poet in the sexual world below "Where green figs gleam / By oyster shells." Pocahontus was a "Princess whose brown lap was virgin May" ("The Dance"), and the poet once thought that accessibility to her lap and the preservation of her virginity were not necessarily incompatible. Now, standing "high in the noon of May," on Prince Street below the tower, he cannot find the elements of his dream-vision. Yet there are "Forget-me-nots at window-panes"—referring to the window of his waking-dream vision in "Harbor Dawn"—and the poet does not finally reject his desire to find a secular Mary so much as he emphasizes the impossibility of attaining his desire on the basis of previous experience. He would still like Mary to let down her golden hair, even though at present he can see her only as an inaccessible employee in the Woolworth Building. The "Saturday Mary" in her modern cathedral is not a realization of the vision he has been seeking, but he chooses to accept her as a means of preserving, if not realizing, that vision.

> Out of the way-up nickel-dime tower shine,
> Cathedral Mary,
> shine!—

## Quaker Hill

In this part of the poem Crane begins his move from dream-vision to "contemporary reality" after his confession in *Three Songs* that his vision of the "nameless Woman" neither "sowed" nor "epitomized 'experience.'" [30] He turns from the visionary woman, whom he did not "experience," to two female writers with whom he has achieved a kind of union in the shared experience he finds expressed in their works. The section is somewhat repetitious in its resignation of his earlier conception of the mythic mode of perception, but there are also indications of the kind of vision toward which he is turning.

*Quaker Hill* begins with the apparently serious assertion that only cows have a true "perspective" of existence, for they

> see no other thing
> Than grass and snow, and their own inner being
> Through the rich halo that they do not trouble

30. Crane to Waldo Frank (June 20, 1926), *Letters of Crane*, p. 260.

> Even to cast upon the seasons fleeting
> Though they should thin and die on last year's stubble.

They do not need to enhance the passing of time or the seasons through a bovine mythopoeia. It is enough for them to see only grass and snow and "their own inner being," to accept what they see and to accept the consequences of their immediate experience without seeking other terms as a reference for their acceptance. The cows are "awkward, ponderous and uncoy," but they do not need to boast of their "store of faith" or to find and affirm a mythic vision in order to accept their existence.[31]

Compared with the cows, the poet's "store of faith" is made to appear hypocritical, yet he continues the exploration of his powers of vision, all in terms of "perspective." The poet expresses his angle of vision as a contrast between the former glories of New England and its dreary present. Where formerly "One's glance could cross the borders of three states," the poet "has seen death's stare in slow survey / From four horizons that no one relates." What was once the "Promised Land" is now promising only to the land agent or to the alien predator Powitsky. Crane must now contemplate the "Adams' auction" which he had anticipated in the first stanza of *Cape Hatteras*. The contrast is expressed in sentimental terms, and perhaps overdone, but the poet's despairing wonderment at what made this pattern of history rings with a true note.

> Who holds the lease on time and on disgrace?
> What eats the pattern with ubiquity?
> Where are my kinsmen and the patriarch race?

He does not know where the Indians and pioneers have gone, and he has to accept the death of the "slain Iroquois" as an irrevocable fact, as the cows accept the grass and snow and their own death. He now feels able to "Shoulder the curse of sundered parentage," to accept the inevitable separation between him and his visionary parent-images, and

31. Crane pushes the human-cow contrast a little further than necessary with his reference in the second stanza to a personal quarrel with the Tates. See Horton, *Hart Crane*, pp. 199–200. Crane's bitterness slips out also in stanza 7 with the reference to his parents' separation—which has direct relevance to his theme—and to the difficulties he had in getting money from his father. The "birthright by blackmail" joins the reference to the Tates in a region outside the main focus of this part of the poem.

to accept the historical sundering of Pocahontas and Maquokeeta. Since the separation was already inherent in the concept of a punishing father, apart and unapproachable, this element alone of Columbus's voyage in *Ave Maria* is still available to the poet as a part of "contemporary reality" and as an epitome of experience.

The poet slowly comes to a realization that, like the cows, like Isadora Duncan and Emily Dickinson, he must accept the limitations of his present existence. It is the same realization already traced in Blake, Wordsworth, and Keats. The poet must create his vision in the present, from the viewpoint of its limitations and his own sufferings.

> So, must we from the hawk's far stemming view,
> Must we descend as worm's eye to construe
> Our love of all we touch, and take it to the Gate
> As humbly as a guest who knows himself too late,
> His news already told? Yes, while the heart is wrung,
> Arise—yes, take this sheaf of dust upon your tongue!
> In one last angelus lift throbbing throat—
> Listen, transmuting silence with that stilly note
>
> Of pain that Emily, that Isadora knew!
> While high from dim elm-chancels hung with dew,
> That triple-noted clause of moonlight—
> Yes, whip-poor-will, unhusks the heart of fright,
> Breaks us and saves, yes, breaks the heart, yet yields
> That patience that is armour and that shields
> Love from despair—when love foresees the end—
> Leaf after autumnal leaf
>                         break off,
>                               descend—
>                                     descend—

"The Gate" to which he must take his humble offering of experienced reality looks forward to the "Gates of Wrath" through which he must pass in *The Tunnel*, as the "last angelus" looks backward to the "Angelus" sung around "the cordage tree" in *Ave Maria* just before Columbus became aware of the "sounding heel" of the Elohim. Crane is now ready to enter the tunnel and find evidence of the sounding heel in his own life. The perspective here is the opposite extreme from that found in *Cape Hatteras* ("Now the eagle dominates our days, is jurist / Of the ambiguous cloud"), and this perspective survives only as the "triple-noted clause of moonlight" sounding "high from dim elm-chancels hung with dew." The poet now sees this error of vision as an experience that both breaks and saves. It "breaks the heart, yet yields / That patience that is armour and that shields / Love from despair." Crane now feels ready for the complete acceptance of the loss of vision which he had prepared himself for in *Cape Hatteras*. The poet's painful experience of the tawdriness of life in contrast to the beauty of his vision, and the similarity of his experience to that of other sensitive individuals, thus has in it a redeeming source of power: it may provide him with a strength of patience to avoid despair.

Each time the poet has relied on the past for his vision he has met an overwhelming source of doubt and despair in the unavoidable disparity between the past, as milieu for the Indian, the pioneer, and Whitman, and his own milieu, the confusing, hostile, and oppressive twentieth century. In *Quaker Hill* the poet expresses the realization that he must look around him in his own experience for a firm basis for his vision and not rely solely on an intuitive empathy with the past which, in spite of all its glory, has led only to the present.

### The Tunnel

> Night and day lie open the gates of death's dark kingdom:
> But to retrace your steps, to find the way back to daylight—
> That is the task, the hard thing
>
> —Vergil, *Aeneid*

> And for the morn of truth they feigned, deep night
> Caught them ere evening.
>
> —Shelley, *Triumph of Life*

The part of the poem called *The Tunnel* expresses Crane's final attempt to find a sustaining vision; as such it is much more closely related to *Quaker Hill* than has generally been acknowledged. The "descend— / descend—" of *Quaker Hill* represents a literal descent into the subway and also a descent "from the hawk's far stemming view . . . as worm's eye to construe" a vision based on the poet's own immediate experience. Vergil reenters the poem by analogy here, for Crane's tunnel is a birdless place like the classical Avernus, and the poet is seeking a Father (as manifested in the "sounding heel") as Aeneas sought his father. Because the earlier parts of the poem indicated that any vision that failed to incorporate all the tawdriness of the present would fail, and because *Quaker Hill* showed the strength that could be found in an acceptance of one's present sufferings, the poet fittingly chooses a twentieth-century analogue of hell as the setting for his vision.[32] It is the subway that now "yawns the quickest promise home."

As a motto for his quest and as an indication of his determination, Crane adopted two lines from Blake: "To Find the Western path / Right thro' the Gates of Wrath." *The Tunnel* begins with a résumé of the earlier, misguided portion of the poem as the poet ironically describes the "nightly sessions" at "Columbus Circle," which he reaches by going "up Times Square." This is ground the poet has covered before, so he can now express the whole process through a few well-chosen puns and highly condensed metaphors. "You shall search them all [the nightly dream sessions]," he says, only to "find the garden in the third act dead," as he found it dead in *Three Songs*. This is all in the past; now he is ready to descend into the subway of the present. But first he dismisses religion from consideration, as he has consistently done before.

> Then let you reach your hat
> and go.
> As usual, let you—also
> walking down—exclaim
> to twelve upward leaving
> a subscription praise
> for what time slays.

His argument against religion (the "twelve" are the Twelve Apostles) is that its direction is "upward," away from the reality of experience. It may have been an acceptable attitude in the past, but it is now reduced to a "subscription praise" for past beliefs or attitudes that time has slain.

The poet hesitates only a moment before entering the subway, considering whether or not he should walk a bit first. The decision is made for him when he finds himself "Preparing penguin flexions of the arms" so as to "be minimum" to meet the crowds or "hiving swarms" of the dead he will find in the subway.[33] The actual descent begins with an

---

32. Cf. Eliot's remarkably similar use of the "underground" in *Burnt Norton*, sect. 3.
33. Crane folds his arms to make himself as small as possible, not because he is cold, as suggested by Dembo (*Crane's Sanskrit Charge*, p. 121), but because he has

intensely subjective description of the poet's entry into the yawning mouth of the subway, where the effects of claustrophobic oppression are suggested by four rhymed lines. As we should expect from the poetic development of Blake and Keats, the transition here is toward an exploration of an inner state of consciousness.[34] The deceptions the poet experienced earlier were due to his looking for a myth in the outward form of things. In this sense, the theme was subjective and pertained to the poet's state of consciousness, but the vision itself was being sought by a "Strange bird-wit" in terms of external symbols alone. He is now ready, like the cows of *Quaker Hill*, to ignore the "snow and grass" and to explore his "own inner being." The distinction between the two processes may be hard to recognize, since both involve inner states of mind *and* symbolic expressions of the inner state. But in one process the symbol, prompted by desire, comes first (rainbow, bridge, etc.) and the attempt is made to fit the mind to the symbol and thereby to achieve a faith in the symbol's significance. In the second, the "interborough fissures of the mind" and "back forks of the chasms of the brain" come first, and the symbol claims to be no more than an expression of the poet's "own inner being." The poet is "boxed alone," the "phonographs of hades" are "in the brain," and when he meets Poe's visage "here" he is referring not to his own image reflected in a window, or the face of a fellow passenger, but to a state of crisis in his own mind which he likens to Poe's crisis of faith on that last night in Baltimore.

Crane sees the state of mind represented by the subway as a consequence of urban life ("And so / of cities you bespeak / subways"), and the poet accentuates his descent into the region of his "own inner being" by contrasting it with snatches of dialogue overheard on the subway which refer to his former quest.

> "Let's have a pencil Jimmy—living now
> at Floral Park
> Flatbush—on the Fourth of July—
> like a pigeon's muddy dream—potatoes

experienced as a subway rider the "swarms" of the dead he is to meet in hell. He may also have been thinking of Vergil's dead, "Multitudinous as the leaves that fall in a forest," or of Eliot's use of Dante: "I had not thought that death had undone so many."

34. Cf. Blake's transition from *The Four Zoas* to *Milton* and from *Milton* to *Jerusalem*, and Keats's transition from *Hyperion* to *The Fall*.

to dig in the field—travlin the town—too—
night after night—the Culver line—the
girls all shaping up—it used to be—"

Each of these apparently random outbursts refers to an earlier part
of the poem. Jimmy was the father of Larry in "Indiana," and the
pioneer he represented is living now in a fallen garden, "Floral Park," in
Flatbush. "On the Fourth of July—" is a flashback to the political beginnings of the nation ("I'm a / Democrat," insists the continuation of
Larry in *Cutty Sark*), and the "pigeon's muddy dream" is a reminder of
the dream-vision of the "Strange bird–wit," or mythic consciousness, of
the earlier poem. The salesman is mobile, like the tramps, and sees
"night after night" his vision of "the girls all shaping up." The whole
passage is a burlesque of vision as "it used to be" for the poet.

The poet must recant this earlier vision—"Our tongues recant like
beaten weather vanes"—in order to find the "answer" that "lives like
verdigris, like hair / Beyond extinction, surcease of the bone," in still
another repetition of the now familiar pattern of affirmation by contrast
begun in the first two stanzas of the poem. The "repetition" in burlesque form of the earlier mistaken vision "freezes." Freezes what? The
implied answer is the poet's blood, in which he had found his passion
or hope for the fulfillment of the dream-vision. The desire was strong,
and partially lingers still (as in the "Virginia" section of *Three Songs*),
so the poet offers still another purgatorial repetition.

"What

"what do you want? getting weak on the links?
fandaddle daddy don't ask for change—IS THIS
FOURTEENTH? it's half past six she said—if
you don't like my gate why did you
swing on it, why *didja*
swing on it
anyhow—"

And somehow anyhow swing—

The last line recalls the poet's desire for *any* fulfillment of the dream-
vision, which is perhaps still not entirely frozen, even after *Three Songs*.
The "nameless Woman" of his dream-vision throws his desire in his

face, taunting him with his eagerness to "swing on her gate" rather than to press through the "Gates of Wrath." These are the sounds of "The phonographs of hades in the brain" that reduce "love" to "A burnt match skating in a urinal." To this musical accompaniment the poet must now "TAKE THE EXPRESS" that "made time" over the land in "The River" section, leaving the poet behind "still hungry on the tracks."

The vision the poet achieves at this point is one he has often had ("why do I often meet your visage here"), but one he has been unable to accept until now. In these "interborough fissures of the mind" Poe replaces Whitman as an index of the poet's experience. He does not reject the acceptance of Whitman so carefully prepared for in *Cape Hatteras,* but he finds in the agony of Poe's last night a closer analogue for his own emotional state.[35]

> —And did their riding eyes right through your side
> And did their eyes like unwashed platters ride?
> And Death, aloft,—gigantically down
> Probing through you—toward me, O evermore!
> And when they dragged your retching flesh,
> Your trembling hands that night through Baltimore—
> That last night on the ballot rounds, did you
> Shaking, did you deny the ticket, Poe?

The poet is hovering on the verge of losing his faith completely, and he wonders—he can never know—if Poe gave up the ticket under comparably agonizing circumstances. Everywhere he turns he finds images of death and despair. "For Gravesend Manor change at Chambers Street. / The platform hurries along to a dead stop."

For a moment he catches a glimpse of hope in the "intent escalator" which "lifts a serenade" upward and in the riders whose eyes shift suddenly from their shoes to the heavens which "Burst suddenly in rain." But as the train begins "taking the final level for the dive / Under the river" the poet is still aboard, still striving to find an acceptable meeting point for his vision and his symbols. In the birdless region of the train

35. In spite of Crane's bold claim that modern machinery was an essential part of the contemporary poet's "material," he had more than a small touch of Poe's fear of machinery. In addition to Poe's "The City in the Sea" (from which Crane adapted a line, "And Death, aloft,—gigantically down"), one might cite the mechanical horror of stories like "The Pit and the Pendulum" and Roderick Usher's strange picture of a fantastic tunnel.

car, "Newspapers wing, revolve and wing" in harsh contrast to the
"seagull's wings . . . shedding white rings of tumult" in the "Proem,"
while blank windows synaesthetically gargle incomprehensible signals
through the roar. He finds only a "Wop washerwoman" with "bandaged
hair" to match against the proud image of Columbus. But the question
he asks her shows that his desire for a consummation of the dream-
vision has not yet been completely frozen. "O Genoese, do you bring
mother eyes and hands / Back home to children and to golden hair?"

The next two stanzas are a condensation of the whole argument that
we have attempted to follow from *Cape Hatteras* on. In the first stanza
Crane finally recognizes that the desire to find his vision, even in the
degraded "Wop washerwoman," is something he cannot purge, even
though he can mock and burlesque it as a form of deception.

> Daemon, demurring and eventful yawn!
> Whose hideous laughter is a bellows mirth
> —Or the muffled slaughter of a day in birth—
> O cruelly to inoculate the brinking dawn
> With antennae toward worlds that glow and sink;—
> To spoon us out more liquid than the dim
> Locution of the eldest star, and pack
> The conscience navelled in the plunging wind,
> Umbilical to call—and straightway die!

His vision of "worlds that glow and sink" is balanced on a "brinking
dawn" that can never become full day. It is an unavoidable working of
his "conscience" that produces visions "Umbilical to call" which must
nevertheless "straightway die." The poet's "shrill ganglia" are "Impas-
sioned with some song we fail to keep." Failure to keep the song is
death, and yet even in death he feels

>                         the slope,
> The sod and billow breaking,—lifting ground,
> —A sound of waters bending astride the sky
> Unceasing with some Word that will not die. . . !

The "Word that will not die," even though every particular vision the
poet finds must die, is the vision of his continually reborn desire to find
a vision. For an instant the poet is able to accept that vision, because
his hands "drop memory" of his failure, leaving only the recognition of

continually reborn desire. But there is a glimpse also of a further step, in which his hands may "be drawn away, to die." This is the ultimate failure of desire, the final "Kiss of our agony" that he would then have to bear. In a last prophetic vision he sees the "Hand of Fire" gathering him into that last agony. The kiss of agony "takest all," everything from the songs "we fail to keep" even to this last vision of reborn desire. "It still interests me to affirm certain things," the poet once said in a less passionate context, but now he is contemplating even the loss of that "interest" as something that must be borne in turn and accepted as part of the cruel "parable of man."

The vision neither finds nor attempts to discover God's holy purpose in the poet's suffering. He can only feel that somehow God is working his plan through that suffering and that ultimately the plan will be realized. The final "Word" is an "incognizable Word," for the "Hand of Fire" here is the same that Crane addressed in *Ave Maria,* and it is still searching "Cruelly" but "with love" for his "parable of man." But the poet has not succeeded, as it once seemed Columbus had, in getting a glimpse of the "dim frontier." He still has only "A needle in the sight, suspended north,— / Yielding by inference and discard, faith."

### Atlantis

I feel an absolute music in the air again, and some tremendous rondure floating somewhere.

—Crane, to Waldo Frank

The infirm glory of the positive hour.

—Eliot, *Ash-Wednesday*

*Atlantis* is a return to the bridge as a symbol, and a final expression of the vision the poet has achieved. Many readers have found the section confusing and overwritten in light of the despair and resignation of *Quaker Hill* and *The Tunnel.* Weber, for example, finds it "quite impossible to be carried away by the animistic vision of The Bridge embodied in these lines." [36] There is a conflict of tone between the nature of the vision expressed and the triumphant enthusiasm which seems to imply that the poet thinks he has successfully found the vision

36. Weber, *Hart Crane,* p. 375.

he hoped to achieve in the beginning of the poem. However, if one accepts as inevitable the discrepancy in tone, it is possible to find in *Atlantis* an accurate summation of the poet's true vision.

*Atlantis*, which Crane originally conceived as "the mystic consummation toward which all the other sections of the poem converge," remained basically unchanged throughout the writing of *The Bridge* as the goal toward which the poem was directed. While Crane continued to see the "contents" of all the parts of the poem as "implicit in its summary," the nature of the summary changed drastically even though the words remained the same.[37] For Crane the poem was "a test of materials as much as a test of one's imagination," but the materials refused, in the light of day, to fit themselves to the pattern of his "waking dream," and he was left with his vision "suspended somewhere in ether like an Absalom by his hair." [38] We should now be able to recognize the full significance of this "suspension" metaphor. Crane is able to resurrect his earliest vision, in *Atlantis*, as an embodiment of his visionary desire. But it is now presented, not as a triumphant, firmly held vision, but as one of those "worlds that sink and glow." It is resurrected only to die again, and the poet is left with only the hope—also prophetically doomed to die—that he can continue to resurrect *Atlantis*, not as a vision held, or a vision lost, but as an embodiment of the *desire* for a vision he hopes will not die.

In the first three stanzas Crane views the bridge as a harp, as is suggested in the "Proem." The harp's song is beautiful but ethereal, speaking in "Sibylline voices" that "flicker, waveringly stream / As though a god were issue of the strings. . . ." The fourth stanza suggests that only the poet, who has suffered and met experience head-on, can hear the bridge's song and read its meaning.

> Sheerly the eyes, like seagulls stung with rime—
> Slit and propelled by glistening fins of light—
> Pick biting way up towering looms that press
> Sidelong with flight of blade on tendon blade
> —Tomorrows into yesteryear—and link
> What cipher-script of time no traveller reads
> But who, through smoking pyres of love and death,
> Searches the timeless laugh of mythic spears.

37. Crane to Otto H. Kahn (Mar. 18, 1926), *Letters of Crane*, p. 240.
38. Crane to Waldo Frank (June 20, 1926), *Letters of Crane*, p. 236.

These lines now have an ironic significance which we can read in them only if we have committed ourselves fully to the logic of the poem and followed it to this point. The poet now knows that he cannot "link" the "cipher-script of time," and turn "Tomorrows into yester-year," even though he has searched "through smoking pyres of love and death . . . the timeless laugh of mythic spears." Yet the desire that leads him to the search can only be preserved by a continuation of the search and by an attempt to reassert the *Atlantis* vision.

The poetic ecstasy increases until Crane makes a claim for his vision palpably at odds with what he has actually experienced. The bridge is assigned a symbolic meaning it cannot bear within the context of the poem as written; it belongs, rather, to the poem the poet hoped to write, to the vision he hoped to achieve.

> Tall Vision-of-the-Voyage, tensely spare—
> Bridge, lifting night to cycloramic crest
> Of deepest day—O Choir, translating time
> Into what multitudinous Verb the suns
> And synergy of waters ever fuse, recast
> In myriad syllables,—Psalm of Cathay!
> O Love, thy white, pervasive Paradigm . . . !

At the height of his vision, the poet feels that "love strikes clear direction for the helm," and that

> *Always* through blinding cables, to our joy,
> Of thy white seizure *springs the prophecy:*
> *Always* through spiring cordage, pyramids
> Of silver sequel, Deity's young name
>     Kinetic of white choiring wings . . . ascends.

> (Italics added)

The original sense of these lines, that the bridge will always be a symbol of the poet's fulfilled desire, must now give way to the new sense forced on them by the poem Crane actually wrote. The "always" refers to the rebirth of the desire rather than to its fulfillment.[39]

Even while making his extravagant claim of having searched "the

---

39. The rhetorical insistence of these lines on an achieved permanency, in a context of ambivalence, should be compared with Wordsworth's use of "habitually," "every," "all," and "endless" in *The Prelude*, bk. 13:105–119.

timeless laugh of mythic spheres," the poet indicates the absence of a firmly assured vision. "Thy pardon for this history," he asks, as if to excuse the doubts his suffering caused. "Hold thy floating singer late!" he pleads, as if conscious that this vision he is trying to sustain is in danger of disappearing once more into the teeming span. "Is it Cathay," he asks in the final stanza, that the "orphic strings" sing?

> Is it Cathay,
> Now pity steeps the grass and rainbows ring
> The serpent with the eagle in the leaves . . . ?

As Orpheus lost Eurydice when he turned to look at her, the poet, we know, must lose this vision after the poetic ecstasy of expression passes; the "arching strands of song," the "humming spars" and "chimes," the vision "terrible of drums" which was "like an organ" do in fact give way when faced with the question, "Is it Cathay?" to ambiguous and undecipherable whispers: "Whispers antiphonal in azure swing." The poet has returned to the "Sibylline voices" that "flicker, waveringly stream," in the confession that he can never know whether or not "a god" is "issue of the strings."

In this survey of the subjective theme of *The Bridge* I have not been attempting the impossible task of finding a prose equivalent for the meaning of Crane's poem, or even for particular lines or words within the poem. I have tried to show, by a pedestrian tour of the most obvious guideposts that it is possible to read it not as a myth or a vision in the usual sense, but as a poem about a poet's *search* for a vision, a vision that would reconcile him to the present and foresee a continuation of the glories of the past. Crane liked to think of himself as the Vergil of the new world, but his true desire was to be its Aeneas, to complete a voyage from the shattered world of Troy to a new beginning in Rome, connecting the two worlds by a "destiny" that made success inevitable if only the voyager held true to the vision of the goal.

The criterion of success for a poem of this kind should not be whether or not the poet actually achieves the vision he seeks, or whether or not the vision is acceptable to the reader. It should be the degree of poetic honesty and skill the poet exhibits in pursuing his quest. The quest itself may end in failure, as did Keats's; it may be a qualified success, as was Wordsworth's; or it may even achieve a momentary conviction of success as in Blake's *Milton*. But regardless of the outcome, the expres-

sion of a man, trying by sheer will and faith to find an acceptable purpose and meaning in his life, is still one of the most inspiring themes a
poet can attempt. It may even be, as I suggested in my introduction,
the heroic argument or epic theme of our age. And it is certainly the
closest we have come to a theme that can excite anything like an epic
response from poets.

Crane may well illustrate the final fate of the visionary poet who
conceives of his vision as a "test of materials," and who pursues the
conception to the bitter end without going beyond his materials to the
concept of a divine grace that will aid him in his search. We may specu-
late that Crane represents a point to which Blake, Wordsworth, and
Keats *might* have come, if we also remain aware of differences in them
that led them to different forms of a prelude to vision.

It was Blake, thinking of Dante, who gave Crane the motto for *The
Tunnel*. And it was Blake, again connected with Dante, who can give
us the last word on Crane's attempt to find the "Western path." After
trying to draw a diagram of the relations between Dante's Paradise,
Purgatory, and Inferno, Blake remarked, "This is Upside Down When
view'd from Hell's gate, which ought to be at top, But right When
View'd from Purgatory after they have passed the Center. In Equivocal
Worlds Up & Down are Equivocal." [40] If viewed only from the "Hell's
gate" of *The Tunnel*, Crane's *Bridge* is upside down in more than
chronology. But past "the Center," if we *can* pass the center in the
tunnel, the poem is "right." The spiritual world of *The Bridge* is an
equivocal world, in which even up and down become equivocal. Crane
recognizes that there are "Two worlds of sleep" (*Atlantis*), but he can
never decide if his visionary world exits through the gate of horn or
through the gate of ivory. It is the vertical equivocation in this world
that permitted Crane to make a significant change in the second stanza
of the "Proem" only a few days before the poem was published, when
he suggested to Caresse Crosby that the line "And elevators heave us
to our day" be changed to "Till elevators drop us from our day." [41]

"I'll leave the choice to you," he said in the letter, for in the end the
larger choice contained in the contrast between the two lines was one
he could not make. In a sense, the spatial and chronological ambiguities
of the whole poem are contained in the contrast between these two
lines; and as *Atlantis* was the beginning of the poem, as well as the

40. "Notes on the Illustrations to Dante," *Poetry and Prose of Blake*, p. 785.
41. (Dec. 26, 1929), *Letters of Crane*, p. 347.

end, so the "Proem," if we read it as containing a choice between these two lines, becomes the end as well as the beginning.

Crane constantly referred to himself, during the period of writing, as being "in the middle of *The Bridge*," and at one point he noted that his *Bridge*, like the physical structure that gives it its name, "is begun from the two ends at once." [42] Implicit in the poem he completed is the corollary recognition that once the bridge is completed, what were its beginnings become its ends.

*The Bridge* is thus not a summary of linear progress toward a goal, sought with difficulty but finally and firmly grasped. It is an attempt to diagram the regions of heaven, hell, and purgatory within the poet's own mind; to find the right perspective from which to view those regions, and to find the proper discipline necessary to achieve that perspective. The quest takes us through time, from Columbus to Brooklyn, and through space, from "infinity's dim marge" to the depths of the tunnel, yet it never leaves the poet's own consciousness, which sounds at first like the music of the spheres, but on closer approach becomes "Whispers antiphonal in azure."

In a later poem, *The Broken Tower*, Crane has expressed in two stanzas much of what I have been trying to say of *The Bridge*.

> And so it was I entered the broken world
> To trace the visionary company of love, its voice
> An instant in the wind (I know not whither hurled)
> But not for long to hold each desperate choice.
>
> My word I poured. But was it cognate, scored
> Of that tribunal monarch of the air
> Whose thigh embronzes earth, strikes crystal Word
> In wounds pledged once to hope—cleft to despair?

*The Bridge* is a record of the poet's attempt "to hold each desperate choice" and is an outpouring of the poet's own "word" rather than the reception of an ultimate "Word." Recognizing it as his own word only, Crane can never know if it is cognate with that other Word. He can only build a broken tower of words up into the "visible wings of silence sown / In azure circles, widening as they dip"; and *The Bridge*, failing its function as a bridge, is that broken tower.

42. Crane to Waldo Frank (Aug. 3, 1926), *Letters of Crane*, p. 270.

## Chapter 7

# The Prelude as Structure

> The common end of all *narrative*, nay, of *all*,
> Poems is to convert a *series* into a *Whole*: to
> make those events, which in real or imagined
> History move in a *strait* Line, assume to our
> Understanding a *circular* motion—the snake with
> its Tail in its Mouth.
>
> —Coleridge

This study began with the observation that many poets since Milton have desired to earn the title of epic poet. Among the attempts these poets have made to write epics, there is a group of poems in which the epic struggle is the attempt to write an epic, or the preparation for writing one, and the crucial effort derives from the need to maintain the hope that poetry can fulfill for modern man and society the function it served when the earlier epics were written. The result of attempts of this sort is a group of long poems concerned more with poetry and with the poet writing than with a "subject" in the traditional sense. I have called these poems "preludes to vision" because the desired function of each is that it enable the poet to achieve or preserve a vision of epic scope. I have tried to substantiate the existence of such poems by detailed readings of four examples—not to determine that we should call them epics, but to suggest that they belong together in some generic sense and can illuminate each other if read together as similar attempts to find in the human imagination a source of power and knowledge. I shall now return to the larger context of the epic considered generally, and shall try to make some concluding remarks about these poems in that context—how it helps us to see certain important elements in the poems and, perhaps more surprising, how these modern poems can help us understand some of the features of earlier poems.

Although I shall talk about structure as if it were a separable entity, the main burden of my argument is that structure, as I see it, is itself a manifestation of the poem's meaning. It is included in the "saying" of the poem and no more separable from that act than any other element of the poem.

So far I have characterized the prelude poem as a preparatory or enabling work. But in a sense, every work is preparatory to its own conclusions. All prepare for the moment of perspective which grows from, yet transcends the particulars of character, plot, and form in their limited space and time. This is even more true of the established epics (of Homer, Vergil, Dante, Spenser, Milton, etc.) which attempt to chart a route for man, through his struggle for intellectual survival, to some kind of hopefully permanent spiritual enlightenment. The epic structure points not to an end, but to a continuation and fulfillment in the future. It must have a linear or chronological dimension in time, but it can't stop *in* time as real events do; it must then be timeless yet in time, and the only way to achieve that effect structurally is to be cyclical, to be complete in a way that real time, or experiential time, can never be. This point lies behind Ortega's reflections on "the absolute gap which exists between the mythical *yesterday* and the real *today*."

> The epic past is not *our* past. Our past is thinkable as having been the present once, but the epic past eludes identification with any possible present, and when we try to get back to it by means of recollection it gallops away from us like Diomedes' horses, forever at the same distance ahead of us. No, it is not a remembered past, but an ideal past.
>
> If the poet asks Mneme, Memory to tell him about the Achaean sufferings, he does not have recourses to his own subjective memory but to a cosmic memory which he supposes to be latent in the universe. Mneme is not the reminiscence of an individual but an elemental power.[1]

This is an important point, but behind it is an even more important one. The epic connects with real life not in time, not as the real past which preceded the real present on the same chronological axis, but in giving the reader a vision of connectedness in his own time and the

1. José Ortega y Gasset, *Meditations on Quixote* (New York: W. W. Norton & Co., 1961), p. 118.

possibility of that time having an epic fulfillment in the future. The epic leads up to the anticipation of a future state; we are not now in that state, but we can share in the anticipation of it generated by the epic poem. It is when an epic can no longer achieve this effect that it becomes an historical document rather than a contemporary poem. Anyone who has tried to teach the ending of the *Odyssey* to a group of students who feel their existential hero has betrayed them by settling down to bourgeois life has experienced the death of an epic.

There are several other insights and problems lurking in Ortega's formulation. Think of Aeneas looking at the frescoes of the Trojan War. For him they are a combination of personal memory and purified memory, memory transformed into art.[2] What Aeneas is doing—what Vergil would have us accept Aeneas as doing—is precisely what Ortega says is impossible. Aeneas is living a personal life, yet is in history, in art. Even though the process he undergoes is the loss of the personal, the absorption into the impersonal, we can see that Vergil is seriously showing this combination in Aeneas, in fact is showing the genesis of Aeneas' move from a limited consciousness of life to the larger consciousness of life as art and history. We ourselves cannot conceive how to do this as individuals, how to do for ourselves what Aeneas does or has happen to him. Cervantes has shown what happens when an individual tries to live his private life as a work of art. One must give way to the other, and either way it is the "saddest and funniest" quest the human mind can undertake. There is an interesting parallel, then, between the passive way in which Aeneas is "visited" by visions, guidance, and mishaps and the way in which he is distinct from and passive in relation to Vergil. If the attempt to live literally as Aeneas is Quixotic or maddening, the attempt to *write* Aeneas, from one's subjective memory, is equally Quixotic. What it amounts to is the artist's wanting to be Vergil, yet to be himself, to have Calliope and Mneme be the same muse, and more, to have them be not cosmic consciousness, filling the mind from outside as the bee fills its hive with honey, but the subjective consciousness of the poet himself. This is the longing behind Coleridge's enigmatic note to himself. "To have a continued Dream, representing visually & audibly all Milton's Paradise Lost."[3] The desire

---

2. Cf. Adam Parry's discussion of this point in "The Two Voices of Virgil's *Aeneid*," *Arion* 2, no. 4 (Winter 1963): 68–80.
3. Quoted in J. B. Beer, *Coleridge the Visionary* (New York: Collier Books, 1962), p. 78.

to experience all of *Paradise Lost* within his own mind is comparable to the desire to "revive within" the symphony and song of the "damsel with a dulcimer" beheld in a vision. To achieve such a mode of vision would be to find a way of experiencing narrative as if it were lyric, to combine in one mental form the first-person tale of the *Ancient Mariner* and the omniscient prose gloss. So far, no poet seems to have succeeded in this attempt, and the common sense of criticism has tended to reject it out-of-hand. Aristotle's requirement that "the poet should say very little *in propria persona*, as he is no imitator when doing that," has been accepted as a rule of epic composition.

The basic attempt of the poems I have been describing, and of many works like them, has been to move from a lyric mode of vision, centered in a moment of perception, toward a larger vision that would retain the immediacy, the quality of felt truth, of the subjective moment. As such it is not a movement away from subjectivity, but an attempt to combine the quality of feeling in the lyric moment with a structure that goes beyond its limitations. The goal is to combine two modes of perception or states of consciousness that are usually kept separate, both in literature and in life.[4]

One of the best characterizations of these two modes is William James's distinction between the "raisin" and the "bill of fare." It is worth quoting at some length.

> The world of our experience consists at all times of two parts, an objective and a subjective part, of which the former may be incalculably more extensive than the latter, and yet the latter can

---

4. There are many similar attempts to find this kind of combination which cannot be explored here. Some poets—Whitman, Yeats, Lowell, Stevens, for example—have stayed with shorter poems but tried to find a way of combining them to make the total effect exceed the sum of the parts. In the novel, a number of approaches have been tried, ranging from Brontë's dialectical approach (see my "Story and History in Wuthering Heights," in *Twentieth Century Views of Wuthering Heights* [Englewood Cliffs, N.J.: Prentice-Hall, 1968]) to the lyric intensity of *Finnegans Wake*. The novelist-narrator has learned, like Melville's Ishmael, that in addition to the "valuable statistics" of the "skeleton dimensions," some part of the body must remain a "blank page for a poem" that can never be completely finished (*Moby Dick*, ch. 102). Henry James rejected the "romantic privilege" of using the first person because "the first person, in the long piece, is a form foredoomed to looseness" (Preface to *The Ambassadors*), but went on to show that what exists, as far as Strether is concerned, is what he can make of it in his own consciousness. Although he never completely achieved it, Hermann Broch was concerned with finding a lyric "super-voice" that could combine "lyrical forms" with the "novelistic form" (see Theodore Ziolkowski, *Hermann Broch* [New York: Columbia University Press, 1964], p. 19).

never be omitted or suppressed. The objective part is the sum total of whatsoever at any given time we may be thinking of, the subjective part is the inner 'state' in which the thinking comes to pass. What we think of may be enormous,—the cosmic times and spaces, for example,—whereas the inner state may be the most fugitive and paltry activity of mind. Yet the cosmic objects, so far as the experience yields them, are but ideal pictures of something whose existence we do not inwardly possess but only point at outwardly, while the inner state is our very experience itself; its reality and that of our experience are one. . . . such a concrete bit of personal experience may be a small bit, but it is a solid bit as long as it lasts. . . . it is of the *kind* to which all realities whatsoever must belong; the motor currents of the world run through the likes of it; it is on the line connecting real events with real events. That unsharable feeling which each one of us has of the pinch of his individual destiny as he privately feels it rolling out on fortune's wheel may be disparaged for its egotism, may be sneered at as unscientific, but it is the one thing that fills up the measure of our concrete actuality, and any would-be exis- tent that should lack such a feeling, or its analogue, would be a piece of reality only half made up.

. . . The axis of reality runs solely through the egotistic places,—they are strung upon it like so many beads. To describe the world with all the various feelings of the individual pinch of destiny, all the various spiritual attitudes, left out from the de- scription—they being as describable as anything else—would be something like offering a printed bill of fare as the equivalent for a solid meal. . . . A bill of fare with one real raisin on it instead of the word 'raisin,' with one real egg instead of the word 'egg,' might be an inadequate meal, but it would at least be a com- mencement of reality.[5]

The problem for the poet is implied in James's distinction without being directly tackled. The "axis of reality" is not as tangible as the moments strung upon it; to deal with the moments, or "beads," does not give you the axis any more than to eat one course of a meal gives you the menu. One is either in the moment or out of it, eating his raisin or reading the menu, and the virtues of one are the deficiencies of the other. The discontinuity of the two states is described more directly by

5. William James, *The Varieties of Religious Experience* (New Hyde Park, N.Y.: University Books, 1963), pp. 498–500.

Merleau-Ponty. "We cannot subject our perception of the world to philosophical scrutiny without ceasing to be identified with that act of positing the world, with that interest in it which delimits us, without drawing back from our commitment *which is itself thus made to appear as a spectacle,* [italics added] without passing from the *fact* of our existence to its *nature*, from the Dasein to the Wesen." [6]

The verdict seems to be that Coleridge's wish can never be fulfilled, that the intensity of a dream can never coexist with the structure of a *Paradise Lost.* If we have a total structure, it will be "made to appear as a spectacle," or as an "ideal picture" we do not "inwardly possess." Thus, although the doubts, hesitations, and problems of Aeneas are Vergil's too, are the problems of the civilized consciousness itself, those problems are put back in time and separated from the author, made into a psychological spectacle of inward possession rather than an *act* of possession. Aeneas himself is similarly denied a present. "His present could not be a moment of passion because it was instead a moment of destiny." [7] The events of his life occur in a linear time separate from, but supposedly like the present. They are revived by Vergil for commemoration and purified contemplation but not as immediate experience, not for participation. We can see the same distinction made even more clearly in the two parts of Coleridge's *Kubla Khan.* In the first part of the poem Kubla Khan decrees the building of a pleasure dome. The action is related in the past tense; it is an act of creation, and a model of the same kind of poetic vision which presents the first part of the poem to us. The dome, like the poem, comes into being and has a recognizable existence as an "other" even though it symbolizes subjective states. In the second part the poet speaks in the first person of a different form of creation "within me," which exists only in the

6. M. Merleau-Ponty, *Phenomenology of Perception*, trans. Colin Smith (London: Routledge & Kegan Paul, 1962), p. xiv. The Preface to this work, which tries "to bring together the celebrated phenomenological themes," defines the "philosopher" as a person remarkably like the poet engaged in the attempt to write a prelude poem. "The philosopher . . . is a perceptual beginner, which means that he takes for granted nothing that men, learned or otherwise, believe they know. It means also that philosophy itself must not take itself for granted, in so far as it may have managed to say something true; that it is an ever-renewed experiment in making its own beginning; that it consists wholly in the description of this beginning; and finally, that radical reflection amounts to a consciousness of its own dependence on an unreflective life which is its initial situation, unchanging, given once and for all" (p. xiv).
7. Brooks Otis, "Introduction" to *The Aeneid*, trans. F. O. Copley (New York: Bobbs-Merrill, 1965), p. xiv. There is a fuller discussion of this point in his *Virgil: A Study in Civilized Poetry* (London & New York: Oxford Univ. Press, 1963).

act of creation itself. It cannot be reported as past; it can only be "revived within." Like music, it exists only while being played, and cannot be located in place or time.

The basic strategy of the kind of poem written by Vergil, Dante and Milton can be seen as a *separation* of what the poets in this study were trying to *combine*. Vergil is distinct from his Aeneas, although they share the same problems. Similarly the consciousness of Vergil the poet is separate from the cosmic consciousness of his Muse, as Dante and Milton are separate from the source of their inspiration. Coleridge was quick to recognize and to criticize Wordsworth's deviations from the direct involvement of the poet as poet in his work. "For all the admirable passages interposed in this narration [*The Excursion*] might, with trifling alterations, have been far more appropriately, and with far greater verisimilitude, told of a poet in the character of a poet; and without incurring another defect which I shall now mention, . . . an undue predilection for the *dramatic* form . . . from which one or other of two evils result. Either the thoughts and diction are different from that of the poet, and then there arises an incongruity of style; or they are the same and indistinguishable, and then it presents a species of ventriloquism, where two are represented as talking, while in truth one man only speaks." [8]

The convention of calling on the Muse for inspiration is worth some attention here. A device that later poets have either rejected or found unavailable, it was more than an arbitrary technical device or a religious superstition. It posited the kind of cosmic consciousness the poet would have and avoided altogether the epistemological problems of his having it. The use of a Muse was similar in this respect to the device of the omniscient author, which has disappeared from fiction as the Muse from poetry. Such a higher form of consciousness is traditionally beyond the human mind, as a text of Revelations is beyond the power of human invention. *What* is known is not crucial, because in an obvious way the mind knows what the Muse speaks through it. What we consider real is determined much more by its happening in a certain manner familiar to us than by what "actually" happens. The Muse convention avoids the problems inherent in a view of mind as the ultimate "container" of reality. For the poet, it avoids the problems inherent in the poetic consciousness itself being the poem.

8. *Biographia Literaria*, ed. J. Shawcross (London & New York: Oxford Univ. Press, 1907), pp. 108–109.

Poets have explored a number of ways to relinquish the Muse and yet keep something like the separation of modes of consciousness. Crane's prose gloss (used early in *The Bridge*, then dropped) echoes Coleridge's device in *The Ancient Mariner*. Eliot unified the fragments of his *Waste Land* in a single consciousness which is neither his own nor that of a Muse.

> Tiresias, although a mere spectator and not indeed a "character," is yet the most important personage in the poem, uniting all the rest. . . . What Tiresias *sees*, in fact, is the substance of the poem.[9]

Eliot's strategy is an interesting continuation of the nineteenth-century attempt to get away from what Arnold called the "allegory of the poet's mind" as the substance of the poem. He is trying to have it both ways—unity within a single consciousness, but also one "other" than the poet himself. It is a vision but not his own. This is comparable to Browning's strategy of presenting "so many utterances of so many imaginary persons, not mine." [10] Although apologizing for it, Tennyson used "Short swallow-flights of song," or lyric moments, as the basis of *In Memoriam*. Browning, in his *Sordello*, also tried to have it both ways, to write a preludelike poem on the growth of a poet's mind, but to have that mind separate in time and identity. Williams in his *Paterson* offers a unique form of indirection. The goal of the poem is to discover the mind-and-man knowing—"For the beginning is assuredly / the end—since we know nothing, pure / and simple, beyond / our own complexities"—but Williams adopts the device "that a man in himself is a city, beginning, seeking, achieving, and concluding his life in ways which the various aspects of a city may embody—if imaginatively conceived—any city, all the details of which may be made to voice his most intimate convictions." [11]

The poets I have looked at in this study tried a more direct attack, beginning with the phenomenon of human consciousness itself. From the conviction that it is "most worthy then of trust when most intense," they attempted to build a poetic structure that would go beyond the

9. T. S. Eliot, "Waste Land," note to line 218, in *The Complete Poems and Plays* (New York: Harcourt, Brace & Co., 1952), p. 52.
10. Browning's qualification added to his *Dramatic Lyrics* (1842).
11. "Author's Note" to *Paterson* (New York: New Directions Publishing Corp., 1948).

limits of the conventional lyric. The completion of such a work would confirm the starting-point, a state of mind, as a sign of what Crane called "the real connective experience" and the work itself would *be* that experience.

> Poetry, in so far as the metaphysics of any absolute knowledge extends, is simply the concrete *evidence* of the *experience* of a recognition (*knowledge* if you like). It can give you a *ratio* [this word is from Blake] of fact and experience, and in this sense it is both perception and thing perceived, according as it approaches a significant articulation or not. This is its reality, its fact, *being*. When you attempt to ask more of poetry,—the fact of man's relationship to a hypothetical god, be it Osiris, Zeus or Indra, you will get as variant terms even from the abstract terminology of philosophy as you will from poetry; whereas poetry, without attempting to logically enunciate such a problem or its solution, may well give you the real connective experience, the very "sign manifest" on which rests the assumption of a god-head.[12]

It is important to realize that the "sign manifest" that Crane is speaking of here is not a sign or portent "given" to the poet from the outside, but something achieved or found within the realm of comprehensible human experience. This attitude toward personal experience and its function in the poem is one of the most radical differences between the prelude poem and the kind of epic written by Vergil, Dante and Milton.

In one of the more interesting studies of the conventional epic, Thomas Greene has adopted a revealing approach. Focusing on "the history of a minor form within a larger, encompassing form," he has chosen as the minor form "the descent of an emissary god or angel from heaven bearing a message to earth. . . . In most respects the celestial descent makes a peculiarly useful point of critical departure. For it does more than describe the swift and dramatic movement of a body through space. It constitutes typically a crucial nexus of the narrative; it represents the intersection of time and the timeless; it points to the human realm of paramount concern to the gods; and it brings divine authority to the unfolding heroic action." [13] Although Greene is not talking

12. Crane to Gorham Munson (Mar. 17, 1926), *The Letters of Hart Crane*, ed. Brom Weber (New York: Hermitage House, 1952), p. 237.
13. Thomas Greene, *The Descent From Heaven* (New Haven: Yale Univ. Press, 1963), p. 7.

about the Muse *per se*, the form or device of a descent from heaven reflects the same state of mind as that which saw the poetic act in relation to a Muse. The descent of an "emissary god or angel" to the hero of an epic poem is comparable to the Muse's entry into the consciousness of the poet. Both turn on something seen as existing outside the poet's or hero's mind which enables him to do things otherwise impossible. Blake is the only poet among those of this study who could claim this enabling device. In *Milton* that which "descends" on Blake from "outside" his own mind is not so much something divine as it is a poetic or prophetic tradition. The descent allegory was a way of revealing his continuation of that tradition which he also created. This is not radically different from Eliot's argument that "the past should be altered by the present as much as the present is directed by the past." [14]

When Wordsworth thinks of a Muse, he does not know what to invoke.

> Urania, I shall need
> Thy guidance, or a greater Muse, if such
> Descend to earth or dwell in highest heaven!

("Prospectus" to *The Recluse*)

Whatever it is, it cannot be outside of himself, because his goal is human life as a state of continuous revelation, to make paradise "A simple produce of the common day." If we look for "the crucial nexus" in Wordsworth, or in the poets I compare him with, it would be the opposite of a descent from the gods, although it would represent the same "intersection of time and the timeless." It would be the moment when consciousness, cut off from the impinging and limiting perceptions of ordinary existence, moves simultaneously inward and upward to a higher consciousness.

> Anon I rose
> As if on wings, and saw beneath me stretch'd
> Vast prospect of the world which I had been
> And was; and hence this song.

(*Prelude*, 13:379)

14. T. S. Eliot, "Tradition and the Individual Talent," in *Selected Essays* (New York: Harcourt, Brace & Co., 1950), p. 5.

It would be an "ascent," and there are, in fact, innumerable images in these poems of rising to a perspective beyond the scope of normal consciousness. But for every ascent, there is a descent, the loss of a way of seeing which for a brief period seemed within the possibilities of unassisted human consciousness.

The model of an inward-ascending movement of mind is of course not new. As noted by Harry Berger, Jr., it had some currency during the late Middle Ages as a conventionalized pattern. "Late medieval poets, mystics, and theologians, accepting the spherical universe as the real picture of the world, felt that to move *inward* in contemplation, to withdraw mentally from the everyday world, was to move *upward*. Withdrawal was not to a radically discontinuous second world, another frame of reference, therefore *upward* was not construed as a metaphoric but as a symbolic adverb: the inward/upward movement of the spirit in contemplation was imagined to be a real *ascensus* of thought through the hierarchies, prefiguring the literal ascent of the saved soul after death. Any true inner withdrawal had to be conceived in a correspondence relation to some aspect of real space or time." [15] But such a model, as Berger points out, "epitomizes the incarnational movement of God down into the core of human life and history, and also into the core of the human soul." It is the model of proper ascent, made possible by the presence of God within.

For Dante (the pilgrim in the poem) there is no ascent to the sunny hill (*Inferno*, canto 1) without first internalizing the Grace offered to him from outside. Poets who rely on human wisdom and genius alone are in the circle of Limbo or designated, as Guido Cavalcante apparently is, for the realm of the heretics. One of Milton's basic distinctions between Adam and Satan is precisely this acceptance of Grace. Adam's intuitive reaction on finding himself in the world is to recognize a "Power / That made us" and to worship and obey that power, his mind ascending to it in prayer. Satan's mind, however, is limited to a narcissistic psychology that can recognize only itself.

> We know no time when we were not as now;
> Know none before us, self-begot, self-rais'd
> By our own quick'ning power.

> (*Paradise Lost*, bk. 5:859–861)

15. "Theatre, Drama, and the Second World: A Prologue to Shakespeare," *Comparative Drama* 2, no. 1 (Spring 1968): 3–20.

"Self-rais'd" is Satan's way of seeing his own reality in the world, and his mistake is man's sin.[16] It is the basis of his appeal to Eve and to many of the Romantic poets. Milton would have seen Wordsworth's "Anon I rose / As if on wings . . ." as the human equivalent of Satan's phenomenology, reflecting the continuation within the human mind of the temptation of Eve.

> Forthwith up to the Clouds
> With him I flew, and underneath beheld
> The Earth outstretcht immense, a prospect wide
> And various: wond'ring at my flight and change
> To this high exaltation.
>
> (*Paradise Lost*, 10:86–90)

For Milton, man's hope, given in the form of Grace to Adam, is that he can recognize an order outside his own mind and worship the creator of that order, reaping the psychological benefits of a "paradise within." [17]

So far I have been speculating on the model of a vertical axis as it is applied to different ways of interpreting the mind in one of James's moments of truth. The crucial point is that there are two radically different ways of interpreting such moments. To take the moment as exhibiting the presence within of a consciousness other than his own (Muse, Grace, inspiration, temptation) is to enable the poet to present it as spectacle without actually participating in it. A reality

16. The logic and rhetoric of Milton's Satan are remarkably close to Merleau-Ponty's formulation. "I am the absolute source, my existence does not stem from my ante-cedents, from my physical and social environment; instead it moves out towards them and sustains them, for I alone bring into being for myself (and therefore into being in the only sense that the word can have for me) the tradition which I elect to carry on, or the horizon whose distance from me would be abolished—since that distance is not one of its properties—if I were not there to scan it with my gaze. Scientific points of view, according to which my existence is a moment of the world's, are always both naïve and at the same time dishonest, because they take for granted, without explicitly mentioning it, the other point of view, namely that of consciousness, through which from the outset a world forms itself round me and begins to exist for me. To return to things themselves is to return to that world which precedes knowledge, of which knowledge always *speaks*, and in rela-tion to which every scientific schematization is an abstract and derivative sign-language, as is geography in relation to the countryside in which we have learnt beforehand what a forest, a prairie or a river is" (*Phenomenology of Perception*, p. ix).
17. Greene (*Descent From Heaven*, pp. 387–411 passim) has an interesting discus-sion of the "vertical imagery" of *Paradise Lost*.

from outside pervades the poet's mind and informs it with a structure, shaping his mind rather than being shaped by it. Similarly, the presentation of mind in the poem will be separate from the poet's own mind (as Dante the pilgrim is separate from Dante the poet, and Satan and Adam are separate from Milton), and although the process of mind in the poem will be exemplary of the poet's mental process and his audience, it will be presented and beheld as that of an "other." On the other hand, to take the human mind as "absolute source" (Merleau-Ponty's phrase) is to change radically the kind of poem that can be written. The poem will *be* the mind of the poet, both in form and content, which means that it will be a continuing self-realization rather than a completed structure in the conventional sense.

A similar comparison can be made with respect to a horizontal, or chronological, model of consciousness as it is present in poetry. If the poem is an allegory of the mind of the poet, then the time of the poem will correspond with the subjective time of the poet's mind. Although this sounds like a kind of phenomenological honesty, it is as much a fiction or convention of poetic structure as the Muse. The continuity of any poetic structure is its most radical fiction. This stems from the fact that the mind itself does not exhibit an unconditioned continuity except for very short periods of time. A poem is written part by part and read line by line, and can never be held in the mind *in toto* as Coleridge desired of *Paradise Lost* or Poe prescribed in his "Poetic Principle." It is possible, however, for the poet who recognizes these short periods of continuity or moments of perception to desire to prolong them, and to undertake a long poem that would be an act of continuous revelation —a poem that would *achieve* such continuity as structural principle. Here we are back in circularity again, for the poem itself is an attempt to achieve continuity, yet its existence depends on the continuity being already present in the mind embodied in the poem. It cannot be willed into being, either as poetic structure or as a state of mind. This point is behind Coleridge's distinction between the "primary IMAGINATION . . . as a repetition in the finite mind of the eternal act of creation in the infinite I AM" and the secondary imagination which coexists with "the conscious will." [18]

If, on the other hand, the poet's mind is not itself the source of the continuity, but merely a vehicle temporarily filled by a consciousness

18. *Biographia Literaria*, 2 vols., ed. J. Shawcross (London & New York: Oxford Univ. Press, 1958), 1:202.

other than his own whose nature is that of continuous revelation, then certain problems do not exist. The chronological axis of the poem can be presented as spectacle, as linear narrative. It does not have to be "lived" as in a dream by the consciousness of the poet. Its continuity is prior to and independent from his, as the past is conventionally prior to and independent from the poet's present state—he can remember it but not change it. The distinction between present and past already presupposes a diachronic conception of reality in which what is real is more a manner of happening than what actually happens. In this case the manner of happening is temporal, events occur in linear time and must be seen in an order that reflects their chronology. Yet the only mind that can really know all time with the unmediated intensity of our experience of the present must be like Mneme, the cosmic historical consciousness, which can know all of history the way we know our own subjective histories.

Wordsworth's *Prelude* is happening while it's being written, even though its subject is ostensibly the past growth of the poet's mind. The main temporal axis is the present-tense address to Coleridge, but the past as well exists on that axis as a present in Wordsworth's mind. *The Prelude* must be read, then, as a present, on-going movement, rather than a view of past and finished action presented as spectacle. The same point holds for *Milton, The Fall of Hyperion,* and *The Bridge.* Wordsworth's regenerative moment, if it can happen, must be happening now in the present. Although the structure of the poem pretends to be chronological in the narrative convention of reporting past actions, the real structure is much more an endlessly repeated situation, a "shapeless eagerness" that keeps making its own beginning and never becomes a completed linear structure.

In the conventional narrative structure, found in most epics, the poet reports events and states of consciousness that are completed and "fixed" in the past. The poet is not participating in them now, and in the terms of the convention he never did. Still, we as interpreters can usually see them as embodiments of his own experience and reflections of his own time, no matter how far back into legendary time they are placed. The point is, to see them clearly, the poet must see them as ideal pattern, as spectacle, as "other," and in the temporal framework this need dictates that they be in the past. They must be seen as past, as fitting into a linear chronology, and in an important sense they are not real (i.e., cannot be understood) until they can be seen that way. Thus the importance of the *in medias res* convention in narrative is not its story-telling convenience, or its generation of suspense, but its entry into the past providing a deeper, more ordered view of already-lived-through experience. Aeneas, seeing his own life as spectacle in the past, is thus reflecting Vergil's strategy in the poem. Present experience cannot be seen in this way (in the way of seeing that confirms its "reality"), and the desire to see one's life *sub specie aeternitatis* reflects the need to be outside, seeing one's life as spectacle in a space-time framework larger and more real than it is. That present experience cannot be seen in this way contributes to tragic irony and the structure of tragedy in which the past slowly catches up with the present. The protagonist operates with false assumptions about the past and about his present situation with respect to the future. His involvement with the present and his concern for the future prevent him from reentering and re-viewing the past, from undertaking the epic discipline that would change his vision and avoid or transcend his tragedy. The temporal problem for the poet who wants to participate in his poem, to possess it inwardly, rather than present it as an ideal picture, is similar to the problem of consciousness discussed in relation to the Muse. The temporal axis of the poem would be the (subjective) time of the poet's thinking it. It would be synchronic, existing outside of time, rather than diachronic existence through time. On this point, Coleridge has another relevant Miltonic phantasy.

> The story of Milton might be told in two pages. It is this which distinguishes an epic poem from a romance in metre. Observe the march of Milton; his severe application; his laborious polish; his deep metaphysical researches; his prayer to God before he began his great work; all that could lift and swell his intellect became his daily food.
>
> I should not think of devoting less than twenty years to an epic poem. Ten years to collect materials and warm my mind with universal science. I would be a tolerable mathematician. I would thoroughly understand Mechanics; Hydrostatics; Optics, and Astronomy; Botany; Metallurgy; Fossilism; Chemistry; Geology; Anatomy; Medicine; then the mind of man; then the minds of men, in all Travels, Voyages and Histories. So I would spend ten years; the next five in the composition of the poem, and the last five in the correction of it. So would I write, haply not unhearing of that divine and nightly-whispering voice, which speaks

to mighty minds of predestined garlands, starry and unwither-
ing.[19]

Coleridge gives Milton a structured mental existence through time, in
which he knows at every point his relative position, where he has been
and where he is going. In Augustine's terms, Milton is to Coleridge the
mind "wonderful beyond belief" that would know "all the past and all
the future . . . as clearly as I know a familiar psalm." [20] If time is "an
extension of the mind itself," such an extension can be imagined only
for the mind of God, and mental existence as a "march" can characterize only such a mind. Human time, the extension of the human
mind, is for Augustine a limited and confusing thing that does not
even know what it is. Coleridge and Wordsworth seem at times to have
thought the human mind could—or *ought* to—will itself a different
extension; but they never succeeded in doing so. For them the "march"
is an ideal pattern, outside the mind, which they desired and sought
but never achieved.[21]

If we look at the temporal structure of *The Prelude* in this light, we
can see that it reflects something like the contrast between a walking
tour and a march. To subject the poem, and with it life, to a goal, is
to violate the present moment. But to make the present moment an end
in itself is to lose the possibility of an overall guiding structure. Again
there are Christian parallels, two opposing routes to God reflecting opposing forms of literary structure. The walk reflects the possibility of
*any* moment being the moment out of time in which all things are
seen clearly, and this is similar to the religious urge to find in the present
moment the lost union with God. The alternate route through time to
God is to make the present moment not an end in itself, but only the
means to some future end, to lay out one's time in preparation for a
happy eternity. If the present moment is both the beginning of the
poem and the desired state completing the poem, then a linear structure
will be irrelevant—the state of renewed vision will be achieved not in a
future union of epic time and real time, but in the apocalyptic present
of the poem. Wordsworth tries repeatedly to find his mind exhibiting

19. Quoted in Joseph Cottle, *Reminiscences* (London, 1847), p. 103.
20. *Confessions*, trans. R. S. Pine-Coffin (Hammondsworth: Penguin, 1961), p. 279.
21. Shortly after he undertook a systematic course of reading in preparation for
writing a series of hymns to the sun, moon, and elements, and an epic on the
origin of evil, Coleridge switched to the *Ancient Mariner* to raise £5 to pay the
expenses of a walking tour (Humphrey House, *Coleridge* [London: Rupert Hart-
Davis, 1969], p. 85).

the heroic pattern of a march, a move forward through time and upward, crossing the alps. But he always returns to an experiential reality
of a completely different nature, to "glimpses" and "spots of time," to
sudden turnings of the path that change his points of view, hoping to
find within himself

> Emotion which best foresight need not fear.
> Most worthy then of trust when most intense.
> Hence chearfulness in every act of life
> Hence truth in moral judgements and delight
> That fails not in the external universe.
>
> (*Prelude,* 13:122–126)

The end of the poem, of course, is a return to the chronological axis
of the ideal pattern. His "history" is brought to its "appointed close,"
and the regeneration will be the grace of Providence "surely yet to
come."

> Oh! yet a few short years of useful life,
> And all will be complete, thy race be run,
> Thy monument of glory will be raised.
> Then, though, too weak to tread the ways of truth,
> This Age fall back to old idolatry,
> Though men return to servitude as fast
> As the tide ebbs, to ignominy and shame
> By nations sink together, we shall still
> Find solace in the knowledge which we have,
> Bless'd with true happiness if we may be
> United helpers forward of a day
> Of firmer trust, joint-labourers in a work
> (Should Providence such grace to us vouchsafe)
> Of their redemption, surely yet to come.
>
> (13:430–443)

The figure of the poet in *The Excursion,* although keeping the
peripatetic motion of a wanderer, has learned the lesson of time's inevitable victory. And there Wordsworth has learned to keep himself
separate from the "other," to point to him as an imaged ideal or spectacle.

In Blake there is no comparable tension between conflicting existence in time. The extension of his mind, which is the time of his poem, has nothing to do with an act of will ordering his daily existence. His *Milton* ends, as poem, the instant he returns from the visionary moment "To Resurrection & Judgment in the Vegetable Body." In *Jerusalem* he gives his "awful Vision" in the present tense because he is seeing it in the "now" of the poem.

> I see the Past, Present & Future existing all at once
> Before me. O Divine Spirit, sustain me on thy wings
>
> (Ch. 1, pl. 15:8–9)

What he sees—which is dependent on how he sees it—unfolds in the now of speaking/seeing; it is not an anticipated state or a reported episode from the past. It may, in Augustine's phrase, be "wonderful beyond belief," but there is no question of how the reader should approach it. To read *The Prelude* as the expression of a state of mind in the present—which we must attempt to do in order to understand it fully as structure—is a much more complicated task, because of Wordsworth's tendency to push it toward an "appointed close" which is "all gratulant."

In *The Fall of Hyperion,* Keats uses the device of a dream to enable him to avoid a stance in conventional reality. He is aware of the idea of ascent through time, up the marble stairs to the "lofty sacrificial fire" of vision. He tries by "patient travail / To count with toil the innumerable degrees" and moves "Towards the altar sober-pac'd." But he cannot mount its "immortal steps" without a radical shift in consciousness presented as a dying into life.

> I strove hard to escape
> The numbness, strove to gain the lowest step.
> Slow, heavy, deadly was my pace: the cold
> Grew stifling, suffocating, at the heart;
> And when I clasp'd my hands I felt them not,
> One minute before death, my iced foot touch'd
> The lowest stair; and, as it touch'd, life seem'd
> To pour in at the toes; I mounted up,
> As once fair angels on a ladder flew
> From the green turf to heaven.
>
> (127–136)

The promise of a vision that is to transcend time does not hold, however. He must bear his vision "Without stay or prop," with his "own weak mortality" which cannot bear the burden of past, present and future all at once. Aeneas had to lose his humanity, his life of passion, in order to take on the burden of destiny. Keats, like Moneta, must "humanize" his "sayings," keep his human consciousness of time-as-destroyer and extend it toward the unbearable consequences.

Time in Crane's work reveals the same tensions inevitably present in the human consciousness that experiences two modes of being. He prefaces the work with the description of Satan from *Job*.

> From going to and fro in the earth,
>     and from walking up and down in it.

We can see in *The Bridge* something of the strategy I have described in *The Prelude*. The poet's motion through the poem is not a linear version of the "myth to God." Diachronic time in the poem, as in the history of the country, is a hostile element, destructive of vision and of faith in those ascendant moments which encompass all time. Crane returns to the country's past and to his past not to discover the chronological pattern that orders events, but to discover a way of seeing that would transcend time as a "River" carrying all experience, all history with it to the oblivion of the sea. Such a discovery could be made only by "going to and fro in the earth, and from walking up and down in it," or the poet's equivalent of walking around in the modern city, waiting for the moment of consciousness that would contain and order all the mind's experience. Walking on Brooklyn Bridge gave Crane the physical sensation of moving both "forward and upward" at the same time. What Crane is seeking through the poem is the mental equivalent of that *ascensus*, a state of mind leading not to an "other" state, a goal in the future, but to a vision of the now of human existence. He expressed this in a letter to Waldo Frank: "The validity of a work of art is situated in contemporary reality to the extent that the artist must honestly anticipate the realization of his vision in 'action' (as an actively operating principle of communal works and faith), and I don't mean by this that his procedure requires any bona fide evidences directly and personally signalled, nor even any physical signs or portents. The darkness is part of his business. It has always been taken for granted, how-

ever, that his intuitions were salutary and that his vision either sowed
or epitomized 'experience' (in the Blakeian sense)." [22] Wordsworth
makes much the same point in *The Prelude*.

> Not in Utopia, subterraneous Fields,
> Or some secreted Island, Heaven knows where,
> But in the very world which is the world
> Of all of us, the place in which, in the end,
> We find our happiness, or not at all.

(10:724–728)

To look in *The Bridge*, then, for a structure comparable to those
found in earlier epics is to look for something which is not there, or
there only as a threat or imposition, something to be avoided. This has
often been held against it, as well as against those other poems whose
mode of existence is the on-going present state of the poet's mind. It is
tempting, to one who respects these poems as poetic achievements, to
try to define a "structure" that will answer the objections held against
them. Such structures, however, tend to be either attempts to define
"mysticism" or readings of the poems as autobiographies. In the former,
meaningful structure gives way to ecstacy, either divine or morbid. In
the latter, the larger goal of spiritual biography, or an allegory of life,
gives way to the reductions of psychology and the irrelevancies of personal detail.

My own notion is that we should approach the problem of structure
in these poems with an alert tentativeness. These poems are radical attempts to understand the mind in a moment of its "true" existence,
and to build from that moment toward a structure. If the result is fragmentary, it may be the result of the particular poem or poet, or the
consequences of the nature of the human mind engaged in such an attempt. It is senseless, merely because these are long poems, to continue
looking in them for conventionalities of fable, plot or narration, or to
reject them because we do not find that their view of human consciousness falls into that kind of pattern. We cannot choose our point
of view if we expect to see anything, and this is especially true if we
expect to see anything new. In addition to Keats's quality of "Negative
Capability," we should read these poems with Eliot's warning in mind.
"For a long time after an epic poet like Milton, or a dramatic poet

22. *Letters of Hart Crane*, p. 260.

like Shakespeare, nothing can be done. Yet the effort must be repeatedly made; for we can never know in advance when the moment is approaching at which a new epic, or a new drama will be possible; and when the moment does draw near it may be that the genius of an individual poet will perform the last mutation of idiom and versification which will bring that new poetry into being." [23]

But we should also beware the dangers inherent in the conventional search for the great poet, which are apparent in this statement by Erwin Edman.

> In our own day there will doubtless in good time arise some imaginative poet or novelist who will be able to make a sustained image, in which all the spiritual tensions and all the daring intellectual hypotheses of our own day will not be made into a system, but transmuted into an artistic coherence like that of a symphony or a great painting. . . . we could imagine there being born, by the good luck of statistical accident, some really great imaginative poet even in our own time, a poet such as Dante, who, having a wide and ranging intellectual vision, should also have the gift of literary art and in one sustained symphonic synthesis, as it were, express rather than state, disclose rather than argue, those relations of appearance to reality, the present to the future, of time to eternity, of the animal basis of human nature to man's spiritual possibilities, of the conflict in our own time between the necessity for security and the human passion for freedom. One could imagine a poet, who, catching these ideas by a kind of osmosis, having the antenna of his imagination—to change the metaphor—stirred or vibrated by those waves of ideas could produce a work that should be at once an esthetic image, a work of art, and a work of philosophy.[24]

On the surface, this would seem like a search for the new philosophic poet of our age, but it is the rhetoric of a misguided and misinformed nostalgia, vainly hoping that the future will repeat the past. Neither "the good luck of statistical accident" nor the sheer exertion of human will can produce this kind of work for our times.

---

23. T. S. Eliot, "Milton II," in *On Poetry and Poets* (New York: Farrar, Straus & Giroux, 1961), p. 171.
24. "Philosophy and the Literary Artist," in *Spiritual Problems in Contemporary Literature*, ed. S. R. Hopper (New York: Harper & Bros., 1952), p. 34.

On the other hand, as Robert Langbaum has pointed out, "it is possible for poets and critics not yet to have generalized the rationale of a new kind of poetry." [25] Anything will look incoherent until we know it has a principle of order; and any coherence will elude us until we know what that principle of order is and understand how it works. To suggest that the mind, or "imagination" or "vision," is not only the subject of these poems but is the form as well, is only to suggest that the principle of order is still an unknown, that we are in the position of having to learn from this poetry that which will enable us to understand it more fully. The task is for the poet to reveal and the reader to understand something like the "argument" of human consciousness. By argument I mean something more than a thematic focus or a tonal unity, more than a unity of subject or attitude. The trick, if I may risk a prediction, will be to find a mode of revealing consciousness that has more scope than the time-bound center of a limited point of view in the novel, and more structure than the psychologically realistic stream-of-consciousness. The nature of consciousness itself is, of course, now being explored from many different vantage points, often with a deliberateness that may be self-defeating, but also with an enthusiasm that makes prophets of the poets. It may turn out that none of the approaches comes close, or that consciousness eludes the kind of self-knowledge we desire, or that consciousness is itself a metaphor for some still undiscovered life-line to reality. Blake may have caught it, or Melville, or Joyce—or someone else whom we do not yet know how to read.

25. Robert Langbaum, *The Poetry of Experience* (New York: W. W. Norton & Co., 1957), p. 33.

# Index